The Habitats D

Yvonne Scannell, Ph.D., LL.D.,
Fellow, Trinity College Dublin

and

Robert Cannon

Martin Clarke, LL.B.

Oran Doyle,
Scholar, Trinity College Dublin

CENTRE FOR ENVIRONMENTAL LAW AND POLICY,
LAW SCHOOL, TRINITY COLLEGE DUBLIN

*Centre for Environmental Law and Policy,
Law School, Trinity College Dublin*

*This publication has received support from the Heritage Council
under the 1998 Publications Grant Scheme.*

© *Yvonne Scannell, Robert Cannon,
Martin Clarke and Oran Doyle 1999*

First published 1999

ISBN 0-9534979-0-9

*Printed by Reprint Ltd,
South Cumberland Street, Dublin 2*

Cover design by Maximilian D. Hills

Dedicated to

Professor Barry Sullivan

and

Frances Lewis

Foreword

This book is a study on the implementation of a Directive. It represents the collective efforts of the authors and is the outcome of a good deal of debate and compromise. Three of the authors were undergraduates in the Environmental Law class of 1997-8 in the Law School, Trinity College, Dublin. Much of the research was undertaken for dissertations which they were required to do as part of their examination exercises. The fourth was their fortunate lecturer in Environmental Law. I hope readers will not be surprised to know that all of the students got first class honours in Environmental Law.

The book is not a comprehensive description of Habitats Law in Ireland: rather it seeks to examine constructively and critically the manner in which the Habitats Directive was implemented in Irish law by the European Communities (Natural Habitats) Regulations, 1997. It does not deal in any depth with the implementation of the related Directive on the conservation of wild birds. This deficiency is regretted but it was decided at the outset to confine our endeavours to a study of the Habitats Directive.

The book begins with chapters devoted to European Community law and to the Irish Constitutional protection of private property by way of background. The purpose of these chapters is solely to put the Habitats Directive, and the implementing Irish Regulations, into their proper context. Readers who wish to know more should consult specialist texts in these areas. This is followed by a substantive discussion of the Habitats Directive and the Habitats Regulations. Individual chapters deal with the process of site designation for *Natura 2000*, the controls on land use imposed to ensure the conservation of designated sites, compensation schemes for restrictions on land use and an examination of measures which protect species directly, other than the creation of sites. The final chapter is a discussion of the various schemes available for funding habitat protection.

Our examination has shown that the manner in which the Habitats Directive has been implemented is less than impressive. The regulations contain anomalies, mistakes and inconsistencies which reflect badly on the State. Modern Irish environmental legislation in general is not noted for its clarity and ease of comprehension, but the Habitats Regulations must mark a new departure for being particularly obtuse and difficult to understand. This is especially regrettable given the length of their gestation and the extensive consultation which preceded their enactment.

One of the most important problems in any regulatory system which regulates land-uses is the extent to which the use of land may be restricted while at the same time ensuring proper protection for constitutional rights, particularly property rights, rights to earn a livelihood and rights to procedural justice. The Habitats Regulations have not addressed this problem in an honest and equitable manner. In particular, it is submitted that they do not implement the specific constitutional obligation to defend and vindicate the property rights of the citizen in so far this is practicable. It is well accepted that property rights may be limited in the interests of environmental protection and a sound constitutional argument could be made that the preservation of important habitats is an objective which justifies restrictions on some constitutional rights. But in securing this objective it is important in a democracy that proper regard be had to the burdens which individuals will have to bear under these regulations, individuals who in most cases are not wealthy or in a position to carry these burdens without disproportionate cost. A fairer system of compensation should be provided for, one which has due regard not only to the interests of farmers, but also to the interests of others who will be required to bear the burdens of habitats protection and one which does not depend on the accidents of which regulatory system imposes the restrictions on property rights. Much more attention should also have been given in implementing the Directive to devising more imaginative means of providing for compensation for restrictions on property rights such as conferring development rights on restricted property owners or purchasing, leasing or accepting gifts of these rights or easements over land. Compensation should be calculated by an independent arbitrator or by a committee representative of all the interests involved. Activities in SACs could be discouraged by legislation providing that no public funding, tax concessions or other publicly funded benefits shall be available in respect of any development which could significantly adversely affect a special area of conservation.

One must also question to what extent it was wise to vest control over development which is not subject to planning legislation in a central government department which has little expertise in land-use regulation. It would surely have been more efficient and democratic to vest all controls on development of any kind which could damage special areas of conservation in planning authorities who are already experienced in doing this and who are usually more attuned to the sensitivities of their constituents than a central government department. This could be simply achieved by de-exempting development in, and adjacent to, special areas of conservation and, if necessary, providing for a simplified procedure for dealing with proposals for private sector development affecting these areas.

Consideration should also be given to providing for a system of independent regulation and control over all public sector activities which could adversely affect special areas of conservation instead of permitting some public authorities to decide for themselves whether or not an activity is consistent with habitat conservation. The lessons of the Mullaghmore and Luggala cases must surely be that there is little justification for providing a less stringent and transparent system of regulatory control for public sector development, except in the most exceptional cases.

Measures for the protection of special areas of conservation are not well integrated into the existing legal framework for land - use control, environmental protection and the provision of infrastructure. The assumption was apparently made that development plans are the only type of environmental management plans which require modification to meet the objectives of the Habitats Directive. This is manifestly not the case and the Directive requires more than this.

Despite of the fact that European Communities (Natural Habitats) Regulations, 1997 are extremely complex and difficult, no Ministerial guidance has been issued on the manner in which they are to be implemented. Administrators in Ireland are incentivised to promote their authority's objectives by an appreciation of the fact that judicial review for unreasonableness is expensive and very likely to be unsuccessful. Those administering these regulations - and other legislation implementing the Directive- should be required to make a careful and reasoned analysis of the types of activities that might be allowed to take place on or near important habitats without impairing ecological values. There could be a temptation to use the regulations to impose blanket and arbitrary prohibitions of a variety of activities which could be permitted without detracting from the values which the Regulations are designed to protect. Judgments on these matters should not be the prerogative of administrators who may be inadequately qualified or trained to implement this new legislation properly.

Having alluded to some of the inadequacies of the Regulations, the authors hope that inadequacies on their part will be attributed to the short time period available for completing this study. It was conceived in May and substantially written by October. Summer holidays intervened. They would be delighted to learn of any inaccuracies. They wish to record their gratitude to the Heritage Council which partly funded this publication, particularly to Beatrice Kelly. They also wish to acknowledge the assistance of Dr Catherine O'Connell of the Irish Peat Conservation Council, Brendan Burgess, Dr Declan Doogue and Shirley Clerkin of the Irish Wildlife Trust, and Frank King, Lily Tangney and Maeve O'Donnell of the Ballyseedy Wood Action Group. For proof reading and invaluable suggestions, they are indebted to Roderick Maguire, Alan Doyle, Rory O'Malley, Ailin Doyle, Eric Gannon, Barry Doyle, Richard Leonard, Philip Cody and especially Brendan Slattery. They would particularly like to thank Sharon Turner for her many valuable suggestions. Max Hills and Barry Brophy deserve credit for the cover design. They would also like to thank their families and the Law School, Trinity College, Dublin for the enormous support and encouragement which they have received from them.

Professor Yvonne Scannell
Law School
Trinity College
Dublin 2
10 December 1998

Contents

Chapter 1	**THE EUROPEAN DIMENSION** HABITAT PROTECTION IN THE CONTEXT OF EUROPEAN ENVIRONMENTAL LAW	1
Chapter 2	**THE CONSTITUTION** THE INTERACTION OF PROPERTY RIGHTS AND LAND USE CONTROLS	39
Chapter 3	**DESIGNATION OF SITES** A BALANCE OF COMMUNITY AND NATIONAL RESPONSIBILITIES	55
Chapter 4	**SITE CONSERVATION MEASURES** CONTROLS OVER DEVELOPMENT AND ACTIVITIES	89
Chapter 5	**THE PAYMENT OF COMPENSATION** AN UNEASY COMPROMISE	139
Chapter 6	**SPECIES CONSERVATION MEASURES** PROTECTING SPECIMENS AS WELL AS SITES	165
Chapter 7	**FINANCING HABITAT PROTECTION**	189
Appendix I	COUNCIL DIRECTIVE 92/43/EEC ON THE CONSERVATION OF NATURAL HABITATS AND OF WILD FAUNA AND FLORA	201
Appendix II	FIRST AND SECOND SCHEDULES TO THE EUROPEAN COMMUNITIES (NATURAL HABITATS) REGULATIONS, 1997	220

Table of Contents

CHAPTER 1: THE EUROPEAN DIMENSION
HABITAT PROTECTION IN THE CONTEXT OF EUROPEAN ENVIRONMENTAL LAW

1.1	INTRODUCTION	1
1.2	THE EMERGENCE OF EC ENVIRONMENTAL LAW AND POLICY	
	The Treaty of Rome	4
	The Single European Act	6
1.3	THE LEGAL BASIS OF *NATURA 2000*	
	The Birds Directive	8
	The Habitats Directive	8
1.4	SOME GUIDING PRINCIPLES OF EUROPEAN ENVIRONMENTAL LAW AND POLICY	
	Sustainable Development	9
	The Precautionary Principle	15
1.5	INTERNATIONAL CONVENTIONS	16
1.6	REMEDIES FOR NON-TRANSPOSITION AND NON-COMPLIANCE WITH THE HABITATS DIRECTIVE	
	Information Gathering	18
	Enforcement in the European Court of Justice	21
	Enforcement in the Irish Courts	24
1.7	INTEGRATION OF THE HABITATS DIRECTIVE INTO THE IRISH LEGAL SYSTEM	
	Supremacy of European Community Law	28
	Directives	29
	Transposition into National Law	31
	Direct Effect	33
	Indirect Effect	36
	Interaction of European Community Law and Irish Constitutional Law	37

CHAPTER 2: THE CONSTITUTION
THE INTERACTION OF PROPERTY RIGHTS AND LAND USE CONTROLS

2.1	INTRODUCTION	39
2.2	THE PROTECTION AFFORDED BY THE CONSTITUTION	
	The Constitutional Text	39
	The Extent of Property Rights	41

2.3	THE PRINCIPLE OF PROPORTIONALITY	
	The Emergence of a New Test	43
	The Application of the Test to Restrictions of Property Rights	45
	The Limits of the Test	46
2.4	COMPENSATION	
	General Principles	47
	The American Approach	47
	A Possible Development of the Irish Approach	49
2.5	THE CONSTITUTIONALITY OF LAND USE RESTRICTIONS	
	General Observations	50
	The Constitutionality of Land-Use Plans	51
	The Constitutionality of Requiring Planning Permission or other Consents for Activities on Land	52

CHAPTER 3: DESIGNATION OF SITES
A BALANCE OF COMMUNITY AND NATIONAL RESPONSIBILITIES

3.1	INTRODUCTION	
	Natura 2000	55
	Natural Habitat Types and Species of Community Interest	55
	Priority Natural Habitat Types and Species	56
	Favourable Conservation Status	57
3.2	NATURAL HABITAT TYPES AND SPECIES PROTECTED BY *NATURA 2000*	
	Community Interest Criteria for Natural Habitat Types	58
	Classifying the Community's Habitats	58
	Significance of the Interpretation Manual	60
	Community Interest Criteria for Species	60
3.3	OVERVIEW OF THE DESIGNATION PROCESS FOR *NATURA 2000* SITES	
	Member State and Community Interaction	61
	Preparation of the National Lists of Sites	61
	Selection of Sites of Community Importance	62
	Designation as Special Areas of Conservation	62
3.4	PREPARATION OF THE CANDIDATE LIST OF SITES	
	Obligation on Member States	62
	Selection of Sites for the Candidate List	63
	Surveillance	64
	Only Scientific Information to be Considered?	65
	Natura 2000 Form	67

3.5	NOTICE	
	Community Law and the Principles of Natural Justice	68
	Notice to those with an Interest in the Land	68
	Contents of the Notice	69
	Public Notification Adopted in Practice	70
	Notice to Ministers, Statutory Authorities and Planning Authorities	71
3.6	OBJECTIONS	
	Submission of Objections	71
	Requests for Review or Modification of the Candidate List	72
	Grounds on which Objections May Be Based	72
	Decision on Objections and Amendment of Candidate List	73
	Appeals Advisory Board	74
	Natural Justice Considerations	75
	Modification of the Candidate List	75
	Informal Appeals	76
3.7	SITES OF COMMUNITY IMPORTANCE (SCIs)	
	Designation of Sites at Community Level	76
	Examination of Sites by Biogeographical Region	77
	Procedure for Selecting SCIs	77
	Candidate List Sites Not Selected as SCIs	79
	Notice of SCI Designation	80
3.8	SPECIAL PROCEDURE FOR SITES NOT ON THE CANDIDATE LIST SUBMITTED TO THE COMMISSION (ARTICLE 5 PROCEDURE)	
	Sites Subject to the Article 5 Procedure	81
	Bilateral Consultation	81
	Council Power to Adopt Site as SCI	82
	Notification and Objection Procedures Must Be Followed	82
	Purpose of the Article 5 Procedure	83
3.9	SPECIAL AREAS OF CONSERVATION (SACs)	
	Final Stage in Designation Process	83
	Priorities in Designation	84
	Notice of SAC Designation	84
	Purpose of the SAC Designation	85
3.10	*NATURA 2000* NETWORK – AN EVOLVING ENTITY	
	Periodic Review of *Natura 2000*	86
	Amendments to Annexes I and II	87
	Declassification of sites	87

CHAPTER 4: SITE CONSERVATION MEASURES
CONTROLS OVER DEVELOPMENT AND ACTIVITIES

4.1	EUROPEAN CONSERVATION OF *NATURA 2000* SITES	
	The Philosophy of the Habitats Directive	89
	Explicit Site Protection Requirements	90
	Implicit Site Protection Requirement	91
	Limits to the Protection	93
	Opinions of the Commission	94
	A Comparison with the Irish Regulations	96
4.2	INTRODUCTION TO THE IRISH REGULATIONS	
	Integrated Habitat Protection	96
	"Neither Directly Connected with nor Necessary to the Management of a European Site"	97
	"Significant Effect" and "Adverse Effect"	98
	"European Site"	98
	"Environmental Impact Assessment"	99
4.3	INTEGRATION OF HABITAT PROTECTION INTO IRISH PLANNING AND ENVIRONMENTAL LAW	
	Existing System of Planning and Environmental Controls	100
	Structure of the Regulations	102
4.4	CONTROL OF OPERATIONS OR ACTIVITIES	
	The Requirement to Obtain Consent	105
	The Minister's Decision	107
	Duty to Give Reasons	108
	Appeals against the Minister's Decision	109
	Enforcement	110
4.5	CONTROL OF LAND USES SUBJECT TO PLANNING PERMISSION, AND OF LICENSABLE ACTIVITIES	
	The Existing Systems	113
	Integration of Habitat Considerations into the Planning System	113
	Decision on Planning Applications	114
	Authorisations under the Second Schedule	115
	Review of Existing Planning Permissions	116
	Reviews of Existing Ministerial Authorisations	119
4.6	PUBLIC AUTHORITY LAND USE	
	Four Systems of Control	121
	Self Regulation of Local Authority Development	122
	Independent Regulation of Local Authority Development	122

		Self Regulation of Ministers' Development and Activities	123
		Public Authority Development and Activities Subject to Full External Control	123
		Review of Decisions to Allow or Undertake Public Authority Projects	124
4.7	PROACTIVE CONSERVATION MEASURES		124
4.8	INADEQUATE IMPLEMENTATION OF THE DIRECTIVE		
		Structure of the Analysis	126
		Irish Protection of SACs	126
		Irish Protection of SPAs	127
		Irish Protection of SCIs	127
		Irish Protection of Article 5 Sites	127
		Irish Protection of Candidate List Sites	128
		Irish Protection of Sites Generally	129
		The Doctrines of Direct and Indirect Effect	129
4.9	PUBLIC PARTICIPATION AND THE REQUIREMENTS OF ADMINISTRATIVE LAW		
		Basic Principles	130
		Compliance of the Habitats Regulations with Administrative Law	132
		A Policy Argument in Favour of Wider Public Participation	133
4.10	THE CONSTITUTIONALITY OF THE RESTRICTIONS		
		Relationship with Administrative Law	134
		Is Species Protection a Legitimate State Activity?	134
		The Payment of Compensation	136
4.11	ENFORCEMENT		
		Criminal Liability	136
		Restoration of Land in a European Site Following Damage	137
		Powers of Enforcement under Planning Law	138

CHAPTER 5: THE PAYMENT OF COMPENSATION
AN UNEASY COMPROMISE

5.1	INTRODUCTION		139
5.2	COMPENSATION PAYABLE FOR REFUSAL OF CONSENT TO THE CARRYING OUT OF OPERATIONS OR ACTIVITIES		
		Definition of Operation or Activity	141
		The General Scheme of Compensation	141
		Circumstances in Which Compensation is Not Payable	142

	Who May Claim Compensation?	145
	The Measure of Compensation	146
	Constitutionality	147
	An Arbitrary Compensation Scheme	148
	Minister's Power to Award Compensation "where it would not be just and reasonable to refuse it"	150
	Community Law and Compensation	151
5.3	COMPENSATION PROVISIONS RELATING TO PLANNING PERMISSIONS AND LICENSABLE ACTIVITIES	
	Habitat Protection in Planning Legislation	152
	Compensation Under the Planning Acts	152
	Development Objectives	154
	Not Just and Reasonable to Deny Compensation	155
	An Alternative View	155
	Planning Permission Revoked or Modified	156
	Compensation for Modification, Revocation or Refusal to Issue an Environmental Licence	157
5.4	THE RURAL ENVIRONMENT PROTECTION SCHEME (REPS)	
	Introduction	158
	Agri-environment Plans	159
	REPS and the Habitats Regulations	161

CHAPTER 6: SPECIES CONSERVATION MEASURES
PROTECTING SPECIMENS AS WELL AS SITES

6.1	INTRODUCTION	
	Background to Protection of Species Measures	165
	The Habitats Directive: Protection of Species Obligations	166
	The Habitats Regulations and the Wildlife Act, 1976	167
	"Specimen"	168
6.2	PROTECTION OF WILD FLORA	
	General Scheme of Protection: Wildlife Act, 1976	169
	Definition of Flora	170
	Prohibited Actions	170
	The Habitats Regulations - Strict Protection of Annex IV(b) Flora Species	171
	The Habitats Regulations - Measures in Respect of Annex V(b) Flora Species	171
	Application of Amended Section 21 of the Wildlife Act	172
	Amended Section 21 as a Possible System of Strict Protection for Annex IV(b) Flora Species?	173
6.3	PROTECTION OF WILD FAUNA	
	General Scheme of Protection: Wildlife Act, 1976	174

	Definition of Fauna	175
	Prohibited Actions	175
	Strict Protection of Annex IV(a) Fauna Species	177
	Prohibition of Deliberate Capture or Killing of Specimens	177
	Prohibition on Keeping, Transport, Sale, etc. of Specimens	178
	Incidental Capture and Killing of Specimens	179
	Measures in respect of Annex V(a) Fauna Species	180
6.4	PROHIBITION OF INDISCRIMINATE MEANS OF CAPTURE AND KILLING	
	General Prohibition	180
	Prohibited Means of Capture and Killing of Wild Mammals	181
	Prohibited Means of Capture and Killing of Wild Fish	184
	Prohibited Modes of Transport	184
6.5	DEROGATIONS	
	Power to Derogate	184
	Grounds for Derogations	185
	Requirements for Derogation	186
	Report to Commission	186
	Habitats Regulations	187
	Consideration of the General Requirements in Article 2(3)	187

CHAPTER 7: FINANCING HABITAT PROTECTION

7.1	INTRODUCTION	189
7.2	PROCEDURAL REQUIREMENTS	190
7.3	THE FINANCIAL INSTRUMENTS	
	The LIFE Programme	191
	The Structural Funds	193
	The Cohesion Fund	198
	The Community Initiatives	198
	Other Sources of Funding	200

Table of National Legislation

CONSTITUTION OF IRELAND, 1937

Article 15.2 .... 37, 38
Article 29.4.7 .... 37, 38, 72, 149
Article 40.3 .... 40, 41, 135, 150
Article 40.3.2 .... 40, 41, 42
Article 43 .... 40, 41, 42, 43, 44, 141

STATUTES

Acquisition of Land (Assessment of Compensation) Act, 1919 146
Air Navigation and Transport Act, 1936 104
Air Pollution Act, 1987 .... 36, 100, 102, 119, 137
Dumping at Sea Act, 1996 100
Environmental Protection Agency Act, 1992 .... 26, 36, 100, 116, 119, 121
European Communities Acts, 1972 - 1995 .... 30, 32, 37
Foreshore Acts, 1933-1992 100
Freedom of Information Act, 1997 .... 20, 108
Harbours Acts, 1946 - 1996 115
Lands Clauses Consolidation Act, 1845 146
Local Government (Planning and Development) Acts, 1963 - 1993 ....
  ....27, 49, 51, 52, 53, 100, 102, 103, 111, 113, 114, 117, 118, 148,
  151, 152, 153, 154, 154, 155, 156
Local Government (Water Pollution) Acts, 1977 - 1990 ....36, 102, 113,
  116, 120
Local Government Act, 1991 114
Roads Act, 1993 .... 122, 124
Waste Management Act, 1996 .... 36, 100, 102, 116, 119
Wildlife Act, 1976 ....2, 20, 29, 36, 70, 84, 97, 102, 106, 125, 142,
  166, 167, 168, 169, 170, 171, 172, 174, 175, 178, 179, 180, 181, 182,
  183, 184, 187

TABLE OF STATUTORY INSTRUMENTS*

European Communities (Conservation of Wild Birds) Regulations, 1985...**2**
European Communities Act, 1972 (Access to Information on the
   Environment) Regulations, 1998 .... **20, 108**
Flora Protection Order, 1987..**169**
Local Government (Planning and Development) Regulations, 1994........**69, 104, 121, 122, 123, 124**

* The Habitats Regulations as amended are not included in this table because their inclusion would be of only limited assistance to the reader.

Table of International Conventions

Bern Convention on the Conservation of European Wildlife and Natural
   Habitats...**17**
Bonn Convention on the Conservation of Migratory Species of Wild
   Animals..**16**
Convention on Biological Diversity...**17**
Convention on International Trade in Endangered Species of Wild Fauna
   and Flora..**16**
European Convention of Human Rights......................................**130**
Ramsar Convention on Wetlands of International Importance...............**17**

Table of Cases

ADBHU (Case 240/83) [1985] ECR 531 .... 6, 33
Al-Jubail Fertilizer Co. and Saudi Arabian Fertilizer Co. v. Council (Case
    49/88) [1991] ECR I-3187; [1991] 3 CMLR 377 133
Amministrazione delle Fianze delle Stato v. Simmenthal SpA (Case
    106/77) [1978] ECR 629; [1978] CMLR 263 .... 26, 28, 33
An Taisce and WWF v. Commission, Court of First Instance (Case T-
    461/93) [1994] ECR II-733, European Court of Justice (Case 325/94P)
    [1996] ECR I-3727 .... 23, 31, 196
Arcaro (Case 168/95) [1996] ECR I-4705; [1997] 1 CMLR 179 34
Association pour la Protection des Animaux Sauvages (Case 435/92)
    [1994] ECR I-67 187
Attorney General (McGarry) v. Sligo County Council [1989] ILRM 768;
    [1991] 1 IR 99 133
Becker v. Finanzamt Munster-Innenstadt (Case 8/81) [1982] ECR 53;
    [1982] 1 CMLR 499 35
Benedetti v. Munari (Case 52/76) [1977] ECR 163 25
Blake v. Attorney General [1982] IR 117 40
Blessington Heritage Trust Ltd. v. Wicklow County Council, unreported,
    High Court, 21 January 1998 26
Borker (Case 138/80) [1980] ECR 1975; [1980] 3 CMLR 638 25
Brasserie du Pécheur S.A. v. Germany and Regina v. Secretary of State for
    Transport, *ex parte* Factortame (No.3) (Joined Cases 46/93 and 48/93)
    [1996] ECR I-1029; [1996] 1 CMLR 889 28
Browne v. An Bord Pleanála [1989] ILRM 865 30
Buckley v. Attorney General [1950] IR 67 41
Central Dublin Development Association v. Attorney General (1970) 109
    ILTR 69 .... 43, 47, 51, 139, 145
Chambers v. An Bord Pleanála [1992] 1 IR 134 26
Chaulk v. Regina (1990) 3 S.C.R. 1303 44
Chief Constable of the North Wales Police v. Evans [1982] 1 WLR 1155 26
CILFIT v. Ministry of Health (Case 283/81) [1982] ECR 3415 26
Comitato di Coordinamento per la Difesa della Cava and Others v. Regione
    Lombardia (Case 236/92) [1994] ECR I-483 35
Commission v. Belgium (Case 102/79) [1980] ECR 1473; [1981] 1 CMLR
    282 30
Commission v. Belgium (Case 239/85) [1986] ECR 3645; [1988] 1 CMLR
    248 30
Commission v. Belgium (Case 247/85) [1987] ECR 3029 .... 8, 32
Commission v. Belgium (Case 42/89) [1990] ECR I-2821; [1992] 1 CMLR
    22 30

Commission v. Belgium (Case 2/90) [1992] ECR 1-4431; [1993] 1 CMLR 365 ....**6, 15**
Commission v. Denmark (Case 302/86) [1988] ECR 4607....................**6, 33**
Commission v. Federal Republic of Germany (Case 131/88) [1991] ECR I-825 ....**32**
Commission v. Germany (Case 29/84) [1985] ECR 1661; [1986] 3 CMLR 579 .... **32, 34**
Commission v. Germany (Case 131/88) ECR [1991] I-825 ....**28**
Commission v. Germany (Case 361/88) [1991] ECR I-2567; [1993] 2 CMLR 821 ....**28, 29, 30**
Commission v. Germany (Case 58/89) ECR [1991] 1-4983 ....**28**
Commission v. Germany (Case 83/97), European Court of Justice, 11 December 1997.. .....**22, 30, 37**
Commission v. Hellenic Republic (Case 329/96) [1997] ECR I-3749.......**22**
Commission v. Italy (Case 91/79) [1980] ECR 1099 ....**5**
Commission v. Italy (Case 42/80) [1980] ECR 3639 ....**32**
Commission v. Italy (Case 145/82) [1983] ECR 711 ....**30**
Commission v. Italy (Case 280/83) [1984] ECR 2361 ....**34**
Commission v. Italy (Case 262/85) [1987] ECR 3073 ....**32**
Commission v. Italy (Case 363/85) [1987] ECR 1733 .... **28, 32**
Commission v. Italy (Case 104/86) [1988] ECR 1799 .... **35, 37**
Commission v. Netherlands (Case 96/81) [1982] ECR 1791 ....**30**
Commission v. Netherlands (Case 339/87) [1990] ECR I-851; [1993] 2 C.M.L.R 360... **30, 189**
Commission v. Netherlands (Case 3/96), European Court of Justice, 19 May 1998..**22**
Commission v. Spain (Case 355/90) [1993] ECR I-4221 .... **22, 66**
Commission v. Spain (Case 242/94) [1995] ECR I-3031 ....**30**
Commission v. United Kingdom (Case 337/89) [1992] ECR I-6103 ....**30**
Coppinger v. Waterford County Council [1996] 2 ILRM 427 .... **27, 28**
Costa v. ENEL (Case 6/64) [1964] ECR 585; [1964] CMLR 425 .... **28, 34**
Daly v. Revenue Commissioners [1995] 3 IR 1; [1996] 1 ILRM 122 .... **46, 148**
Danielsson v. Commission (Case T-219/95) [1995] ECR II-3051 ....**23**
Dori Faccini v. Recreb Srl (Case 91/92) [1994] ECR I-3325; [1994] 1 CMLR 665 ....**34**
Dreher v. Irish Land Commission [1984] ILRM 94 ....**41**
Dublin County Council v. Eighty-Five Developments Ltd [1993] 2 IR 292 ....**153**
E.S.B. v. Gormley [1985] IR 129; [1985] ILRM 494 .... **41, 150**
East Donegal Co-op v. Attorney General [1970] IR 317; (1970) 104 ILTR 81 ....**46, 107, 134**
Emmott v. Minister for Social Welfare [1991] ILRM 387 ....**27**

Florida Rock Industries Inc v. United States 791 F 2d 893 (Fed Cir 1986) **48**
Foster v. British Gas plc (Case 188/89) [1990] ECR I-3313; [1990] 2 CMLR 833 ....**34**
Francovich and Others v. Italy (Cases 6,9/90) [1991] ECR I-5357; [1993] 2 CMLR 66 ....**28**
Fratelli Costanzo v. Comune di Milano (Case 103/88) [1989] ECR 1839; [1990] 3 CMLR 239 .... **29, 34**
Gourmetterie Van den Burg (Case 169/89) [1990] ECR I-2143 ....**32**
Greene v. Minister for Agriculture [1990] 2 IR 17; [1990] ILRM 364 .....**39**
Greenpeace v. Commission (Case T-585/93) European Court of First Instance, 9 August 1995 ....**23**
Harz v. Deutsche Tradex GmbH (Case 79/83) [1984] ECR 1921 .... **27, 36**
Hauer v. Land Rheinland-Pfalz (Case 44/79) [1979] ECR 3727; [1980] 3 CMLR 42 .... **50, 130, 139**
Heaney v. Ireland [1994] 3 IR 593, [1994] ILRM 420 ....**44**
Heineken Brouwarfen (Joined Cases 91,127/83) [1984] ECR 3435, [1985] 1 CMLR 389 ....**25**
Iarnrod Eireann v. Ireland [1995] 2 ILRM 161 ....**45**
Inter-Environment Wallonie ASBL v. Region Wallonne (Case 129/96) [1997] ECR I-7411 ....**31**
Internationale Handdelgesellschaft v. Einfuhr-und Vorratsstelle fur Getreide und Futtermittel (Case 11/70) [1970] ECR 1125; [1972] CMLR 225 ....**29**
Irish Creamery Milk Suppliers Association v. Ireland (Joined Cases 36,71/80) [1981] ECR 735 ....**25**
Johnston v. Chief Constable of the RUC (Case 222/84) [1986] ECR 1651; [1986] 3 CMLR 240 ....**36**
Keogh v. Galway County Council [1995] 1 ILRM 142............................**132**
Lancefort v. An Bord Pleanála [1998] 2 ILRM 401 .... **26, 134**
Lawlor v. Minister for Agriculture [1990] 1 IR 356 .... **52, 107, 139**
Lucas v. South Carolina Coastal Commission, 120 S.Ct. (l.Ed..2d.) 798 (1992)..**147**
Malahide Community Council Ltd. v. Fingal County Council [1997] 3 IR 383 ....**26**
Marleasing S.A. v. La Commercial International de Alimentation S.A. (Case 106/89) [1990] ECR I-4135; [1992] 1 CMLR 305 ....**37**
Marshall v. Southampton and South-West Hampshire Area Health Authority (Case 152/84) [1986] ECR 723; [1986] 1 CMLR 688.. **30, 34**
McBride v. Galway County Council, High Court, 4 February 1997; Supreme Court, 24 March 1998 ....**26**
McDonagh v. Galway Corporation [1995] 1 IR 191................................**51**
McNamara v. An Bord Pleanála [1995] 2 ILRM 125 ....**27**

McPharthalain v. Commissioners of Public Works [1992] 1 IR 111; [1994] 3 IR 353 .... **51, 132**
Meagher v. Minister for Agriculture [1994] 1 IR 329; [1994] 1 ILRM 1..... .... **31, 37, 152, 156**
Molkerei-Zentrale Westfalen v. Hauptzollamt Paderborn (Case 28/67) [1968] ECR 143; [1968] CMLR 187 ....**35**
Murphy v. Attorney General [1982] IR 241 ....**46**
Murphy v. Bord Telecom [1982] ILRM 53 ....**36**
Ni hEilí v. E.P.A. [1997] 2 ILRM 458 ....**75**
Nold v. Commission (Case 41/73) [1974] ECR 49; [1974] 2 CMLR 338 .... **130, 139**
Norbrook Laboratories Ltd. v. Ministry of Agriculture Fisheries and Food (Case 127/95) European Court of Justice, 2 April 1998 ....**28**
Nordsee v. Reederei Mond Hochseefischerei Nordstein A.G. (Case 102/81) [1982] ECR 1095 ....**25**
O'Callaghan v. Commissioners of Public Works [1985] ILRM 364..........**49**
O'Keefe v. An Bord Pleanála [1993] 1 IR 39 ....**26**
Oberkreisdirektor des Kreises Borken v. Handelsonderreming Moormann B.V. (Case 190/87) [1988] ECR 4689 ....**28**
Penn. Central Transportation Co. v. City of New York (1978) 438 US 104; 57 L Ed 2d 631, 88 S Ct 264 ....**49**
Pennsylvania Coal Co. v. Mahon 260 US 393, 43 S Ct. 158 ....**48**
Peralta (Case 379/92) [1994] ECR I-3453 ....**33**
Pine Valley v. Minister for the Environment [1987] IR 23.........................**42**
Pretore di Salo v. Persons Unknown (Case 14/86) [1987] ECR 2545; [1989] 1 CMLR 71 ....**25**
Regina v. H.M. Treasury, *ex parte* British Telecommunications plc (Case 392/93) [1996] ECR I-1631; [1996] 2 CMLR 217 ....**28**
Regina v. Secretary of State for the Environment *ex parte* Royal Society for the Protection of Birds (Case 44/95) [1996] ECR. I-3805 ....**66**
Regina v. Secretary of State for Transport, *ex parte* Factortame Ltd (No.1) (Case 213/89) [1990] 1 ECR 2433; [1990] 3 CMLR 375 ....**27**
Rewe Zentralfinanz eG and Rewe-Zentral A.G. v. Landwirtschaftskammer fur das Saarland (Case 33/76) [1976] ECR 1989; [1977] 1 CMLR 533 ....**27**
Rheinmuhlen Dusseldorf v. Einfuhr-und Vorratstelle fur Gertreide und Futternittel (Case 166/73) [1974] ECR 33; [1974] 1 CMLR 523 ....**25**
Royer (Case 48/75) [1976] ECR 497; [1976] 2 CMLR 619 ....**31**
Shannon Regional Fisheries Board v. An Bord Pleanála, unreported, High Court, 17 November 1994 ....**36**
SPUC v. Grogan (Case 159/90) [1991] ECR I-4685; [1991] 3 CMLR 849 ....**29**
State (FPH Properties Ltd.) v. An Bord Pleanála [1989] ILRM 98 ..... **42, 51**
State (Gleeson) v. Minister for Defence [1976] IR 280 ....**131**

State (Murphy) v. Johnston [1983] IR 235 .... **112, 137**
Steenhorst-Neerings v. Bestuur van de Bedrijfsvereniging vour
 Detailhandel, Ambachten en Huisvrouiven (Case 338/91) [1993] ECR
 I-5475 .... **37**
Tuohy v. Courtney [1994] 3 IR 1 .... **41**
TV3 v. Independent Radio and Television Commission [1994] 2 IR 439 **132**
Vaassen v. Management of the Beambtenfonds voor het Mijnbedrijf (Case
 61/65) [1966] ECR 261; [1966] CMLR 508 .... **25**
Van Duyn v. Home Office (Case 41/74) [1974] ECR 1337; [1975] 1
 CMLR 1 .... **33, 35**
Van Gend en Loos v. Nederlandse Administratie der Belastingen (Case
 26/62) [1963] ECR 1; [1963] CMLR 105 .... **33, 35**
Verbond van Nederlandse Onderneminger v. Inspecteur der Invoerrechten
 en Accijnzen (Case 51/76) [1977] ECR 113 ....**30**
Von Colson v. Land Nordrhein-Westfalen (Case 14/83) [1984] ECR 1891;
 [1986] 2 CMLR 430 .... **36**
Webb v. EMO Air Cargo [1992] 4 All ER 929 ....**36**
WWF-UK and Royal Society for the Protection of Birds v. Secretary of
 State for Scotland, The Times, 20 November 1998 .... **66, 72**
XJS Investments Ltd. v. Dun Laoighaire Corporation [1986] IR 750 ......**153**

Table of European Community Legislation

TREATY OF ROME..4, 5, 6, 8, 9, 10, 11, 13, 15, 18, 19, 21, 22, 23, 24, 30, 33, 92, 189, 190, 193, 195, 196, 197, 198

Article 3b	13
Article 3c	11
Article 5	19
Article 100	5, 6, 8
Article 130r	6, 8, 9, 11, 15, 18, 92, 189, 190, 193
Article 130s	6, 8, 189, 191
Article 130t	6
Article 138c	24
Article 138d	23
Article 138e	24
Article 169	21, 23, 63
Article 170	23
Article 171	22
Article 173	23
Article 177	24, 25
Article 189	18, 29, 30
Article 189c	8
Article 235	5, 6, 8

SINGLE EUROPEAN ACT..5, 6, 8

TREATY ON EUROPEAN UNION.....6, 8, 9, 10, 11, 13, 15, 30, 190, 198

Article A	13
Article B	10
Article G(60)	30

TREATY OF AMSTERDAM................................6, 10, 11, 12, 13

REGULATIONS

Commission Regulation 2772/95/EEC	158, 197
Commission Regulation 2773/95/EEC	197
Commission Regulation 231/96/EEC	197
Commission Regulation 746/96/EEC	158, 197
Commission Regulation 1962/96/EEC	158, 197

Commission Regulation 938/97/EEC 16
Commission Regulation 2307/97/EC 16
Commission Regulation 767/98/EC 16
Council Regulation 2052/88/EEC of 24 June 1988 on the tasks of the Structural Funds and their effectiveness and on coordination of their activities between themselves and with the operations of the European Investment Bank and the other existing financial instrument **193, 195, 196, 198**
Council Regulation 4253/88/EEC of 19 December 1988 laying down provisions for implementing Regulation 2052/88/EEC as regards coordination of the activities of the different Structural Funds between themselves and with the operations of the European Investment Bank and the other existing financial instruments **193, 198**
Council Regulation 4254/88/EEC of 19 December 1988 laying down provisions for implementing Regulation 2052/88/EEC as regards the European Regional Development Fund **196, 198**
Council Regulation 4255/88/EEC of 19 December 1988 laying down provisions for implementing Regulation 2052/88/EEC as regards the European Social Fund **195**
Council Regulation 4256/88/EEC of 19 December 1988 laying down provisions for implementing Regulation 2052/88/EEC as regards the European Agricultural Guidance and Guarantee Fund **196**
Council Regulation 1210/90/EEC of 7 May 1990 on the establishment of the European Environment Agency and the European Environment Information and Observation Network **18**
Council Regulation 1973/92/EEC of 21 May 1992 establishing a financial instrument for the environment **192**
Council Regulation 2078/92/EEC of 30 June 1992 on agricultural production methods compatible with the requirements of the protection of the environment and the maintenance of the countryside **158, 161, 197**
Council Regulation 2079/92/EEC of 30 June 1992 instituting a Community aid scheme for early retirement from farming **197**
Council Regulation 2080/92/EEC of 30 June 1992 instituting a Community aid scheme for forestry measures in agriculture **197**
Council Regulation 2080/93/EEC of 20 July 1993 laying down provisions for implementing Regulation 2052/88/EEC as regards the Financial Instrument for Fisheries Guidance **196**
Council Regulation 2081/93/EEC **193, 198**
Council Regulation 2082/93/EEC **193, 198**
Council Regulation 2083/93/EEC **196, 198**
Council Regulation 2084/93/EEC **195**
Council Regulation 2085/93/EEC **196**
Council Regulation 1164/94/EC of 16 May 1994 establishing a Cohesion Fund **198**

Council Regulation 1404/96/EEC **192**
Council Regulation 338/97/EC of 9 December 1996 on the protection of species of wild fauna and flora by regulating trade therein **16**
Council Regulation 950/97/EC of 20 May 1997 on improving the efficiency of agricultural structures **197**
Council Regulation 951/97/EC of 20 May 1997 on improving the processing and marketing conditions for agricultural products **197**

DIRECTIVES (not including the Habitats Directive)

Commission Directive 85/411/EEC **2**
Commission Directive 97/49/EC **2**
Council Directive 79/409/EEC of 2 April 1979 on the conservation of wild birds **2, 3, 6, 7, 8, 12, 14, 17, 19, 20, 22, 32, 35, 55, 66, 89, 90, 91, 93, 94, 98, 105, 129, 130, 142, 163, 168, 184, 185, 190, 192**
Council Directive 81/854/EEC **2**
Council Directive 85/337/EEC **12, 109**
Council Directive 86/122/EEC **2**
Council Directive 90/656/EEC **2**
Council Directive 94/24/EEC **2**
Council Directive 97/11/EC **12, 109**

DECISIONS

Commission Decision 93/701/EEC **10**
Commission Decision 97/150/EC of 24 February 1997 on the setting up of an European consultative forum on the environment and sustainable development **10**
Commission Decision 97/266/EC of 18 December 1996 concerning a site information format for proposed Natura 2000 sites **20**
Council Decision 82/72/EEC of 3 December 1981 concerning the conclusion of the Convention on the conservation on European wildlife and natural habitats **17**
Council Decision 82/461/EEC of 24 June 1982 on the conclusion of the Convention on the conservation of migratory species of wild animals ... **16**
Council Decision 93/626/EEC of 25 October 1993 concerning the conclusion of the Convention on Biological Diversity **17**

RECOMMENDATIONS

Commission Recommendation 75/66/EEC of 20 December 1974 to Member States concerning the protection of birds and their habitats **17**
Council Recommendation 75/436/EEC on cost allocation and action by public authorities on environmental matters **189**

Acronyms and Abbreviations

1963 Act	Local Government (Planning and Development) Act, 1963
1994 Regs	Local Government (Planning and Development) Regulations, 1994
All ER	All England Reports
ASI	Area of Scientific Interest
CMLR	Common Market Law Reports
CAP	Common Agricultural Policy
CFP	Common Fisheries Policy
CITES	Convention on International Trade in Endangered Species of Wild fauna and Flora
CORINE	Co-ordination of Information on the Environment
CSF	Community Support Framework
DG V	Directorate-General for Employment, Industrial Relations and Social Affairs
DG VI	Directorate-General for Agriculture
DG XVI	Directorate-General for Regional Policy and Cohesion
DGXI	Directorate-General for the Environment, Nuclear Safety and Civil Protection
DGXIV	Directorate-General for Fisheries
ECR	European Court Reports
EAGGF	European Agriculture Guidance and Guarantee Fund
EC	European Community
EEA	European Environment Agency
EIA	Environmental Impact Assessment
EIB	European Investment Bank
EIONET	European Environment Information and Observation Network
EIS	Environmental Impact Statement
EPA	Environmental Protection Agency
ERDF	European Regional Development Fund
ESF	European Social Fund
ETC/NC	European Topic Centre on Nature Conservation

EU	European Union
FAIR	Fisheries, Agriculture and Agro-industry Programme
FIFG	Financial Instrument for Fisheries Guidance
GDP	Gross Domestic Product
GNP	Gross National Product
ILM	International Legal Materials
ILRM	Irish Law Reports Monthly
ILTR	Irish Law Times Reports
IR	Irish Reports
NGO	Non-Governmental Organisation
NHA	proposed National Heritage Area
NPWS	National Parks and Wildlife Service
OJ	Official Journal of the European Communities
OPW	Office of Public Works
REPS	Rural Environment Protection Scheme
RSPB	Royal Society for the Protection of Birds
SAC	Special Area of Conservation
SCI	Site of Community Importance
SPA	Special Protection Area
SPD	Single Programming Document
UNCED	United Nations Conference on Environment and Development
US	United States Reports
WLR	Weekly Law Reports
WWF	Worldwide Fund for Nature

ERRATA

On page 75, footnote, 78 should read "but the constitutional rights to private property and to earn a livelihood were NOT at issue in that case.

On page 141, Section 5.2.1 (I) what might be termed exempted development should read what might be termed UN exempted development

Page 118, last line ".... licenses, consents and other authorisations ..." should read Planning permissions

Chapter 1

The European Dimension

Habitat Protection in the Context of European Community Law

1.1 Introduction

On 21 May 1992, the Council of Ministers of the European Community adopted Directive 92/43/EEC on the conservation of natural habitats and of wild fauna and flora, hereinafter referred to as "the Habitats Directive" or "the Directive" where convenient.[1] The object of the Directive is "to contribute towards ensuring biodiversity through the conservation of natural habitats of wild fauna and flora" in the European territory of the European Community.[2] Measures taken pursuant to the Directive must be designed to "maintain or restore, at a favourable conservation status, natural habitats and species of wild fauna and flora of Community interest."[3] The Directive provides for the creation of protected sites known as Special Areas of Conservation (hereinafter referred to as "SACs" where convenient) for certain natural habitat types and certain species of flora and fauna. It also contains provisions for the protection of specific species of wild flora and fauna. The implementation of the Directive is overseen by the European Commission's Directorate-General for the Environment, Nuclear Safety and Civil Protection (DG XI). The Directive is implemented into Irish law by the European Communities (Natural Habitats)

---

[1] Council Directive 92/43/EEC of 21 May 1992 on the conservation of natural habitats and wild fauna and flora, OJ L206/7, 22 July 1992 amended by Council Directive 97/62/EC, OJ L305/42, 8 November 1997.
[2] Habitats Directive, Article 2.
[3] *Ibid.*

Regulations, 1997, as amended,[4] hereinafter referred to as "the Habitats Regulations", "the Irish Regulations" or simply "the Regulations" where convenient.

The Habitats Directive builds upon the Community's existing role in nature conservation under Directive 79/409/EEC on the conservation of wild birds, hereinafter referred to as "the Birds Directive" where convenient.[5] This directive was the Community's first major involvement in legislating on nature conservation. The Birds Directive established a comprehensive scheme of protection for the Community's wild bird species and, in particular, for the conservation of the most important bird habitats through the designation of a network of protected sites known as Special Protection Areas, hereinafter referred to as "SPAs" where convenient. In addition, it introduced a system of controls on hunting and other forms of exploitation. The strong protection afforded to SPAs by the Birds Directive was reduced by an amendment to the Birds Directive introduced by the Habitats Directive.[6] The Birds Directive is implemented into Irish law mainly by the Wildlife Act, 1976 and the European Communities (Conservation of Wild Birds) Regulations, 1985 as amended,[7] hereinafter referred to as "the Birds Regulations" where convenient.

Together, SACs designated under the Habitats Directive and SPAs designated under the Birds Directive will constitute a coherent European ecological network of sites known as *Natura 2000*.[8] The Birds Directive and the Habitats Directive represent the

---

[4] European Communities (Natural Habitats) Regulations, 1997, SI No. 94 of 1997 amended by the European Communities (Natural Habitats) (Amendment) Regulations, 1998, SI No. 233 of 1998.
[5] Council Directive 79/409/EEC of 2 April 1979 on the conservation of wild birds, OJ L103/1, 25 April 1979 amended by Council Directive 81/854/EEC, OJ L319/3, 7 November 1981, Commission Directive 85/411/EEC, OJ L233/33, 30 August 1985, Council Directive 86/122/EEC, OJ L100/22, 16 April 1986, Council Directive 90/656/EEC, OJ L353/59, 17 December 1990, Commission Directive 91/244/EEC, OJ L115/41, 8 May 1991, Council Directive 92/43/EEC, OJ L206/7, 22 July 1992, Council Directive 94/24/EEC, OJ L164/9, 30 June 1994 and Commission Directive 97/49/EC, OJ L223/9, 13 August 1997.
[6] See section 4.1.4.
[7] European Communities (Conservation of Wild Birds) Regulations, 1985, SI No. 291 of 1984 as amended by SI Nos. 48 of 1986; 59 and 349 of 1994; 31, 284, 285, 286 and 287 of 1995; 269, 298 and 305 of 1996; 210 of 1997 and 154 of 1998.
[8] Habitats Directive, Article 3.

two most significant pieces of nature conservation legislation adopted by the European Community to date. The process of designating SPAs under the Birds Directive has operated in parallel with the process of selecting proposed SACs under the Habitats Directive. The latest phase of SPA designations should have been completed in 1998. The programme of SAC designations is not due to be completed until 5 June 2004. This is due to the fact that, while SPAs are designated by the Member States acting alone, the designation of SACs involves a substantially more complex Community procedure. Each Member State must propose a national list of sites and transmit it to the European Commission. In Ireland, the national list is referred to as the "candidate list of European sites."[9] The Commission then adopts a list of sites of Community importance (hereinafter referred to as "SCIs" where convenient) which, for the most part, are selected from amongst the sites on the national lists submitted by the Member States.[10] The most significant controls on land use come into operation at this point. Finally, each Member State must designate all SCIs as SACs before 5 June 2004. Certain natural habitats types and certain species of flora and fauna which are in danger of disappearance, or for which the Community has a particular responsibility, are classified as priority natural habitats types and priority species respectively and are subject to a higher level of protection.

The Habitats Directive is perhaps the European Community's most ambitious undertaking in relation to the environment and is a strong indication of the extent to which environmental policy has emerged as a discrete policy area within the Community. The primary focus of this book is the Habitats Directive and its implementation in Ireland by the European Communities (Natural Habitats) Regulations, 1997. Reference will be made to the provisions of the Birds Directive and to provisions of Irish environmental legislation only where this is of relevance to the primary discussion. In this chapter, it is proposed, first, to outline the framework of EC environmental law and policy within which the Habitats Directive was adopted, secondly, to examine some of the guiding principles underlying the Directive, thirdly, to examine the main mechanisms for enforcement of European Community law

---

[9] Habitats Regulations, Regulation 3(1).
[10] Habitats Directive, Article 4(2).

which have been, and may be, used in the enforcement of the Directive and, finally, to examine briefly the source of the Directive's force in Irish law from both the EC law perspective and the Irish law perspective.

1.2 The Emergence of EC Environmental Law and Policy

1.2.1 The Treaty of Rome

The original Treaty of Rome of 1957 contained no reference to the environment. However, by the 1970s it became clear that the Community should adopt a policy on the environment.[11] Community policy on the environment began to develop for two reasons: first, an acceptance of the interrelationship between economic growth and environmental degradation and, secondly, the emergence of the environment as a significant political issue.

European Community environmental policy dates from the Paris Declaration issued by the Heads of State of the Member States in October 1972.[12] The Declaration stated:

> Economic expansion is not an end in itself. Its first aim should be to enable disparities in living conditions to be reduced. It must take place with the participation of all the social partners. It should result in an improvement in the quality of life as well as in standards of living. As befits the genus of Europe, particular attention will be given to intangible values and to protecting the environment, so that progress may really be put to the service of mankind.

The Declaration requested that a Community environmental policy be drawn up by the European Commission. The Commission's

---

[11] See Jans, *European Environmental Law* (Kluwer Law International, 1995), at 1; Bell and Ball, *Environmental Law*, (4th ed., Blackstone Press, 1997), at 73; Kramer, *Focus on European Environmental Law*, (2nd ed., Sweet and Maxwell, 1997), at 113 and 319; Turner, *Northern Ireland Environmental Law* (Gill and MacMillan, 1997), at 32.
[12] Bull. EC 10-1972.

response, the *First Community Action Programme on the Environment*,[13] was adopted in 1973.

Since then, EC environmental law has developed in two phases: before and after the Single European Act of 1986. Before the ratification of the Single European Act, the legal basis of Community environmental law was not entirely clear. All EC legislation must have a legal basis in the Treaty of Rome. Two articles of the Treaty of Rome were relied upon. These were Article 100 (will be renumbered as Article 94 upon the entry into force of the Treaty of Amsterdam),[14] relating to the harmonisation of national laws in order to further the establishment of the common market, and Article 235 (renumbered Article 308) which gives the Community residual powers to adopt measures in order to achieve one of the objectives of the Community for which there are no specific powers in the Treaty.[15] These articles did not provide a solid legal basis for environmental directives. Environmental directives imposing common standards which affected the establishment or functioning of the common market tended to be justified on the basis of Article 100. In *Commission v. Italy* (Case 91/79)[16] the European Court of Justice explained:

> Provisions which are necessary by considerations relating to the environment and health may be a burden on the undertakings to which they apply, and if there is no harmonisation of national provisions on the matter, competition may be appreciably distorted.

On the other hand, directives of purely environmental content, such as the Birds Directive, were justified on the basis of Article 235. In

---

[13] OJ C112/1, 20 December 1973.

[14] Where an article of the Treaty of Rome or the Treaty on European Union is first mentioned, its number following the entry into force of the Treaty of Amsterdam is also given since the Treaty of Amsterdam is likely to come into force some time in 1999.

[15] Article 235 provides: "If action by the Community should prove necessary to attain, in the course of the common market, one of the objectives of the Community and this Treaty has not provided the necessary powers, the Council shall, acting unanimously on a proposal from the Commission and after consulting the European Parliament, take the appropriate measures."

[16] [1980] ECR 1099.

ADBHU (Case 240/83)[17] the European Court of Justice declared that environmental protection is "one of the Community's essential objectives", thereby implicitly endorsing the use of Article 235 as a basis for environmental legislation.[18] In many instances both Article 100 and Article 235 were cited as legal justification for environmental directives.

1.2.2 The Single European Act

The Single European Act, which entered into force on 1 July 1987, added a new Environmental Title (Title XVI: Article 130r (renumbered Article 174), Article 130s (renumbered Article 175) and Article 130t (renumbered Article 176)) to the Treaty of Rome. These articles introduced a specific basis for Community law-making in relation to the environment, thereby regularising the *de facto* situation. The Treaty on European Union (the Maastricht Treaty), which entered into force on 1 November 1993, amended Title XVI and considerably strengthened the basis for EC action on the environment. Article 2 of the Treaty of Rome, as amended by the Treaty on European Union, sets out the objectives of the Community including the task of promoting "sustainable and non-inflationary growth respecting the environment" throughout Community. Article 3, as amended by the Maastricht Treaty, recognises for the first time that the development of "a policy in the sphere of the environment" is one of the EC's main activities. These provisions give environmental policy a position of central importance within the Community and reflect the EC's increasing commitment to policy sectors beyond those of purely economic concern. The Treaty of Amsterdam, signed on 2 October 1997, will introduce further changes to the Treaty of Rome when in force.[19]

Article 130s of the Treaty of Rome, as amended by the Treaty on European Union, provides for the adoption by the Council of Ministers of environmental action programmes and for the implementation of measures to achieve the objectives set out in these programmes. To date the Commission has adopted five *Action*

---

[17] [1985] ECR 531.
[18] [1985] ECR 538. See also *Commission v. Denmark* (Case 302/86) [1988] ECR 4607 and *Commission v. Belgium* (Case 2/90) [1992] ECR I-4431; [1993] 1 CMLR 365.
[19] See section 1.4.1.

Programmes on the Environment: 1973-1976,[20] 1977-1981,[21] 1982-1986,[22] 1987-1992[23] and 1993-2000.[24] These *Action Programmes* set out the Commission's proposals for the adoption of specific pieces of environmental legislation and its views on the future direction of EC environmental policy. They are not legally binding documents. The Habitats Directive was adopted pursuant to the *Fourth Action Programme*.[25]

EC policy on the environment underwent a major shift in focus with the adoption, in September 1992, of the *Fifth Action Programme, Towards Sustainability*.[26] This Action Programme sets the themes for EC action in relation to the environment in the run-up to the millennium and attempts to set out a new approach which reconciles economic development and environmental protection. Instead of addressing specific environmental media, this *Action Programme* identifies five principal "target sectors" of the economy which have a particular impact on the environment: manufacturing industry, energy, transport, agriculture and tourism. It identifies a list of extremely serious environmental problems which have a Community dimension either because of the effects they have on the operation of the single market, cross-border relations or the sharing of resources, or because every Member State has to cope with them. These problems include the impoverishment of biological diversity.

---

[20] *Supra*, fn 13.
[21] OJ C139/1, 13 June 1977.
[22] OJ C46/1, 17 February 1983.
[23] OJ C328/1, 7 December 1987.
[24] OJ C138/1, 17 May 1993.
[25] See Habitats Directive, Second Recital to the Preamble. This Programme raised environmental policy to a position of central importance in the Community and envisaged the adoption of measures aimed at the conservation of nature and natural resources.
[26] *Supra*, fn 24.

1.3 The Legal Basis of *Natura 2000*

1.3.1 The Birds Directive

As discussed in the preceding section, the Birds Directive was adopted solely pursuant to Article 235 of the Treaty of Rome.[27] In *Commission v. Belgium* (Case 247/85)[28] the European Court of Justice endorsed the necessity for the Birds Directive on the basis of the principles set out in the third recital to the directive's preamble, namely that bird species constitute a "common heritage" and that their protection is a "trans-frontier environment problem entailing common responsibilities." However, as Wils points out, the Court has never explicitly been asked to rule on the validity of the Birds Directive's legal basis.[29] Due to Danish objections to the use of Article 235 as the basis of conservation legislation, it was accepted after the Birds Directive that no further legislation would be passed on wildlife unless it related to trade, for which Article 100 could be invoked. This lacuna was removed by the Single European Act of 1986 but it was another six years until the type of protection afforded to wild birds was extended to flora and fauna other than birds.

1.3.2 The Habitats Directive

The Habitats Directive was adopted unanimously[30] by the Council of Ministers on the basis of Article 130 of the Treaty of Rome. Article 130r contains several objectives, principles and policies. Article 130s permits the Council of Ministers to take action to achieve any objective referred to in Article 130r(1). The environmental objectives in Article 130r(1) include "preserving, protecting and improving the quality of the environment." The Treaty contains no definition of "the environment." However, it is

---

[27] The Birds Directive is one of few directives not adopted pursuant to both Article 235 and Article 100.
[28] [1987] ECR 3029.
[29] Wils, "The Birds Directive, 15 Years Later: A Survey of the Case Law and a Comparison with the Habitats Directive", (1994) 6 *Journal of Environmental Law*, 219, at 223.
[30] As required at that time. At present, Article 130s of the Treaty of Rome, as amended by the Treaty on European Union, provides that environmental legislation may, in general, be adopted by qualified majority in the Council of Ministers according to a procedure set out in Article 189c of the Treaty of Rome (renumbered Article 252).

considered likely that this broad objective includes the protection of habitats and species.[31] The principles in Article 130r(2) should be taken into account when framing policy and legislation. The principle that Community policy on the environment should aim at a high level of protection was introduced by the Treaty on European Union. It is unclear at this time whether the Habitats Directive complies with this guiding principle. However, as noted by Jans, it seems hardly conceivable that a court would accept the argument that a Community measure is invalid on the basis that it does not achieve a high level of protection.[32]

In the next section, we shall discuss some of the principles underpinning the philosophy of the Habitats Directive. When adopted in 1992, the Directive was a sign of things to come in two important respects. First, the third recital to the preamble to the Habitats Directive states that it was adopted as a contribution to the general objective of sustainable development. Secondly, a year after the Habitats Directive was adopted, the Treaty on European Union introduced the precautionary principle into Article 130r.

1.4 Some Guiding Principles of European Environmental Law and Policy

1.4.1 Sustainable Development

The Treaty on European Union introduced the principle of sustainable growth to the Treaty of Rome.[33] The Community's *Fifth Action Programme on the Environment* established "sustainable development" as an objective of Community environmental policy.[34] The Programme states that the policy of sustainable development entails:

> an appreciation that natural resources are finite and that one individual's consumption or use of these resources must not be at the expense of another's; and that neither should one

---

[31] Jans, *op. cit.*, at 14.
[32] Jans, *op. cit.*, at 19.
[33] Article 2.
[34] *Supra*, fn 24.

generation's consumption be at the expense of those following.[35]

Sustainable development has been defined elsewhere as:

[D]evelopment that meets the needs of the present without compromising the ability of future generations to meet their own needs. The use of sustainable development principles is justified in order to achieve or maintain a healthy environment and a healthy economy.[36]

When the Treaty of Amsterdam enters into force, Article 2 of the Treaty of Rome will provide that:

The Community shall have as its task ... to promote throughout the Community a harmonious, balanced and sustainable development of economic activities ....[37]

The Habitats Directive has the potential to contribute significantly to sustainable land management and sustainable development as envisaged in the amended Treaty of Rome. The intention of the Directive is not to prohibit economic activities in, or in the vicinity of, SCIs, SPAs or SACs, but to ensure that such activities are compatible with the maintenance of each site at a favourable conservation status. Indeed, the third recital to the Preamble states that the maintenance of bio-diversity may, in certain circumstances, "require the maintenance, or indeed the *encouragement,* of human activities."[38] This is consistent with the view of the EC's *General Consultative Forum on the Environment,*[39] which has stated that

---

[35] *Ibid.,* chapter 2, at para. 2. The Department of the Environment has published a national sustainable development strategy, *Sustainable Development: A Strategy for Ireland* (Government Publications Office, 1997).

[36] *Report of the World Commission on Environment and Development (Brundtland,* 1987).

[37] Similarly, Article B (renumbered Article 2) of the Treaty on European Union will provide: "The Union shall set itself the following objectives: to promote economic and social progress and ... to achieve balanced and sustainable development .... "

[38] Emphasis added.

[39] Created by Commission Decision 93/701/EEC of 7 December 1993, OJ L328/53, 29 December 1993, later replaced by Commission Decision 97/150/EC

economic and social development and environmental protection are interdependent and should not be considered in isolation from each other.[40] It remains to be seen to what extent development will be permitted within *Natura 2000* sites.

The *Fifth Action Programme* states that two major guiding principles underpin the implementation of sustainable development throughout the Community. These are, first, the integration of environmental provisions into all major policy areas of the Community and, secondly, the replacement of the command and control approach with the principle of shared responsibility between the various actors.

(a) Integration of Environmental Provisions into Other Community Policies

The *Fourth Action Programme on the Environment*, under which the Habitats Directive was adopted, repeated the principle that potential effects on the environment should be taken into account at the earliest possible stage in the decision-making process and stressed the need to integrate environmental protection into other EC policies. The Treaty on European Union incorporated into Article 130r(2) of the Treaty of Rome the legal obligation that "environmental protection requirements must be integrated into the definition and implementation of other Community policies."[41] The Treaty of Amsterdam will delete this provision and insert a new Article 3c (renumbered Article 6) into the Treaty of Rome. This provision will read:

---

of 24 February 1997 on the setting up of an European consultative forum on the environment and sustainable development, OJ L58/48, 27 February 1997.

[40] *Principles of Sustainable Development* (1995).

[41] In June 1993, the Commission approved a series of measures intended to ensure the integration of environmental considerations into its proposals regarding other areas of EC policy making. The *Commission Work Programme* indicates proposals likely to have an environmental impact and annual reports on progress in integrating environmental considerations into other policies have been made. Sustainable development now forms a significant part of the Community's *Fourth Research Framework Programme* which operates in, *inter alia*, the field of research in agriculture and the environment. In its vision of the Community as it approaches the millennium, *Agenda 2000* (COM(97) 2000 final), the Commission proposed a continuation and consolidation of the Community's strategy of integrating environmental and agricultural concerns.

> Environmental protection requirements must be integrated into the definition and implementation of the Community policies and activities referred to in Article 3, in particular with a view to promoting sustainable development.[42]

This requirement would appear to be met by the Habitats Directive which requires the adoption of appropriate statutory, administrative and contractual measures and, if need be, management plans or appropriate provisions in development plans to ensure that the potential effects of projects on SACs are taken into account in the initial decision-making process by regulatory authorities.[43] The Birds Directive does not contain a provision of this nature.

The Habitats Directive requires an appropriate assessment of *any* plan or project likely to have a significant effect on the conservation objectives of an SCI[44] or an SAC.[45] This provision also applies in relation to SPAs due to the amendment of the Birds Directive by the Habitats Directive.[46] It is envisaged that an Environmental Impact Assessment will constitute an appropriate assessment in many instances.[47] It would appear that, if a given objective could be adequately achieved in a variety of ways, the integration principle requires a choice of the least environmentally harmful. It is uncertain whether the legitimacy of actions of the Commission or Council can be reviewed by the Court of Justice in light of the integration principle. Jans notes that the present formulation of the principle, that environmental protection

---

[42] Treaty of Amsterdam, Article 2(4).
[43] Article 6(1).
[44] Article 4(5).
[45] Article 6(3). The principle that the exploitation of nature or of natural resources causing significant damage to the ecological balance must be avoided can be traced back to the *First Action Programme on the Environment, supra,* fn 13.
[46] Birds Directive, Article 4(4) as amended by Habitats Directive, Article 7.
[47] Council Directive 85/337/EEC of 25 June 1985 on the assessment of the effects of certain public and private projects on the environment, OJ L175/40, 5 July 1985 amended by Council Directive 97/11/EC, OJ L73/5, 14 March 1997. See section 4.2.5.

requirements "*must* be integrated"[48] into other policies, would seem to indicate that judicial review could be possible.[49]

The *Fifth Action Programme* envisaged the extension of the range of instruments used in Community environmental law and policy. However, despite the fact that the Habitats Directive was adopted little more than a year before the *Fifth Action Programme* and the fact that the Programme identifies the protection of nature and bio-diversity as one of its key themes, the Directive makes no provision for, nor reference to, the use of alternative mechanisms for environmental protection. This is regrettable in light of the fact that the Directive will not be fully effective until 2004 and that it presented a unique opportunity for the use of alternative mechanisms, for example, the levy of an environmental tax on developments permitted to establish within SACs for imperative reasons of overriding public interest or the creation of incentives to encourage conservation easements or the dedication of lands to habitat use.[50]

(b) Subsidiarity and Shared Responsibility

The Treaty on European Union established the concept of subsidiarity as a principle of central importance and general application. Article A of the Treaty on European Union (renumbered Article 1) refers to the process of creating an ever-closer union among the peoples of Europe, in which decisions are taken as closely as possible to the citizen. Article 3b of the Treaty of Rome (renumbered Article 5), as inserted by the Treaty on European Union, elaborates on what this entails:

> [T]he Community shall take action in accordance with the principle of subsidiarity, only if and in so far as the objectives of the proposed action cannot be sufficiently

---

[48] Emphasis added.
[49] Jans, *op. cit.*, at 29. The author argues at 26 that the integration principle must respect the principle of proportionality and must not entail restrictions on other policies which go beyond what is strictly necessary for the protection of the environment.
[50] The *Progress Report on the Implementation of the Fifth Community Action Programme on the Environment* (COM(95) 624 final, 10 January 1996) highlighted the lack of progress in introducing market-based instruments to change environmentally damaging behaviour.

achieved by the Member States and can therefore, by reason of the scale or effects of the proposed action, be better achieved by the Community.[51]

The *Fifth Action Programme* states that the principle of subsidiarity must be considered in the context of the broader and more informal principle of *shared responsibility* since the objective of sustainable development can only be achieved by concerted action on the part of all the relevant actors working together in partnership.[52] Shared responsibility involves a mixing of actors and instruments at the appropriate levels, without calling into question the division of competencies between the Community, the Member States and regional and local authorities. The success of this approach depends on the creation and maintenance of effective dialogue between the various actors.

The Birds Directive required Member States themselves to select and designate the most suitable sites as SPAs. Despite the fact that the Member States' discretion in selecting sites for designation as SPAs is limited to designating the most suitable areas, Member States have sometimes failed to comply with this obligation.[53] The Habitats Directive, in building upon this experience, introduced the procedure whereby Member States propose sites which may, in turn, be adopted as SCIs by the Commission, and later be designated as SACs by the Member State to form part of *Natura 2000*.[54] This procedure would appear to be consistent with the principle of subsidiarity and, in particular, with the principle of shared responsibility.[55] Article 2(3) of the Habitats Directive requires that account be taken of economic, social and cultural requirements and regional and local characteristics when measures are taken pursuant to the Directive. In short, it would appear that the Commission should exercise restraint and that each Member State

---

[51] See also Treaty of Amsterdam, Protocol on Subsidiarity.
[52] OJ C138/1, 17 May 1993, chapter 8, at para. 2.
[53] See section 3.4.4.
[54] See section 3.9.5.
[55] In addition, the consultation procedure between the Member State and the Commission provided for in Article 5 of the Habitats Directive is a particularly important instance of the practical significance of these principles. See section 3.8.

should participate meaningfully in the implementation of the Habitats Directive.

1.4.2 The Precautionary Principle

Article 130r(2) of the Treaty of Rome, as amended by the Treaty on European Union, provides that Community policy on the environment "shall be based on the precautionary principle." The *Fifth Action Programme* acknowledges the central role of this principle.[56] The principle allows consideration of scientifically based pessimistic predictions thereby allowing measures to be taken even before a causal link has been established between pollution and environmental harm.[57] Principle 15 of the *Rio Declaration on Environment and Development*[58] explains the principle as follows:

> The precautionary approach shall be widely applied by States according to their capabilities. Where there are threats of serious or irreversible damage, lack of full scientific certainty shall not be used as a reason for postponing cost-effective measures to prevent environmental degradation.

The Habitats Directive, in line with the precautionary principle, focuses not only on habitat types which are in danger of disappearance but also on habitat types which have a small natural range and habitat types which present outstanding examples of the typical characteristics of one or more of the six biogeographical regions of the Community.[59] It also focuses not merely on species

---

[56] OJ C138/1, 17 May 1993, chapter 2, at para. 4. See also *Commission v. Belgium* (Case 2/90) [1992] ECR I-4431; [1993] 1 CMLR 365.

[57] The principle is probably justiciable. See Doyle and Carney, "MMDS Technology and the Environment: A Legal Framework", (1998) 14 *Irish Law Times*, 213, at 217. See also *Commission v. Belgium* (Case 2/90), *supra*, fn 56 and *Commission v. Germany* (Case 422/92) [1995] ECR I-1097; [1996] 1 CMLR 383 in which the Court of Justice applied the principle that environmental damage should as a priority be rectified at source as the basis of its decision. This principle, like the precautionary principle, appears in Article 130r(2) of the Treaty of Rome. *Cf.* Hession and Macrory, "Maastricht and the Environmental Policy of the Community: Legal Issues of a New Environment Policy", in O'Keele and Twomey (eds), *Legal Issues of the Maastricht Treaty* (Wiley Chancery, 1994), 151, at 156.

[58] (1992) 31 ILM 874.

[59] Article 1(c). See section 3.2.1.

which are currectly endangered but species which are "vulnerable", i.e. believed likely to become endangered in the future if existing factors persist.[60] The Directive also protects endemic species in need of particular attention by reason of the *potential* impact of the exploitation of their habitat on their conservation status.[61] In this respect, the Habitats Directive is supplemented by the *European Community Biodiversity Strategy*, administered by DGXI, which aims to anticipate, prevent and attack the causes of significant reduction or loss of biodiversity within the European Union at source.[62] The precautionary principle is likely to allow for a much more proactive approach to EC environmental law in general, and conservation law in particular, as well as to the overall objective of achieving sustainable development. In this regard, the EC's *General Consultative Forum on the Environment* has stated that the precautionary principle is consistent with a policy of sustainable development because, where there is a threat of serious or irreversible damage, lack of full scientific certainty should not be used as a reason for postponing precautionary measures which have merit in their own right.

1.5 International Conventions

The Habitats Directive reflects wider efforts at international level to safeguard the natural heritage and bio-diversity. It will operate alongside regulations applying the Convention on International Trade in Endangered Species of Wild Fauna and Flora (CITES) within the Community.[63] The Directive implements into EC law the Bonn Convention on the Conservation of Migratory Species of Wild

---

[60] Article 1.
[61] See section 3.2.4.
[62] COM(98) 42 final, 4 February 1998.
[63] Council Regulation 338/97/EC of 9 December 1996 on the protection of species of wild fauna and flora by regulating trade therein, OJ L61/1, 3 March 1997 amended by Commission Regulation 938/97/EEC, OJ L140/1, 30 May 1997, Commission Regulation 2307/97/EC, OJ L325/1, 27 November 1997 and Commission Regulation 767/98/EC, OJ L109/7, 8 April 1998. The Community however is not a party to the Convention. An amendment to the Convention allowing Community accession was adopted in 1983. As yet, this amendment has not received sufficient ratifications to enter into force.

Animals of 1979 to which the Community is a party.[64] The Community is also a party to the Berne Convention on the Conservation of European Wildlife and Natural Habitats of 1979, a Council of Europe Convention, which aims to safeguard endangered habitats and species throughout Europe.[65] The Habitats Directive and the Birds Directive implement this Convention in the Community and *Natura 2000* constitutes the Community's contribution to the EMERALD Network of Areas of Special Conservation Interest established under the Convention.[66]

The Habitats Directive was partly adopted to give force in EC law to provisions of the Ramsar Convention on Wetlands of International Importance of 1971, to which the EC is not a party but to which Member States are recommended to adhere by the Commission.[67] The Directive was adopted in the year in which the United Nations Conference on Environment and Development (UNCED) was held in Rio de Janeiro, Brazil.[68] The adoption of the directive also coincided with the accession by the European Community to the Convention on Biological Diversity of 1992 signed at the Rio conference.[69] The Directive constitutes the

---

[64] For an account of the Community's perspective on the Bonn Convention, see Council Decision 82/461/EEC of 24 June 1982 on the conclusion of the Convention on the conservation of migratory species of wild animals, OJ L210/11, 19 July 1982.

[65] For an account of the Community's perspective on the Berne Convention, see Council Decision 82/72/EEC of 3 December 1981 concerning the conclusion of the Convention on the conservation on European wildlife and natural habitats, OJ L38/1, 10 February 1982.

[66] See Recommendation 16 (1989) and Resolution 3 (1996) of the Standing Committee of the Berne Convention. Individual Member States are free to designate further EMERALD sites.

[67] See Commission Recommendation 75/66/EEC of 20 December 1974 to Member States concerning the protection of birds and their habitats, OJ L21/24, 28 January 1975. The protection of wetlands of international importance is a priority under the Birds Directive (Article 4(2)) while active raised bogs and blanket bogs are priority habitats under the Habitats Directive.

[68] The Community's *Fifth Action Programme on the Environment* adopted many of the principles endorsed by the main result of the Conference, *Agenda 21*. See section 1.4.

[69] Entered into force on 29 December 1993.

Community's main mechanism for the implementation of this Convention.[70]

1.6 Remedies for Non-Transposition and Non-Compliance with the Habitats Directive

1.6.1 Information Gathering

The Habitats Directive is binding on each Member State.[71] Member State transposition of the Directive and compliance with its provisions have been, and are likely to continue for some time to be, the subject of enforcement proceedings by the European Commission. The Community has established a number of mechanisms to ensure the efficient compilation of compatible and comparable data which can be used in the enforcement of the Directive.

Article 130r(3) of the Treaty of Rome states that the Community shall take account of available scientific and technical data in preparing its policy on the environment. In order to ensure the availability and reliability of information on the environment the Council of Ministers established the European Environment Agency (EEA).[72] The EEA has the task of recording, collating and assessing environmental data and providing the Community and Member States with "objective, reliable and comparable information at European level"[73] enabling them to take the requisite measures to protect the environment and to assess the results of such measures. It also has the task of providing uniform assessment criteria for the environment to be applied to all Member States, thereby providing the Commission with information which can be used to ensure the implementation of Community legislation on the environment.[74]

---

[70] See Council Decision 93/626/EEC of 25 October 1993 concerning the conclusion of the Convention on Biological Diversity, OJ L309/1, 13 December 1993.
[71] Treaty of Rome, Article 189 (renumbered Article 249).
[72] Council Regulation 1210/90/EEC of 7 May 1990 on the establishment of the European Environment Agency and the European Environment Information and Observation Network, OJ L120/1, 11 May 1990. The Agency opened to the public in 1994.
[73] *Ibid.*, Article 1.
[74] *Ibid.*, Article 2(iii).

One of the EEA's tasks is the establishment and co-ordination of the European Environment Information and Observation Network (EIONET). EIONET is comprised of, *inter alia*, a number of Topic Centres. The European Topic Centre on Nature Conservation (ETC/NC) was appointed in 1994 to carry out specific tasks including the updating of the Community's nature databases and the provision of technical support to the Commission in handling incoming data from the Member States on sites proposed for the *Natura 2000* network.[75] In this regard, the ETC/NC is required to continue the CORINE programme (Co-ordination of Information on the Environment) which focused on the collation of information in relation to, *inter alia*, biotypes in need of conservation. CORINE formed the basis of the classifications used in the original Annexes to the Habitats Directive.[76] It is envisaged that the ETC/NC will eventually develop a new database, EUNIS (European Nature Information System), for use in the *Natura 2000* process.

Article 5 of the Treaty of Rome (renumbered Article 10) requires Member States to notify the Commission of national provisions adopted in transposition of a Community directive.[77] Article 23 of the Habitats Directive requires each Member State to inform the Commission of laws, regulations and administrative provisions implemented to comply with the Directive. A similar obligation exists under the Birds Directive.[78] Regulation 37 of the Irish Regulations requires the Minister for Arts, Heritage, the Gaeltacht and the Islands to prepare a report every six years on the implementation of measures taken pursuant to the Habitats Directive.[79] Article 17(1) of the Directive requires the State to forward this report to the Commission. The report must include information concerning the conservation measures which the State has taken in relation to SACs under Article 6(1) of the Directive and

---

[75] *Ibid.*, Article 3(2) provides that the EEA shall give priority to, *inter alia*, work relating to the state of flora and fauna and biotopes.
[76] See section 3.2.2.
[77] Article 5 provides that "Member States shall take all appropriate measures, whether general or particular, to ensure fulfilment of the obligations arising out of this Treaty or resulting from action taken by the institutions of the Community. They shall facilitate the achievement of the Community's tasks."
[78] Birds Directive, Article 18.
[79] See Habitats Directive, Article 17(1).

must provide an evaluation of the impact which measures undertaken have had on the conservation status of the species and natural habitat types listed in the Annexes to the Directive.[80] The results of surveillance undertaken pursuant to Regulation 7 of the Habitats Regulations must be included in the report.[81] The State must make the report accessible to the public.[82] The Commission is required to produce a composite report based on the various national reports. This report must include an evaluation of progress achieved and, in particular, an evaluation of the contribution of *Natura 2000* to the achievement of the objectives of the Directive.[83] Under the Birds Directive, Member States are required to forward a report on the implementation of national provisions under that directive to the Commission every three years.[84] Again, the Commission is required to prepare a composite report.[85]

Regulation 25(2) requires the Minister to forward to the Commission every two years a report on any derogations she may have licensed from the prohibitions contained in Regulations 23 and 24 and section 21 of the Wildlife Act, 1976 on the capture, killing or disturbance of species of flora and fauna set out in the First Schedule to the Habitats Regulations.[86] The Birds Directive requires each Member State to send a report to the Commission each year on any derogations it has invoked from a similar system of protection established by that directive in relation to all species of naturally occurring birds.[87]

In December 1996, the Commission issued a Decision setting out the format in which site information for proposed *Natura 2000* sites is to be supplied by the Member States in submitting their

---

[80] Habitats Regulations, Regulation 37(2); Habitats Directive, Article 17(1).
[81] Habitats Directive, Article 11. See section 3.4.3.
[82] Article 17(1). The Habitats Regulations omit to transpose this obligation, but it is submitted that the provision satisfies the test for direct effects and is binding on the State. See section 1.7.4. In any case, reports would usually be available under the Freedom of Information Act, 1997 or the European Communities Act, 1972 (Access to Information on the Environment) Regulations, 1998, SI No. 125 of 1998.
[83] Article 17(2).
[84] Birds Directive, Article 12(1).
[85] *Ibid.*, Article 12(2).
[86] Habitats Directive, Article 16. See section 6.5.4.
[87] Birds Directive, Article 9(3).

national lists.[88] This Decision will increase the Commission's ability to identify non-compliance. It is clear that the Commission has a right to a wide range of information relating to actions of the Member States in connection with the Directive. The following is a brief outline of the main mechanisms available at European and national level for the enforcement of the Habitats Directive. Specialist texts should be consulted for further information.[89]

1.6.2 Enforcement in the European Court of Justice

Given that *Natura 2000* is the EC's flagship contribution to the protection of global bio-diversity, the European Commission is especially determined to ensure full, effective and timely implementation of the Habitats Directive by the Member States. If a Member State fails to implement the Directive properly by the deadline for transposition, or maintains in force a law which conflicts with the Directive, the Commission can take enforcement proceedings in the European Court of Justice pursuant to Article 169 of the Treaty of Rome (renumbered Article 226) seeking a declaration that the Member State has contravened a provision of Community law. These formal proceedings are normally preceded by informal notification of the alleged breach to the Member State and by non-contentious negotiations with the Member State as to how the situation can be resolved. If the Commission is not satisfied with the Member State's response it can deliver a letter of formal notice to the State. Having given the State an opportunity to submit its observations on the matter, the Commission may invoke the formal procedures in Article 169 and deliver a Reasoned Opinion to the State, setting out the main features of the alleged non-compliance and giving a minimum of two months to the State to

---

[88] Commission Decision 97/266/EC of 18 December 1996 concerning a site information format for proposed Natura 2000 sites, OJ L107/1, 24 April 1997. See section 3.4.5. Previously, the Council adopted Directive 91/692/EEC of 23 December 1991 standardising and rationalising reports on the implementation of certain directives relating to the environment, OJ L377/48, 13 December 1991. This directive harmonised the form of reports which must be submitted to the Commission periodically outlining the implementation measures adopted in relation to certain environmental directives relating to water, air and waste.

[89] Steiner and Woods, *Textbook on EC Law*, (5th ed., Blackstone Press, 1996), at 383 and 409; Wyatt and Dashwood, *European Community Law*, (3rd ed., Sweet and Maxwell, 1993), at 109 and 142; Weatherill and Beaumont, *EC Law*, (2nd ed., Penguin, 1995), at 192 and 279.

fulfil its obligations. If the State fails to comply with the Opinion, the Commission may bring the matter before the Court of Justice. The Commission's decision whether or not to initiate proceedings, or to terminate a proceeding that has already been started, is not open to review by the Court.[90] Neither individuals nor groups can compel the Commission to initiate infringement proceedings. However, the Commission has, to date, vigorously pursued failures to implement the Habitats Directive by national legislation.

Although Ireland did not transpose the Habitats Directive until 26 February 1997, which was more than two and a half years after the deadline for the transposition of the Directive (5 June 1994), the Commission did not make an application to the Court of Justice under Article 169. However, it did make applications in respect of a number of other Member States.[91] In October 1997, the Commission sent Reasoned Opinions to France, Finland, Germany, Luxembourg, the Netherlands, Denmark, Spain, Italy, the United Kingdom and Ireland for failure to send complete lists of proposed *Natura 2000* sites to the Commission. In April 1998, the Commission decided to make applications to the Court of Justice against France, Finland, Germany, Luxembourg, the Netherlands and Ireland in this regard. The Commission's enforcement of the Birds Directive has generated a body of caselaw which is useful when interpreting provisions of the Habitats Directive.[92] Enforcement actions under the Birds Directive are ongoing.[93]

If the Court of Justice gives judgment condemning a Member State for non-compliance with the Directive, the State is required to take the necessary measures to comply with the judgment.[94] Article 171 of the Treaty of Rome (renumbered Article 228), as amended

---

[90] *Commission v. Germany* (Case 422/92) [1995] ECR I-1097; [1996] 1 C.M.L.R 383.
[91] See e.g. *Commission v. Hellenic Republic* (Case 329/96) [1997] ECR I-3749 and *Commission v. Germany* (Case 83/97), European Court of Justice, 11 December 1997, not yet reported, concerning non-transposition of the Directive into Greek and German national law respectively. The Commission succeeded in both actions.
[92] See e.g. *Commission v. Germany* (Case 57/89) [1991] ECR I-883; *Commission v. Spain* (Case 355/90) [1993] ECR I-4221; *Commission v. Italy* (Case 334/89) [1991] ECR I-93. See sections 3.4.4 and 4.1.4.
[93] See e.g. *Commission v. Netherlands* (Case 3/96) European Court of Justice, 19 May 1998, not yet reported.
[94] Treaty of Rome, Article 171(1).

by the Maastricht Treaty, provides that if, having heard the submissions of the State concerned, the Commission is of the opinion that the State has failed to comply with the Court's judgment, it may issue a Reasoned Opinion specifying the points on which the State has not complied with the judgment and setting out a timescale within which the State must comply. If the State does not comply within this period, the Commission can bring the matter before the Court of Justice. The Court of Justice can impose a penalty fine on the Member State if it finds that the State has failed to comply with its judgment.[95] The level of the financial penalty will depend upon the gravity and duration of the violation. The Commission has also withheld, and threatened to withhold, Community funds from Member States which have failed to comply with the obligation to implement and adhere to EC environmental standards.[96]

A Member State can bring the matter of another Member State's non-compliance with the obligations in a directive before the Court of Justice.[97] Non-governmental organisations (NGOs) have a right, in certain circumstances, to appear before the Court of Justice to support a case which has been brought to the Court by a party empowered to do so under the Treaty if the Court decides that the NGO has a legal interest in the case.[98] Article 173 of the Treaty of Rome (renumbered Article 230) in effect provides that individuals or legal persons (which may include NGOs) can, in certain circumstances, sue in the European Court of Justice to challenge the legality of certain EC measures of direct and individual concern to them. Standing to invoke this article has been interpreted restrictively by the Court.[99] Individuals can, however, complain to the Commission, which may, as a result, decide to take enforcement action against the State under Article 169. Indeed, the Commission depends greatly on information received by this means, particularly

---

[95] Treaty of Rome, Article 171(2).
[96] See fn 145 *infra*, and section 7.3.2.
[97] Treaty of Rome, Article 170 (renumbered Article 227).
[98] Statute of the Court of Justice of the European Communities, Article 37.
[99] See *An Taisce and WWF v. Commission,* Court of First Instance (Case T-461/93) [1994] ECR II-733, European Court of Justice (Case 325/94P) [1996] ECR I-3727; *Danielsson v. Commission* (Case T-219/95) [1995] ECR II-3051; *Greenpeace v. Commission* (Case T-585/93) European Court of First Instance, 9 August 1995, not yet reported.

from NGOs. Alternatively, individuals may petition the European Parliament.[100] Petitions are reviewed by the Parliament's Committee on Petitions and acted upon if considered admissible. The main result of a petition is political pressure for reform.

Complaints concerning maladministration by a European Community institution or body, except the Court of Justice and the Court of First Instance when acting in their judicial capacities, may be made to the Ombudsman of the European Parliament by any individual or group in accordance with Article 138e of the Treaty of Rome (renumbered Article 195). The Ombudsman may raise the matter with the institution concerned and request it to give an opinion on the complaint. She will then present a report on the matter to the European Parliament and to the institution concerned. The European Parliament has power under Article 138c of the Treaty (renumbered Article 193) to set up a temporary Committee of Inquiry to investigate contraventions or maladministration in the implementation of EC law. These committees may investigate action taken by an EC institution, by a public administrative body in a Member State or by persons empowered by EC law to implement that law.

1.6.3 *Enforcement in the Irish Courts*[101]

(a) The Preliminary Ruling Procedure
Where a question arises in a court or tribunal of a Member State of the Community as to, *inter alia*, the interpretation of the Treaty of Rome or as to the validity or interpretation of acts of the institutions of the Community, including directives, that court or tribunal may, if it considers that a decision on the question is necessary to enable it to give judgment, request the European Court of Justice to give a ruling thereon pursuant to Article 177 (renumbered Article 234) of the Treaty of Rome.[102] The preliminary ruling procedure is designed

---

[100] Treaty of Rome, Article 138d (renumbered Article 194) and Rules of Procedure of the European Parliament, Rules 156-158.

[101] The enforcement provisions of the Habitats Regulations are discussed in sections 4.4.5 and 4.11.

[102] However, where the answer to the question raised could not affect the outcome of the case or if the point has already been decided by a previous decision of the Court of Justice or if the correct application of EC law is so obvious as to leave no scope for reasonable doubt as to the manner in which the

to ensure that EC law is interpreted uniformly throughout the Community. The Court of Justice has interpreted the notion of "court or tribunal" as encompassing all organs of the Member State which exercise a judicial function.[103] The issue of whether a Community act, including a directive, has direct effects is regarded by the Court of Justice as an aspect of interpretation falling within Article 177.[104] Although a reference can be made at any stage in the proceedings in the national court, the Court of Justice has stated that the facts of the case should be established and questions of purely national law settled before a reference is made.[105] The reference may be requested by one of the parties or be made by the judge of her own volition.[106] If a reference is requested by one of the parties before a court from whose decision there is no further appeal, e.g. the Supreme Court of Ireland, the court is obliged by Article 177(3) to make the application for a preliminary ruling since there is no judicial remedy under national law against its decision.

When the Court of Justice has delivered its ruling, it will refer the case back to the national court which can then decide the case with the benefit of the Court of Justice's interpretation of the relevant Community provision. The Court of Justice will not rule on the application of the law to the specific facts of the case or on the compatibility of a provision of national law with the requirements of Community law.[107] However, a ruling given by the Court of Justice under Article 177 "is binding on the national courts as to the interpretation of the Community provisions and acts in question."[108] Therefore, the national court must refuse to apply conflicting

---

question raised is to be resolved, the court or tribunal can refuse to make a reference (the *acte clair* doctrine) *CILFIT v. Ministry of Health* (Case 283/81) [1982] ECR 3415.
[103] *Vaassen v. Beambtenfonds voor het Mijnbedrijf* (Case 61/65) [1966] ECR 261; [1966] CMLR 508; *Pretore di Salo v. Persons Unknown* (Case 14/86) [1987] ECR 2545; [1989] 1 CMLR 71. *Cf: Borker* (Case 138/80) [1980] ECR 1975; [1980] 3 CMLR 638; *Nordsee v. Reederei Mond Hochseefischerei Nordstein A.G.* (Case 102/81) [1982] ECR 1095.
[104] See section 1.7.4.
[105] *Irish Creamery Milk Suppliers Association v. Ireland* (Joined Cases 36,71/80) [1981] ECR 735.
[106] *Rheinmuhlen Dusseldorf v. Einfuhr-und Vorratstelle fur Getreide und Futtermittel* (Case 166/73) [1974] ECR 33; [1974] 1 CMLR 523.
[107] *Heineken Brouwarfen* (Joined Cases 91,127/83) [1984] ECR 3435; [1985] 1 CMLR 389.
[108] *Benedetti v. Munari* (Case 52/76) [1977] ECR 163.

provisions of national law, even if adopted subsequent to the Community provision.[109]

(b) Remedies in the Irish Courts

Decisions of, *inter alia*, the Minister for Arts, Heritage, the Gaeltacht and the Islands,[110] other Ministers,[111] local authorities,[112] An Bord Pleanála[113] and the Environmental Protection Agency[114] can be challenged in the High Court by means of a judicial review.[115] Judicial review is not an appeal from a decision, but a review of the manner in which the decision was made.[116] An application for leave to apply for judicial review must be made promptly and, in any event, normally within three months from the date of the decision, or six months where the relief sought is *certiorari* (order quashing the decision).[117] The applicant must satisfy the court that she has a "sufficient interest in the matter to which the application relates" (*locus standi*) and that she has an arguable case.[118] In the case of an application for judicial review of a decision of the Environmental Protection Agency to grant or refuse a licence,[119] or of a decision of a planning authority or An Bord Pleanála on an application for planning permission or on an appeal of a planning decision respectively, applications for judicial

---

[109] *Amministrazione delle Finanze dello Stato v. Simmenthal SpA* (Case 106/77) [1978] ECR 629; [1978] CMLR 263.
[110] Habitats Regulations, Regulations 14-18.
[111] *Ibid.*, Regulations 28, 30 and 31.
[112] *Ibid.*, Regulations 27 and 32.
[113] *Ibid.*, Regulations 27 and 32.
[114] *Ibid.*, Regulation 32.
[115] See generally Hogan and Morgan, *Administrative Law in Ireland*, (3rd ed., Round Hall Sweet and Maxwell, 1998), at 691; Galligan, *Irish Planning Law and Procedure* (Round Hall Sweet and Maxwell, 1997), at 256.
[116]*Per* Lord Brightman in *Chief Constable of the North Wales Police v. Evans* [1982] 1 WLR 1155 at 1160. Quoted with approval by Finlay CJ in *O'Keefe v. An Bord Pleanála* [1993] 1 IR 39 at 71.
[117] Rules of the Superior Courts, SI No. 15 of 1986, Order 84, Rule 21(1).
[118] *Ibid.*, Order 84, Rule 20(4). See cases *Chambers v. An Bord Pleanála* [1992] 1 IR 134; *McBride v. Galway County Council,* unreported, High Court, Laffoy J, 4 February 1997, Supreme Court, 24 March 1998; *Malahide Community Council Ltd. v. Fingal County Council* [1997] 3 IR 383; *Blessington Heritage Trust Ltd. v. Wicklow County Council,* unreported, High Court, McGuinness J, 21 January 1998 and *Lancefort v. An Bord Pleanála* [1998] 2 ILRM 401.
[119] Environmental Protection Agency Act, 1992, section 85(8).

review must be made within two months of the decision.[120] In the last two instances, the applicant must satisfy the court that there are "substantial grounds" for contending that the decision ought to be quashed.

Each Member State is obliged under EC law to provide judicial remedies for breaches of EC legislation which comply with the principles of effectiveness and equivalence. Therefore, national procedural rules must not be framed in such a way as to render it virtually impossible to exercise the EC law rights in practice and the procedural conditions governing the enforcement of EC law rights must not be less favourable than those which apply to comparable actions based on national law.[121] It appears that damages should be made available for a breach of a directly effective EC law obligation if a breach of a similar duty under domestic law would receive a payment of damages.[122] Furthermore, the principle of effectiveness may require that new remedies be created under national law in order to ensure the effective enforcement of EC provisions.[123] Traditional common law causes of action such as trespass, nuisance, *Rylands v. Fletcher*,[124] negligence or actions for breach of statutory duty or breach of contract may, in appropriate circumstances, also be used to remedy interferences with *Natura 2000* sites.

The European Court of Justice has recently developed the principle that, in certain circumstances, an individual may have an EC law right to damages against a Member State for harm caused to

---

[120] Section 82 (3A) and (3B) of the Local Government (Planning and Development) Act, 1963 as inserted by Section 19(3) of the Local Government (Planning and development) Act, 1992. In *McNamara v. An Bord Pleanála* [1995] 2 ILRM 125, Carroll J stated that "in order for a ground to be substantial it must be reasonable, it must be arguable, it must be weighty. It must not be trivial or tenuous."

[121] *Rewe Zentralfinanz eG and Rewe-Zentral A.G. v. Landwirtschaftskammer fur das Saarland* (Case 33/76) [1976] ECR 1989, [1977] 1 CMLR 533.

[122] In *Harz v. Deutsche Tradex GmbH* (Case 79/83) [1984] ECR 1921 the Court of Justice stated that sanctions for breach of the requirements of directives in national law must have "a real deterrent effect ... they must be such as to guarantee full and effective judicial protection." See also *Regina v. Secretary of State for Transport, ex parte Factortame Ltd* (No.1) (Case 213/89) [1990] 1 ECR 2433; [1990] 3 CMLR 375; *Emmott v. Minister for Social Welfare* [1991] ILRM 387 and *Coppinger v. Waterford County Council* [1996] 2 ILRM 427.

[123] *Regina v. Secretary of State for Transport, ex parte Factortame Ltd.* (No. 1), *ibid.*

[124] (1865) 3 H&C 774, (1868) LR 3 HL, 37 LJ Ex 161, 19 LT 220 HL.

her by the Member State's breach of Community law.[125] It is unlikely that this principle, as it stands at present, could be used by individuals against a State for failure to implement properly the Habitats Directive as the Directive does not appear to confer rights on individuals as required by the Court of Justice. However, it is not inconceivable that the Court of Justice will develop the principle so that it eventually encompasses the field of nature conservation.[126]

1.7 Integration of the Habitats Directive into the Irish Legal System

1.7.1 Supremacy of European Community Law

The legal system of the European Community is fundamentally different to the traditional model of international law. Unlike international law, EC Law is supreme over the national laws of the Member States.[127] National courts are required to give precedence

---

[125] *Francovich and Others v. Italy* (Cases 6,9/90) [1991] ECR I-5357; [1993] 2 CMLR 66 (failure to implement a directive); *Brasserie du Pêcheur S.A. v. Germany* and *Regina v. Secretary of State for Transport, ex parte Factortame (No.3)* (Joined Cases 46/93 and 48/93) [1996] ECR I-1029; [1996] 1 CMLR 889 (Member State adopts legislation incompatible with EC law); *Regina v. H.M. Treasury, ex parte British Telecommunications plc* (Case 392/93) [1996] ECR I-1631; [1996] 2 CMLR 217 (Member State incorrectly implemented the provisions of a directive into national law); *Norbrook Laboratories Ltd. v. Ministry of Agriculture Fisheries and Food* (Case 127/95) European Court of Justice, 2 April 1998, not yet reported. The principle of State liability for damages for failure to properly implement a Community directive was accepted by the High Court in *Coppinger v. Waterford County Council* [1996] 2 ILRM 427.

[126] While the Court has stated that in order for the principle to arise the directive in question must confer rights on individuals, it has, in effect, held that a general interest, such as the protection of groundwater against pollution, confers rights upon individuals if non-compliance might endanger the health of persons, *Commission v. Germany* (Case 131/88) [1991] ECR I-825; *Commission v. Germany* (Case 58/89) [1991] ECR I-4983; *Commission v. Germany* (Case 361/88) [1991] ECR I-2567; [1993] 2 CMLR 821; *Commission v. Italy* (Case 363/85) [1987] ECR 1733.

[127] *Oberkreisdirektor des Kreises Borken v. Handelsonderreming Moormann B.V.* (Case 190/87) [1988] ECR 4689; *Costa v. ENEL* (Case 6/64) [1964] ECR 585; [1964] CMLR 425; *Amministrazione delle Finanze dello Stato v. Simmenthal SpA* (Case 106/77) [1978] ECR 629; [1978] 3 CMLR 263.

to EC law over conflicting provisions of national law[128] and national Parliaments must refrain from enacting any new conflicting measures. Even the *Constitution of Ireland* is subordinate to a provision of European Community law as demonstrated in *SPUC v. Grogan* (Case 159/90).[129] Accordingly, the Habitats Regulations cannot be challenged in the Irish courts as being repugnant to the Constitution in so far as they are necessary to give effect to EC law.[130] The following is an outline of the main features of EC law relevant to the implementation of the Habitats Directive into the Irish legal system.[131]

1.7.2 Directives
There are two basic sources of EC law, namely "primary legislation" (Treaty law) and "secondary legislation" consisting of regulations, decisions and directives adopted by the Community institutions under Article 189 (renumbered Article 249) of the Treaty of Rome. A directive is a legislative measure binding as to the result to be achieved. The Habitats Directive applies to the European territory of the Member States.[132] In Ireland, implementation of the Directive extends to the exclusive fishing limits of the State.[133] Therefore, provisions relating to SCIs and SACs will apply to the marine environment.

Directives must be incorporated into the national law of a Member State by means of formal legislation. New legislation must be adopted unless the objectives contained in the directive are already reflected in existing legislation.[134] Pre-existing Irish legislation, such as the Wildlife Act, 1976 and subordinate legislation made under it, did not reflect fully the objectives of the

---

[128] *Fratelli Costanzo v. Comune di Milano* (Case 103/88) [1989] ECR 1839; [1990] 3 CMLR 239.
[129] [1991] ECR I-4685; [1991] 3 CMLR 849. See also *Internationale Handelsgesellschaft v. Einfuhr-und Vorratsstelle fur Getreide und Futtermittel* (Case 11/70) [1970] ECR 1125; [1972] CMLR 225.
[130] See section 1.7.6.
[131] For further information, refer to Steiner, *op. cit.*, at 38, Weatherill and Beaumont, *op. cit.*, at 337, Wyatt and Dashwood, *op. cit.*, at 52, Turner, *op. cit.*, at 51.
[132] Habitats Directive, Article 2(1).
[133] Habitats Regulations, Regulation 2.
[134] *Commission v. Germany* (Case 361/88) [1991] ECR I-2567; [1993] 2 CMLR 821.

Habitats Directive. Ireland was, therefore, under a European Community law obligation to transpose the Directive by legislative means. A directive will not be adequately implemented if the national provisions are not effectively enforced.[135] Actual as well as formal compliance is required.[136] Conversely, actual implementation by mere changes in administrative practice without incorporation into the legislation of the State is insufficient to implement a directive because administrative measures can be changed at any time.[137] Ireland chose to implement the Habitats Directive by adopting regulations under the European Communities Act, 1972 as amended.[138]

Directives are binding on the Member State only as to the result to be achieved and leave to the national authorities the choice of form and methods as to how to achieve the prescribed results.[139] The choice of form and methods is subject to two limitations. First, Ireland must implement a directive in the manner most in

---

[135] *Commission v. Belgium* (Case 42/89) [1990] ECR I-2821; [1992] 1 CMLR 22 and *Commission v. Germany* (Case 361/88) [1991] ECR I-2567; [1993] 2 CMLR 821.

[136] *Commission v. United Kingdom* (Case 337/89) [1992] ECR I-6103. The European Court of Justice effectively equated non-compliance in fact with non-compliance in law.

[137] *Commission v. Belgium* (Case 102/79) [1980] ECR 1473; [1981] 1 CMLR 282; *Commission v. Netherlands* (Case 339/87) [1990] ECR I-851; [1993] 2 C.M.L.R 360; *Commission v. Belgium* (Case 239/85) [1986] ECR 3645; [1988] 1 CMLR 248; *Commission v. Italy* (Case 145/82) [1983] ECR 711; *Commission v. Netherlands* (Case 96/81) [1982] ECR 1791; *Commission v. Spain* (Case 242/94) [1995] ECR I-3031 and *Commission v. Germany* (Case 83/97), European Court of Justice, 11 December 1997, not yet reported. See also *Browne v. An Bord Pleanála* [1989] ILRM 865.

[138] European Communities Act, 1972 as amended by the European Communities (Amendment) Act, 1973; European Communities (Amendment) Act, 1985; European Communities (Amendment) (No. 2) Act, 1985; European Communities (Amendment) Act, 1986; European Communities (Amendment) Act, 1992; European Communities (Amendment) Act, 1993; European Communities (Amendment) Act, 1994 and the European Communities (Amendment) Act, 1995.

[139] Article 189, Treaty of Rome as amended by Article G(60), Treaty on European Union. See also *Verbond van Nederlandse Ondernemingen v. Inspecteur der Invoerrechten en Accijnzen* (Case 51/76) [1977] ECR 113; *Marshall v. Southampton and South-West Hampshire Area Health Authority* (Case 152/84) [1986] ECR 723; [1986] 1 CMLR 688 and *Kraaijeveld and Others v. Gedeputeerde Staten van Zuid-Holland* (Case 72/95) [1996] ECR I-5403.

conformity with national constitutional requirements. Therefore, as noted by Temple Lang, a directive must be implemented in a manner consistent with the Constitution, unless it cannot be so implemented.[140] Secondly, Member States are obliged to choose the most appropriate forms and methods of implementation.[141] Normally, implementation is required within a specified period of time. In the case of the Habitats Directive, Member States had two years from the date of notification of the Directive (5 June 1992) in which to bring into force the laws, regulations and administrative provisions necessary to implement it, i.e. until 5 June 1994.[142] The Minister for Arts, Culture and the Gaeltacht (now the Minister for Arts, Heritage, the Gaeltacht and the Islands) made the Habitats Regulations on 26 February 1997, more than two and a half years after the deadline for the transposition of the Directive.[143] In *Inter-Environment Wallonie ASBL v. Region Wallonne* (Case 129/96)[144] the Court of Justice ruled that Member States must refrain from adopting measures liable to seriously compromise the result prescribed by a directive during the period prescribed for its transposition. Consequently, Ireland was obliged from 5 June 1992 to refrain from enacting legislation or carrying out activities which would seriously prejudice the aims of the Habitats Directive.[145]

1.7.3 Transposition into National Law

The transposition of a directive into national law does not require the provisions of the directive to be enacted *verbatim* in a specific

---

[140] Temple Lang, "*Constitutional Aspects of Irish Membership of the EEC*" (1972) 9 CMLR 167, at 175; *Meagher v. Minister for Agriculture* [1994] 1 IR 329; [1994] 1 ILRM 1.
[141] *Royer* (Case 48/75) [1976] ECR 497; [1976] 2 CMLR 619.
[142] Article 23.
[143] The significance of this late transposition is now moot and is not addressed here.
[144] [1997] ECR I-7411.
[145] This argument was used in *An Taisce and WWF v. Commission*, Court of First Instance (Case T-461/93) [1994] ECR II-733, European Court of Justice (Case 325/94P) [1996] ECR I-3727 as part of the case against the granting of EC funding for an interpretative centre at Mullaghmore, County Clare but the European Court of First Instance and the European Court of Justice found that the application was inadmissible and did not deal with the merits of the case.

provision of national law.[146] However, the European Court of Justice does require implementation in a "sufficiently clear and precise manner."[147] In *Commission v. Italy* (Case 262/85),[148] concerning Italy's transposition of Articles 6 and 7 of the Birds Directive, the Court of Justice stated that "a faithful transposition becomes particularly important in a case such as this in which the management of the common heritage is entrusted to the Member States in their respective territories." It is submitted that a similar obligation arises to transpose faithfully the Habitats Directive which, like the Birds Directive, was adopted with the object of protecting the "natural heritage" of the Community.[149] However, the Habitats Regulations repeat many of the opaque terms of the Directive without attempting to define the precise scope or meaning of the terms used. Bell and Ball, commenting upon the equivalent English regulations, argue that this may not constitute full and effective implementation of the Directive as it is contrary to the requirement of legal certainty.[150] The exact implications of many of the Regulations must await either a decision of the courts or administrative guidance. In addition, transposition of the Directive into Irish law by means of statutory instrument can be criticised for its lack of transparency, immunity from political commentary or debate and the weakness of the penalties which can be imposed for breach of a provision in a regulation.[151]

Article 14 of the Birds Directive provides that a Member State may introduce stricter measures than those which that directive prescribes. There is no comparable provision in the Habitats Directive, yet the Habitats Regulations go beyond the requirements of the Directive most notably by protecting non-

---

[146] *Commission v. Italy* (Case 42/80) [1980] ECR 3639; *Commission v. Italy* (Case 363/85) [1987] ECR 1733; *Commission v. Germany* (Case 29/84) [1985] ECR 1661; [1986] 3 CMLR 579.

[147] *Commission v. Federal Republic of Germany* (Case 131/88) [1991] ECR I-825, at para. 6.

[148] [1987] ECR 3073, at para. 9. See also *Commission v. Belgium* (Case 247/85) [1987] ECR 3029.

[149] Habitats Directive, Fourth Recital to the Preamble. See also Birds Directive, Third Recital to the Preamble; *Gourmetterie Van den Burg* (Case 169/89) [1990] ECR I-2143.

[150] See Bell and Ball, *op. cit.*, at 92.

[151] European Communities Act, 1972, section 3(3). See e.g. Habitats Regulations, Regulation 39. See also section 1.7.6.

priority sites on the Irish candidate list of European sites.[152] However, the general principle is that a Member State may adopt stricter measures than those prescribed at Community level to the extent that they are not incompatible with other Community objectives.[153] For example, a Member State cannot adopt stricter protection for a species not occurring within its territory through the imposition of a prohibition on imports and marketing of the species unless similar protections are provided by the legislature of the Member State on the territory of which the species occurs.[154] To do otherwise would be to create a likely restriction of trade and a distortion of competition within the Community. It is submitted that provision for the protection of non-priority sites on the Irish candidate list of European sites is not incompatible with other Community objectives.[155]

1.7.4 Direct Effect

Certain provisions of EC law create rights for individuals which national courts must uphold.[156] Such provisions are said to be directly effective. While some Treaty provisions are directly effective, it is generally considered that the Treaty provisions on the environment are not. Given that the language of Title XVI is of policy and thereby requires further action on the part of the Community institutions, it is reasonably certain that its articles are not directly effective. However, provisions in directives, including environmental directives, can have direct effect. In *Van Duyn v. Home Office* (Case 41/74)[157] the European Court of Justice held that directives could have direct effect if national implementing measures have not been adopted on or before the deadline for implementation. Other cases established the principle that

---

[152] Regulations 14 -18. See section 4.1.3.
[153] Treaty of Rome, Article 130t. Such provisions must be notified to the Commission. See also *Peralta* (Case 379/92) [1994] ECR I-3453.
[154] *Gourmetterie Van den Burg, supra,* fn 149. See also *ADBHU* (Case 240/83) [1985] ECR 531, at paras. 13-15 and *Commission v. Denmark* (Case 302/86) [1988] ECR 4607 at paras. 11-12.
[155] However, this has implications in Irish constitutional law. See section 4.10.2.
[156] *Van Gend en Loos v. Nederlandse Administratie der Belastingen* (Case 26/62) [1963] ECR 1; [1963] CMLR 105; *Costa v. ENEL* (Case 6/64) [1964] ECR 585; [1964] CMLR 425; *Amministazione delle Finanze dello Stato v. Simmenthal SpA, supra,* fn 109. See Kramer, *op. cit.,* at 78.
[157] [1974] ECR 1337; [1975] 1 CMLR 1.

provisions in directives can be directly effective when their implementation is defective, including instances where conflicting provisions of national law are retained in force.[158] An individual cannot rely on the direct effect of a directive against the State or a State authority until the time-limit for its implementation has passed, as prior to that date the State is not in default.[159]

The Court of Justice has held that the doctrine of direct effect of directives applies only to the enforcement of rights and duties in EC law by individuals against the State and Community institutions,[160] i.e. vertical direct effect. However, the concept of *State* is widely interpreted and would appear to include local authorities, An Bord Pleanála, the Environmental Protection Agency and regional government.[161] The term may also include nationalised industries and companies in which the State has a majority shareholding.[162] The enforcement of rights or duties against other individuals not part of the State, i.e. horizontal direct effect, was ruled out in respect of directives in *Marshall v. Southampton and South-West Hampshire Area Health Authority* (Case 152/84).[163] Consequently, a provision of an EC directive which has direct effect may be enforced against the State and any public body but not against a private body or private individual. Accordingly, private bodies may have greater protection than public bodies from the provisions of environmental directives. It should be noted that the direct enforcement of a directive against the State may sometimes have an impact on private parties, for example by requiring the revocation of authorisations granted to them by the State. It is widely considered that this does not amount to

---

[158] *Commission v. Germany* (Case 29/84) [1985] ECR 1661; *Commission v. Italy* (Case 280/83) [1984] ECR 2361; *Commission v. Italy* (Case 41/82) [1982] ECR 4213.
[159] *Publico Ministero v. Ratti* (Case 148/78) [1979] ECR 1629; [1980] 1 CMLR 96.
[160] *Arcaro* (Case 168/95) [1996] ECR I-4705; [1997] 1 CMLR 179.
[161] *Fratelli Costanzo v. Comune di Milano* (Case 103/88), *supra*, fn 128. In this case the Court said that all organs of the administration, including decentralised authorities such as municipalities are covered.
[162] *Foster v. British Gas plc* (Case 188/89) [1990] ECR I-3313; [1990] 2 CMLR 833.
[163] [1986] ECR 723, [1986] 1 CMLR 688. The Court confirmed this decision in *Dori Faccini v. Recreb Srl* (Case 91/92) [1994] ECR I-3325; [1994] 1 CMLR 665.

enforcement against private parties although they may in fact be more seriously affected by the outcome of enforcement proceedings than the State authorities themselves. The direct effect of a provision of Community law will not release a Member State from its obligation to implement the provisions into its national legislation.[164] Not all directives and not all provisions of directives can have direct effect.

Traditionally, in order to confer right on individuals which could be enforced in the national courts a provision in a directive had to be clear and concise, unconditional and of such a kind that no further action was required on the part of the Community institutions or the Member States or, if the measure required such action, that it left no discretion to the Member State in the execution of the measure.[165] At present, the formulation used most frequently by the Court of Justice is that the provision must be "unconditional and sufficiently precise."[166] The issue of whether or not provisions of the Habitats Directive are directly effective is of considerable significance since the Irish Regulations fail to adequately transpose a number of provisions of the Directive. It is probable, based on the experience of Member States with the implementation of substantially similar provisions in the Birds Directive, that some of its provisions are directly effective. See section 4.8.8.

---

[164] *Commission v. Italy* (Case 104/86) [1988] ECR 1799.

[165] *Van Gend en Loos, supra,* fn 156; *Molkerei-Zentrale Westfalen v. Hauptzollamt Paderborn* (Case 28/67) [1968] ECR 143; [1968] CMLR 187.

[166] *Publico Ministero v. Ratti, supra,* fn 159, at para. 23; *Becker v. Finanzamt Munster-Innenstadt* (Case 8/81) [1982] ECR 53, at para. 25; [1982] 1 CMLR 499, at para. 25. In *Comitato di Coordinamento per la Difesa della Cava and Others v. Regione Lombardia* (Case 236/92) [1994] ECR I-483 the Court of Justice stated that a provision is "sufficiently precise" when the obligation which the provision imposes is set out in "unequivocal terms." The Court also said, in citing its judgment in *Molkerei-Zentrale Westfalen v. Hauptzollamt Paderborn, supra,* fn 165, that "a Community provision is unconditional where it is not subject, in its implementation or effects, to the taking of any measure either by the Community or by the Member States." The Court has subsequently taken a wide interpretation of the term "unconditional", see *Van Duyn v. Home Office* (Case 41/74), *supra,* fn 157.

1.7.5 Indirect Effect

The European Court of Justice in *Von Colson v. Land Nordrhein-Westfalen* (Case 14/83)[167] and *Marleasing S.A. v. La Comercial Internacional de Alimentacion S.A.* (Case 106/89)[168] developed the doctrine of "indirect effect" otherwise known as the doctrine of harmonious interpretation.[169] The doctrine provides that, in the event of a conflict between national law and a provision of EC law, the national courts must interpret national law so as to give effect to the spirit and purpose of the EC legal provision, including a directive, even where a provision of a directive is not sufficient to give rise to direct effect. This judicial interpretation of national law is dependent on the existence of some provision of national law which can plausibly be interpreted so as to give effect to a directive.[170] The obligation exists irrespective of whether the national legislation pre-dates or post-dates a directive.[171] Therefore, if a provision of the Habitats Directive is not adequately implemented by the Habitats Regulations, there is an obligation on the State, including local authorities and the courts, to construe existing provisions of national law, such as the Wildlife Act, 1976,[172] the Waste Management Act, 1996, the Air Pollution Act, 1987, the Local Government (Water Pollution) Acts, 1977-1990 or the Environmental Protection Agency Act, 1992 to remedy the deficiency. See section 4.8.8. This principle of interpretation cannot

---

[167] [1984] ECR 1891; [1986] 2 C.M.L.R 430.

[168] [1990] ECR I-4135; [1992] 1 CMLR 305. See also *Harz v. Deutsche Tradex GmbH* (Case 79/83), supra, fn 122, and *Murphy v. Bord Telecom* [1982] ILRM 53. An example of a purposive interpretation of implementing legislation in Ireland is *Shannon Regional Fisheries Board v. An Bord Pleanála,* unreported, High Court, 17 November 1994 in which Barr J held that a pregnant gilt was a "sow" for the purpose of the European Communities (Environmental Impact Assessment) Regulations, 1989.

[169] The doctrine was developed partly to ameliorate the arbitrariness of denying directives horizontal direct effect.

[170] The European Court of Justice in *Johnston v. Chief Constable of the RUC* (Case 222/84) [1986] ECR 1651; [1986] 3 CMLR 240 limited this obligation to the extent that it is "possible" to construe national law in a manner consistent with a non-directly effective directive. See also the decision of the House of Lords in *Webb v. EMO Air Cargo* [1992] 4 All ER 929.

[171] *Marleasing S.A. v. La Comercial Internacional de Alimentacion S.A.,* supra, fn 168.

[172] It should be noted that Regulation 1 of the Habitats Regulations states that the Regulations and the Wildlife Act, 1976 are to be construed as one.

release a Member State from its obligation to amend its national law.[173]

1.7.6 Interaction of European Community Law and Irish Constitutional Law

Article 29.4.7[174] of the Constitution of Ireland provides that no provision of the Constitution shall invalidate laws enacted, acts done or measures adopted by the State which are *necessitated* by the obligations of membership of the European Union or of the Communities and no provision of the Constitution shall prevent the above laws, acts or measures from having the force of law in the State.[175] Therefore, as a matter of Irish law, only legislative provisions *necessary* to implement a directive are free from Constitutional challenge.[176] Section 2 of the European Communities Act, 1972 gives force to European Community law in the State. Section 3 of the 1972 Act provides that a Minister of State may introduce regulations in order to give effect to section 2. It is this provision which gives legal force to the Habitats Regulations. The effect of the 1972 Act was considered by the Supreme Court in *Meagher v. Minister for Agriculture*.[177] The Court held that the power in section 3 to make regulations was solely a power to give effect to section 2. Denham J, with whom Finlay CJ, O'Flaherty J and Egan J agreed,[178] stated that the basic principle in Article 15.2, that the sole and exclusive power of making laws for the State is vested in the Oireachtas, had been restricted by the then Article 29.4.5 (now Article 29.4.7). However, she stated that an attempt should be made to reconcile them as far as possible. Accordingly, primary legislation (by Act of the Oireachtas) is required if a

---

[173] *Steenhorst-Neerings v. Bestuur van de Bedrijfsvereniging vour Detailhandel, Ambachten en Huisvrouwen* (Case 338/91) [1993] ECR I-5475; *Commission v. Italy* (Case 104/86) [1988] ECR 1799; [1988] 3 CMLR 25 and *Commission v. Germany* (Case 83/97), European Court of Justice, 11 December 1997, not yet reported.
[174] Formerly Article 29.4.5 and Article 29.4.3.
[175] See Kelly (Hogan and Whyte), *The Irish Constitution*, (3rd ed., Butterworths, 1994), at 281 and Phelan, *Revolt or Revolution: at the Constitutional Boundaries of the European Community* (Round Hall Sweet and Maxwell, 1997), at 338.
[176] This is particularly significant in relation to provisions of the Habitats Regulations which place restrictions on the exercise of property rights.
[177] [1994] 1 IR 329; [1994] 1 ILRM 1.
[178] Blaney J delivered a separate concurring judgment.

directive leaves matters of principle or policy to be decided. If not, secondary legislation is an acceptable means of implementing the directive. She explained:

> If the regulations contained material exceeding the policies and principles of the directives then they are not authorised by the directives and would not be valid under section 3 unless the material was incidental, supplementary or consequential.[179]

The Habitats Directive left a number of matters of principle and policy to the State's discretion, including the degree of public participation, if any, to be allowed in reaching a decision to permit operations or activities,[180] the nature and form which notification to, and consultation with, landowners should take, the circumstances in which it may be considered necessary to maintain or develop features of the landscape which are of major importance for wild fauna and flora[181] and whether or not to provide compensation.[182] It is, therefore, submitted that the Habitats Directive should have been implemented by Act of the Oireachtas. In addition, it will be submitted in Chapters 4 and 5 that certain provisions of the Habitats Directive have not been implemented in the manner most in conformity with national constitutional requirements. Most notably the Regulations include provisions not prescribed nor necessitated by the Directive.[183] Provisions of this nature do not receive the immunity of Article 29.4.7 and must be judged in accordance with Irish constitutional standards.[184] They may therefore conflict with, *inter alia*, Article 15.2 of the Constitution.[185]

---

[179] [1994] 1 IR 329, at 366; [1994] 1 ILRM 1, at 27.
[180] Article 6(4).
[181] Article 3(3) and Article 10.
[182] Regulation 20.
[183] See sections 4.4.5, 4.10 and 5.2.6.
[184] See chapter 2.
[185] See generally *Greene v. Minister for Agriculture* [1990] 2 IR 17; [1990] ILRM 364.

Chapter 2

The Constitution

The Interaction of Property Rights With Land Use Controls

2.1 Introduction

The Constitution's protection of private property rights is the fundamental norm against which the legitimacy of all land use restrictions must be tested. One of the major concerns about the Habitats Regulations is the manner in which they impose restrictions on the exercise of private property rights. In this Chapter, some observations are made on the nature and extent of the Constitutional guarantee of private property. The opinions expressed reflect the views of the authors as to the present constitutional position. These opinions are not necessarily shared by other writers in this area and they should not be read as a political endorsement of the values of the Constitution. The objective is to state the applicable law as simply as possible, so as to place controls on property rights in their proper constitutional context.

2.2 The Protection Afforded by the Constitution

2.2.1 *The Constitutional Text*
Article 40.3.2 provides that:

> The State shall, in particular, by its laws protect as best it may from unjust attack and, in the case of injustice done, vindicate the life, person, good name and property rights of every citizen.

Article 43 deals more extensively with the protection of private property, providing that:

1.1 The State acknowledges that man, in virtue of his rational being, has the natural right, antecedent to positive law, to the private ownership of external goods.

1.2 The State accordingly guarantees to pass no law attempting to abolish the right of private ownership or the general right to transfer, bequeath and inherit property.

2.1 The State recognises, however, that the exercise of the rights mentioned in the foregoing provisions of this Article ought, in civil society, to be regulated by the principles of social justice.

2.2 The State, accordingly, may as occasion requires delimit by law the exercise of the said rights with a view to reconciling their exercise with the exigencies of the common good.

The fact that property rights are protected in two different ways in different articles (Article 40.3 and Article 43) has been the cause of some confusion. For present purposes, it is not necessary to trace the protracted course of judicial thought on this matter. Nevertheless, some comments should be made on more recent judicial pronouncements. In *Blake v. Attorney General*,[1] the Supreme Court attempted to impose a workable legal structure onto the protection of property by reasoning as follows:

> There exists, therefore, a double protection for the property rights of a citizen. As far as he is concerned, the State [under Article 43] cannot abolish or attempt to abolish the right of private ownership as an institution or the general right to transfer, bequeath and inherit property. In addition, he has the further protection under Article 40 as to the exercise by him of his own property rights in particular items of property.[2]

In a number of cases following *Blake*, the distinction between Article 40.3.2 rights and Article 43 rights seems to have collapsed.

---

[1] [1982] IR 117.
[2] *Ibid.*, 135, *per* O'Higgins CJ.

In *Dreher v. Irish Land Commission*[3] and in *E.S.B. v. Gormley*,[4] the courts assessed whether there had been an "unjust attack" (concept of Article 40.3.2) by reference to the requirements of "social justice" and "common good" (concepts of Article 43). In *Tuohy v. Courtney*,[5] Finlay CJ appeared to accept that the distinction between Article 40.3 property rights and Article 43 property rights. The conclusion of the Constitution Review Group, that the courts have "found it more or less impossible to adhere to a strict categorisation of Article 40.3.2 in contrast with Article 43 property rights",[6] is well founded. For present purposes, it suffices to note that a person's property rights over particular items of property are protected under one or other Article.

2.2.2 The Extent of Property Rights

In the seminal case of *Buckley v. Attorney General*,[7] O'Byrne J (for the Supreme Court) noted the natural law origins of the property rights contained in Article 43. However, the Court did not feel it necessary to examine the philosophical debate concerning property rights, either to determine the origin of the rights or to identify their extent:

> It is sufficient for us to say that this State, by its Constitution, acknowledges that the right to private property is such a [natural] right and that this right is antecedent to all positive law.[8]

O'Byrne J further explained:

> [Antecedent to positive law] means that man by virtue, and as an attribute, of his human personality is entitled to such a right and that no positive law is competent to deprive him of it and we are of opinion that the entire Article is informed by, and should be construed in the light of, this fundamental conception.

---

[3] [1984] ILRM 94.
[4] [1985] IR 129; [1985] ILRM 494.
[5] [1994] 3 IR 1.
[6] *Report of the Constitution Review Group* (1996), at 361.
[7] [1950] IR 67.
[8] *Ibid.*, 82.

What is clear from these statements, and indeed from the text of the Constitution itself, is that the right to private property vests automatically in individual persons.[9] Legislation which purports to restrict the ways in which land is used is an encroachment on property rights.[10] In terms of land use restrictions, this may be contrasted with the position in the United Kingdom where land use was effectively nationalised in 1947.[11] In the UK, the grant of planning permission represents an *expansion* of a person's property rights and a refusal to grant planning permission must be viewed in that context. Conversely, in Ireland a refusal to grant planning permission represents a *restriction* of a *pre-existing right*: the constitutional right to private property exists independently of State action.[12] The distinction, although subtle, is crucial as it defines the fundamental bias of the development code: in Ireland the Constitution requires a presumption in planning legislation (and *a priori* in other legislation which purports to restrict property rights) in favour of development.

---

[9] Mr Justice Costello writing extra judicially stated in *Natural Law, the Constitution and the Courts* (1987) at 108, "It can clearly be inferred that the Constitution rejects legal positivism as a basis for the protection of human rights, and suggests instead a theory of natural law from which these rights can be derived."

[10] See *State (FPH Properties Ltd.) v. An Bord Pleanála* [1989] ILRM 98, at 103 where the Supreme Court *per* McCarthy J (Finlay CJ and Walsh J concurring) stated "... the requirement for planning permission constitutes an encroachment on property rights."

[11] The right to compensation for adverse planning decisions was in effect abolished by the Town and Country Planning Act, 1947. This Act effectively nationalised development rights and any development value which could arise on a grant of planning permission. Provision to compensate persons who had bought land with investment backed expectations was incorporated in the 1947 Act and finally abolished in 1991. However, even in England, compensation is payable for revoking or discontinuing an authorised use of land if it results in loss. See Rowan - Robinson and Ross "Compensation for Environmental Protection in Britain: a Legislative Lottery" 5 *Journal of Environmental Law* 245.

[12] In *Pine Valley v. Minister for the Environment* [1987] IR 23, Finlay CJ stated *obiter* that the grant of outline permission "enhanced and enlarged" the property rights of the plaintiff. It is submitted that this was stated *per incuriam* and that the Chief Justice described the position under English law but not, it is confidently submitted, under Irish law.

The Supreme Court in *Buckley v. Attorney General*[13] held that Article 43 was not only prevents the total abolition of private property but also exists:

> to enshrine and protect the property rights of the individual citizen of the State and that the rights of the individual are thereby protected, subject to the right of the State, as declared in clause 2, to regulate the exercise of such rights in accordance with the principles of social justice and to delimit the exercise of such rights so as to reconcile their exercise with the exigencies of the common good.

It is clear from this and many other constitutional cases that the State is permitted to "delimit" private property rights in the above circumstances. Kenny J in *Central Dublin Development Association v. Attorney General*[14] held that "delimit" means "restrict" and that it most probably does not encompass the complete acquisition of all the rights of ownership. In his view, the complete acquisition of all the rights, which together make up ownership, without compensation "would in almost all cases" be an unjust attack.

2.3 The Principle of Proportionality

2.3.1 The Emergence of a New Test

It is clear from the preceding paragraphs that limitations may be placed on the exercise of property rights. In practical terms, the most important question is whether any particular legislative restriction is constitutionally permissible. In the past, the test favoured by the courts was whether the restriction constituted an "unjust attack".[15] This concept was obviously somewhat amorphous and prone to a large degree of judicial subjectivity. In recent years the proportionality principle, which originated in European law, has emerged in Irish law as a more structured way of testing the constitutionality of legislative restrictions of constitutional rights,

---

[13] [1950] IR 67.
[14] (1975) 109 ILTR 69, at 84.
[15] *Ibid.*

including property rights. In a recent article,[16] Hogan has described the test as "a workable judicial methodology" and as "a badly needed analytical framework". Indeed he goes so far as to argue that the judicial invention of proportionality has become more important than the actual words of Articles 40.3 and 43 themselves.[17] Clearly for any litigant, the importance of the judicial decisions on the proportionality test cannot be overestimated.

In *Heaney v. Ireland*,[18] Costello J stated the rationale of the proportionality principle and formulated a new method for testing the legitimacy of restrictions on property rights. Given the crucial importance of this test, it is useful to quote at length from his judgment:[19]

> In considering whether a restriction on the exercise of rights is permitted by the Constitution the courts in this country and elsewhere have found it helpful to apply the test of proportionality, a test which contains the notions of minimal restraint on the exercise of protected rights, and of the exigencies of the common good in a democratic society.... The objective of the impugned provision must be of sufficient importance to warrant overriding a constitutionally protected right. It must relate to concerns pressing and substantial in a free and democratic society. The means chosen must pass a proportionality test. They must:
> (a) be rationally connected to the objective and not be arbitrary, unfair or based on irrational considerations;
> (b) impair the right as little as possible, and
> (c) be such that their effect on rights are proportional to their objective: see *Chaulk v. R.*[20]

Only where (a), (b) and (c) are satisfied can it be said that an attack on property rights will be deemed a "just attack" and accordingly

---

[16] Hogan, "The Constitution, Property Rights and Proportionality" (1997) 33 (ns) *Irish Jurist* 373.
[17] Whether the courts are entitled to take this activist approach is a point of some contention. Nevertheless, it is difficult to disagree with Hogan's observation that such an activist approach is being taken.
[18] [1994] 3 IR 593; [1994] 1 ILRM 420.
[19] *Ibid.*, 607; *ibid.*, 431-2.
[20] (1990) 3 SCR 1303, 1335-1336.

constitutionally legitimate. A restriction which does not serve a legitimate aim, or which is disproportionate, or which is arbitrary, is an "unjust attack". It follows from the fact that the legislation itself must not be arbitrary that any restrictions imposed on the basis of that legislation must not be applied in an arbitrary manner.[21] Restrictions which proportionately serve a legitimate aim must be applied in a consistent manner in order to be acceptable.

2.3.2 The Application of the Test to Restrictions of Property Rights

In two High Court cases the proportionality principle has been applied to the issue of property rights. In *Daly v. Revenue Commissioners*,[22] Costello P was prepared to strike down a provision of the tax statutes. While the High Court accepted that it was permissible for the Oireachtas to impose tax, there were two factors of this particular tax which made it a disproportionate restriction of Dr Daly's property rights. First, by operating as a form of double taxation, it was "manifestly unfair". Secondly, although the problem which the section sought to remedy was once off and only affected certain persons, the section applied permanently and to all self-employed persons receiving payments from the State. Costello P concluded that the restriction was "in a manner out of proportion to the objective which the measure is designed to achieve".[23]

In *Iarnrod Eireann v. Ireland*,[24] Keane J approved the proportionality test but emphasised that the Oireachtas had a margin of appreciation in imposing restricitons on property rights. It was thus legitimate for the Oireachtas, in enacting the joint and several liability rule, to favour the interests of plaintiffs at the expense of defendants. This means that the courts will usually defer to the Oireachtas, where it legislates to restrict property rights, on the basis that it is better constitutionally placed to make an assessment of what the common good requires. Only where that assessment of the common good appears unreasonable would a court be likely to

---

[21] This is particularly relevant when we consider the Habitats Regulations which give the power to many competent authorities to impose land use restrictions.
[22] [1995] 3 IR 1; [1996] 1 ILRM 122.
[23] *Ibid.*, 11; *ibid.*, 132. Accordingly, the scheme of restrictions could be classified as "arbitrary", failing to meet the second limb of the proportionality test.
[24] [1995] 2 ILRM 161.

strike down a provision. However, it is worth noting that the same level of respect is not afforded to the actions of a Government Minister,[25] or, by analogy, to the actions of any other administrative authority.

2.3.3 The Limits of the Test

In *Daly*, Costello P emphasised that it was not for the courts to decide if the Oireachtas could have framed a better provision.[26] It is difficult, however, to see how the courts can decide that a provision "impaired the right as little as possible" (as they are obliged to do, under Costello P.'s formulation of the test) if they are prohibited from considering to what extent other suggested provisions (which would achieve the same end) might impair the right. It is impossible to answer a relative question without reference to other legislative measures which could have been taken instead. In practice however the courts seem to prefer this minimalist approach, probably out of respect for the Oireachtas as another organ of government, thus depriving the proportionality test of some of its vigour.[27] However, where, as happens under the Habitats Regulations, different compensation mechanisms apply according to which regulatory regime governs a particular land-use, it should not be difficult for the courts to make a comparative analysis of the various compensation schemes available.[28]

In addition, it should be noted that the Legislature might impose a restriction on a property right, not in the interests of the common good, but rather to regulate the interaction of two competing property rights. In such circumstances it is suggested that the test should be one of balance and not one of proportionality. Notwithstanding these two caveats, the proportionality test is

---

[25] See *East Donegal Co-op v. Attorney General* [1970] IR 317; (1970) 104 ILTR 81.
[26] [1995] 3 IR 1, at 13; [1996] 1 ILRM 122, at 132.
[27] Here one heeds the warning of Mr. Justice Holmes in *Pennsylvania Coal Co. v. Mahon* 260 US 393, at 416; 43 S Ct 158, at 160 who, in referring to the police power qualification on protections for private property in the US Constitution, stated that, "We are in danger of forgetting that a strong desire to improve the public condition is not enough to warrant achieving the desire by a shorter cut than the constitutional way of paying for the change".
[28] See section 5.2.7. The Supreme Court performed a similar task in comparing the tax advantages available to married couples with those available to unmarried couples in *Murphy v. Attorney General* [1982] IR 241.

currently the preferred judicial method of assessing the legitimacy of legislative interferences with property rights. In assessing the constitutionality of the Regulations later in this book, reference will be made to this principle of proportionality.[29]

2.4 Compensation

2.4.1 General Principles
Interferences with property rights may be remedied by the provision of compensation. Indeed the formulation of the right in the United States Constitution focuses specifically on the need for compensation.[30] Although the Irish Constitution does not specifically mention compensation, the courts have focused on the provision of compensation in assessing the legitimacy of restrictions of property rights. One does not have a *right* to compensation as such. Compensation is rather a device which may render constitutional an otherwise invalid delimitation of property rights. The courts' approach to the issue has been somewhat confused. An attempt will be made to set out the judicial position as well as an alternative rationale for the provision of compensation.

In *Central Dublin Development Association v. Attorney General*,[31] Kenny J stated that compensation should usually be given where there is an outright appropriation of property, as this amounts to an acquisition of all the rights of property over an item and is not merely a restriction on the exercise of some of those rights. The kernel of this approach is that it is acceptable for the State to regulate the exercise of property rights, but not for the State to confiscate items of property.

2.4.2 The American Approach
While Kenny J's exposition on property rights would appear to limit the scope for requiring compensation to situations where something akin to an outright appropriation occurs, the approach of the American courts in this area should be noted. In the case of

---

[29] See section 4.10.2.
[30] The Fifth Amendment to the US Constitution provides that "private property may not be taken for public use without just compensation".
[31] *Supra*, fn 14.

Pennsylvania Coal Co. v. Mahon,[32] the Supreme Court stated that a regulation which goes "too far" will be recognised as a "taking", thus justifying a claim for compensation. This phrase, although ambiguous as to what constitutes "too far", clearly shows that regulation of land-use can be classified as acquisition of land if the regulation goes "too far". In the context of environmental regulation, the American courts have evolved a two-pronged test as to what constitutes a "taking". In *Nollan v. California Coastal Commission* and in *Lucas v. South Carolina Coastal Commission*,[33] it was held that a regulation goes "too far" if it fails to advance a legitimate State interest or denies an owner any economically viable use of property. It is submitted that a regulation which fails to advance a legitimate State interest would in any case be invalid under the Irish proportionality test, but there remains scope for the incorporation of the "denial of economically viable use" test into Irish law.

In order to assess whether any economically viable use of the land remains, the American courts question whether the regulation affects the parcel of land as a whole or only part of the land. At present, two lines of authority compete for attention. The traditional view was that the land could not be subdivided so as to assess whether economically viable use of one tract of land had been denied: the land had to be viewed as one parcel. More recently, the United States Supreme Court has questioned this view,[34] and has been prepared to narrow their inquiry to the affected tract of land, where it was merely a portion of the whole land, and question whether that particular tract of land had been deprived of any economically viable use. This probably reflects a more libertarian approach in general by the American courts and, were the Irish courts to adopt the "regulation which goes too far" line of authority, it is suggested that they would, as it would be relevant in assessing proportionality, prefer the "parcel as a whole" approach, thus reducing the scope for a finding of unconstitutionality.

If the courts find no "categorical taking", they must then apply a balancing test examining the character of the governmental regulation, the economic impact and the effect of the regulation on

---

[32] (1922) 260 US 393.

[33] (1987) 483 US 825; 97 L 2ed 677, 107 S Ct 3141: 112 S Ct 2886 (1992).

[34] See for instance, *Florida Rock Industries Inc v. United States* 791 F 2d 893 (Fed Cir 1986).

the owner's reasonable investment based expectations.[35] It is suggested that these factors, the latter two being the most important, should also be relevant for an Irish court in assessing whether compensation should be payable.[36] Thus the courts should question what value the land has lost as a result of the regulation. If the landowner bought the land with notice of the restriction, a claim for compensation should not succeed as the market value at the time of purchase should have reflected the devaluation imposed by the restriction.[37] A restriction might be upheld if the landowner could still put the land to a reasonably beneficial use despite the restriction.

The American approach to assessing the constitutionality of land-use restrictions has been described here because it demonstrates the potential for expansion of the "outright appropriation" test.

2.4.3 A Possible Development of the Irish Approach

When the Oireachtas imposes taxes, it effects an outright appropriation of certain items of property (moneys); yet

---

[35] See for instance, *Penn. Central Transportation Co. v. City of New York* (1978) 438 US 104; 57 L Ed 2d 631, 88 S Ct 264. In the context of the Irish Regulations, it is worth noting that they provide that designation as an SAC may be registered as a burden on land.

[36] Indeed, implicit Irish recognition of the relevance of investment backed expectations may be seen in three instances. First, the Local Government (Planning and Development) Act, 1990, Section 12 provides that compensation may be refused where planning permission is denied on the basis that it would contravene a development objective contained in the development plan. However, where the development objective is changed in the five years immediately preceding the imposition of the restriction, compensation will be paid unless the applicant had acquired the land after the change was made. This represents a recognition by the Oireachtas that compensation is not appropriate where a person acquires land with notice of the restriction. Secondly, the Habitats Regulations themselves provide for a comparable compensation provision in Regulation 20(5). The Regulations also allow the designation of land to be registered as a burden on the land thus giving people an opportunity to discover the status of land before they expend money. Finally, in *O'Callaghan v. Commissioners of Public Works* [1985] ILRM 364, the Supreme Court stated that the fact that the applicant had purchased the land *with notice of the restriction*, was one of the factors which made the restriction legitimate. Accordingly, the relevance of investment backed expectations already appears to be accepted in Irish law.

[37] See *O'Callaghan v. Commissioners of Public Works* [1985] ILRM 364.

compensation would clearly be inappropriate. For this reason the "outright appropriation" test is unsatisfactory. It is suggested that compensation is only required where the public good is achieved at the disproportionate and/or unfair expense of an individual. Thus, it is submitted that restrictions of property rights should be permissible if they proportionately and consistently serve a legitimate State interest. This is a test which has also been applied by the European Court of Justice.[38] However, if such a legitimate restriction imposes a particular burden on one individual, a burden which in all justice and fairness should be borne by the taxpayers in general, compensation should be payable to that individual. This recognises the distinction between the legitimacy of the restriction and the requirement to pay compensation. Much of the American authority, which was cited in the previous paragraphs, may be relevant in assessing whether such an unfair burden has been imposed on an individual.[39]

It is true that Walsh J in the Supreme Court held *obiter* in *Dreher v. Irish Land Commission*[40] that "it may well be that in some particular cases social justice may not require the payment of compensation upon a compulsory acquisition that can be justified by the State as being required by the exigencies of the common good". However, it is submitted that such cases must be rare and that this *dictum* still requires a case by case analysis.

2.5 The Constitutionality of Land Use Restrictions

2.5.1 *General Observations*[41]

The Habitats Regulations primarily[42] operate by imposing restrictions on the manner in which land may be used. This reflects the general scheme of planning law which prescribes certain circumstances in which planning authorities may interfere with the

---

[38] See *Hauer v. Land Rheinland Pfalz* (Case 44/79) [1979] ECR 3727; [1980] 3 CMLR 42.
[39] The "regulation which goes too far" approach could be of use here.
[40] [1984] ILRM 94 at 96.
[41] In this section, the emphasis is on substantive constitutional law. Issues of procedural constitutional law (or administrative law) will be considered further in section 4.9.
[42] With the exception of Part III of the Regulations which deals with species protection. See chapter 6.

property rights of land users. It is therefore necessary to consider the constitutionality of the planning system so as to be able to suggest some views as to the constitutionality of the restrictions imposed by the Habitats Regulations.[43] In assessing the constitutionality of any restriction of land use, two inquiries must be made. First, it must be ascertained whether or not the general facility to impose the restriction is constitutional. Secondly, even if the general facility is constitutional, it must further be questioned whether the restriction actually imposed on the basis of that general facility adequately respects the property rights of those involved.[44]

2.5.2 The Constitutionality of Land-Use Plans

Only two Irish cases to date have examined the constitutionality of land-use plans or designations.[45] In *Central Dublin Development Association v. Attorney General*,[46] Kenny J examined the constitutionality of the Dublin Corporation development plan. He accepted that a development plan restricts property rights in that it provides that only certain types of development may proceed on certain sites. In this regard, the question is whether such a restriction constitutes an unjust attack. Kenny J was of the opinion that it did not. He saw a development plan as necessary in the interest of the common good; accordingly, it did not constitute an unjust attack. It is clearly in the interests of all that a town or city develop in a rational fashion, and so Kenny J's actual decision was unsurprising. It should be noted that, while Kenny J's judgment did affirm the constitutionality of the requirement, contained in section 19 of the Local Government (Planning and Development) Act, 1963, to formulate a development plan, it also, in line with the observations made in the previous paragraph, considered and affirmed the validity of the plan in question. It thus remains open to a litigant to challenge any future development/land-use plan on the basis that it

---

[43] See section 4.10.

[44] For example, while it is clearly permissible for a statute to allow conditions to be imposed on the grant of planning permission, it does not follow that every condition which is imposed is permissible. See *State (FPH Properties SA) v. An Bord Pleanála* [1987] IR 698 and also *McDonagh v. Galway Corporation* [1995] 1 IR 191.

[45] *McPharthalain v. Commissioners of Public Works* [1992] IR 111; [1994] 3 IR 353 and *Central Dublin Development Association v. Attorney General, supra*, fn 14.

[46] *Supra*, fn 14.

was made in a manner which violated constitutional procedural rights[47] or that it represents a disproportionate or arbitrary delimitation of constitutional rights. Although it is constitutionally permissible to impose restrictions on land use, not *all* such restrictions are necessarily constitutional. Moreover, in *Cental Dublin*, Kenny J expressly referred to the fact that that the planning authority had considered and heard objections to the draft plan as a relevant factor in upholding the constitutionality of development plans generally.[48]

2.5.3 The Constitutionality of Requiring Planning Permission or other Consents for Activities on Land

Under section 24 of the Local Government (Planning and Development) Act, 1963, unauthorised development constitutes an offence. The development plan would be largely ineffective if there were no requirement to seek planning permission before carrying out development. Thus, the planning permission system should be seen as the logical corollary of the development plan and, to that extent, constitutional.[49]

Support for this approach may be found in the judgment of Murphy J in *Lawlor v. Minister for Agriculture*.[50] In that case, the plaintiff argued, inter alia, that he had a property right over a milk quota. Murphy J rejected this contention, observing that the entire milk quota scheme represented an interference with private property rights in the interests of the common good. As such, one could not have a property right in the quota: the quota was instead the means by which one's right was restricted. It is submitted that this approach should be applied, *mutatis mutandis*, to the question both of planning permission and of other restrictions of land use, such as those contained in the Habitats Regulations, made in the context of environmental management plans. The requirement to obtain planning permission for development constitutes a restriction of property rights in the interests of the common good. (Indeed, it is merely the logical corollary of the development plan.) Planning

---

[47] See *McPharthain v. Commissioners of Public Works supra*, fn 45, see section 4.9.
[48] *Supra*, fn 14, at 90.
[49] Likewise other provisions in legislation requiring consents for carrying out activities.
[50] [1990] 1 IR 356.

permission may be granted, refused or granted subject to conditions. Whichever of these occurs, it is still the legal manifestation of the restriction of one's property rights. It is illogical to argue that one has a property right to the legal mechanism which is in fact the means of delimiting one's property rights.

The essential point being made here is that there is functional unity between the development plan and subsequent restrictions imposed in the interests of the common good. Restrictions may only be imposed and assessed by reference to the existing plan: if the plan is defective, that defect may be amplified in the restriction. Accordingly, an applicant may be able to challenge the validity of a restriction by reference to a defect in the original plan.

As discussed earlier,[51] there is a further question which needs to be considered: is any particular instance of the refusal of planning permission, or the imposition of a condition, unconstitutional? Each decision must strike a proper balance between consideration of the common good and consideration of the property rights of those involved. In *State (FPH Properties SA) v. An Bord Pleanála*,[52] the Supreme Court held that a condition requiring a developer to restore a Georgian House adjacent to his development was invalid. In interpreting section 26(2)(a) of the Local Government (Planning and Development) Act, 1963 Act to this effect, the court relied on the fact that the Constitution obliged it to protect the developer's property rights. Thus, it is submitted that any judicial examination of an administrative decision restricting property rights must take proper account of the constitutional rights of persons affected.

---

[51] See section 2.5.1.
[52] [1987] IR 698.

Chapter 3

Site Designation

A Balance between Community and National Responsibilities

3.1 Introduction

3.1.1 Natura 2000

The stated aim of the Habitats Directive is to "contribute towards ensuring" bio-diversity through the conservation of natural habitats and of wild fauna and flora in the European territory of the Member States of the Community.[1] The primary means of fulfilling this aim is the creation of *Natura 2000*, a network of sites hosting natural habitat types and habitats of species.[2] Once the designation process is complete, the title Special Areas of Conservation (SACs) is applied to these sites. Sites designated as Special Protection Areas (SPAs) under the Birds Directive[3] also form part of *Natura 2000*.[4]

3.1.2 Natural Habitat Types and Species of Community Interest

The Habitats Directive does not require the designation of sites for every natural habitat type and species present in the Community territory. There are many species, and to a lesser extent, natural habitat types, which are prolific within the Community and in respect of which no conservation measures need be taken.

Only sites which host natural habitat types of Community interest and/or species of Community interest (together with SPAs

---

[1] Habitats Directive, Article 2(1). The term "Community territory" will be used below to refer to the area to which the Directive applies, although strictly speaking the term would include the French overseas territories and other non-European territories which form part of the Community but to which the Habitats Directive does not apply.
[2] Habitats Directive, Article 3(1).
[3] Directive 79/409/EEC on the conservation of wild birds, OJ L103/1, 25 April 1979.
[4] Habitats Directive, Article 3(1), second subparagraph.

designated under the Birds Directive) form part of *Natura 2000*.[5] The natural habitat types of Community interest are listed in Annex I to the Directive[6] and the species of Community interest are listed in Annex II.[7] The listing of a natural habitat type or species as one of Community interest is generally[8] an indication that it is in danger of extinction or disappearance, or that factors such as a small natural range or very specific environmental needs make it especially vulnerable to extinction or disappearance should conditions become adverse.[9]

3.1.3 Priority Natural Habitat Types and Species

Some of the natural habitat types and species of Community interest are given the superior classification of "priority". These are natural habitat types and species which are in danger of extinction or disappearance and for which the Community has particular responsibility in view of the proportion of their natural range which falls within the Community territory.[10] These priority natural habitat types and priority species are indicated by an asterisk (*) in Annex I and Annex II. Sites hosting priority natural habitat types and/or priority species are more likely to be designated as SACs than other proposed sites[11] and, once designated, are afforded a higher level of protection from adverse activities than other SACs.[12] Such sites are hereinafter referred to as "priority sites" where convenient.

---

[5] Habitats Directive, Article 3(1), first subparagraph.

[6] Annex I lists 252 natural habitat types (increased from the 164 in the original Annex I by the Accession Act of Austria, Finland and Sweden (OJ L1/1, 1 January 1995)).

[7] Annex II lists 634 species, of which 200 are fauna species and 434 are flora species.

[8] But not always. Habitats Directive, Article 1(c) provides that natural habitat types which "present outstanding examples of typical characteristics" of one of the biogeographical regions of the Community are of Community interest. This is irrespective of whether or not the natural habitat types in question are in danger of disappearance.

[9] See section 3.2.

[10] Article 1(d) and 1(h).

[11] Annex III (Stage 2) to the Habitats Directive, Article 1: "All the sites identified by the Member States in Stage 1 which contain priority natural habitat types and/or species will be considered as sites of Community importance."

[12] Habitats Directive, Article 6(4) allows certain activities to be carried out in designated sites for imperative reasons of overriding public interest. The public interest considerations justifying such activities are narrower for sites hosting

3.1.4 Favourable Conservation Status

The concept of "favourable conservation status" is fundamental to the Habitats Directive and to the operation of the *Natura 2000* network. "Conservation status" is a reference to the viability of the natural habitat type or species within the ecosystem. The stated purpose of the *Natura 2000* network is the maintenance of the natural habitat types and species of Community interest at a "favourable conservation status".[13] The Directive sets out the circumstances in which the conservation status of natural habitat types and species can be considered "favourable".[14] This involves reference to various factors. In the case of a natural habitat, the conservation status will be taken as "favourable" when:
(a) its natural range and areas it covers within that range are stable and increasing, and
(b) the specific structure and functions which are necessary for its long-term maintenance exist and are likely to continue to exist for the foreseeable future, and
(c) the conservation status of its typical species is favourable.

The conservation status of a species will be considered favourable when:
(a) population dynamics data on the species concerned indicate that it is maintaining itself on a long-term basis as a viable component of its natural habitats, and
(b) the natural range of the species is neither being reduced nor is likely to be reduced for the foreseeable future, and
(c) there is, and will probably continue to be, a sufficiently large habitat to maintain its populations on a long-term basis,

The Irish Regulations use the terms "conservation status" and "favourable conservation status",[15] yet do not specifically define them. Regulation 2(2) provides that a word or expression used in the Regulations shall, unless the contrary intention is expressed, have the same meaning as in the Directive. This is a common provision in Irish legislation implementing Community directives. It is regrettable that it should be used in such important regulations as

---

priority natural habitat types and/or priority species than for those hosting non-priority habitat types and species.
[13] Habitats Directive, Article 3(1).
[14] Article 1(e) and (i)
[15] See, *inter alia*, Regulations 7(5)(a) and 36(1).

the Habitats Regulations as it can result in uncertainty and impede access to information in cases where the reader of the Regulations does not have a copy of the Directive. Arguably, it also amounts to inadequate implementation of the Directive as a failure on the part of the State to ensure legal clarity.[16]

3.2 Natural Habitat Types and Species Protected by Natura 2000

3.2.1 Community Interest Criteria for Natural Habitat Types

Article 1(c) of the Habitats Directive defines natural habitat types of Community interest, establishing three basic categories:

(i) Those which are *in danger of disappearance* in their natural range. All of the priority natural habitat types fall into this category.[17]

(ii) Those having *a small natural range* following their regression or by reason of their intrinsically restricted area.

(iii) Those presenting *outstanding examples of the characteristics of their biogeographical region*. This category appears to be quite limited as the focus of the Directive is on protecting endangered and vulnerable sites.

3.2.2 Classifying the Community's Habitats
(a) The CORINE Biotopes Project

The habitats of the Community do not naturally fall into a series of discrete habitat types. The first stage was to devise a classification system for the Community's habitats. A hierarchical classification of European habitats was developed by the CORINE Biotopes project in 1989.[18] The Commission, on the basis of the criteria identified in the CORINE project, then drew up a draft list of habitat types of Community interest. After discussions with the national experts, this eventually resulted in the version published in Annex I to the Directive which includes references to the habitat type codes used in the *CORINE Biotopes Technical Handbook*.

---

[16] See section 1.7 (text accompanying footnote 139).
[17] See section 3.1.3.
[18] *CORINE Biotopes - Technical Handbook, Volume 1*, at 73-109. Corine/ Biotopes/89-2.2, 19 May 1988, partially updated 14 February 1989.

However, in December 1991, while the Directive was being adopted, a revised version of the CORINE classification was published.[19] This made changes in the classification of habitat types and their codes. The new codes and descriptions did not always correspond to those used in both the original 1989 CORINE classification and in Annex I to the Directive. In order to deal with this problem, the European Environment Agency published a paper reconciling the habitat codes of Annex I with those of the 1991 CORINE classification.[20]

(b) Interpretation Manual of EU Habitats

In May 1992, in light of the difficulties discussed above, a Scientific Working Group set up by the Habitats Committee suggested the preparation of a manual for the interpretation of Annex I. The work was directed primarily at the priority natural habitat types. An interpretation manual for these was approved by the Habitats Committee in 1994. This consisted of descriptive sheets for each habitat, with a scientific definition of the habitat type, using pragmatic descriptive elements (e.g. characteristic plants) and taking into consideration any regional variations.

A set of 36 non-priority habitat types causing interpretation problems was then identified. In April 1995 the Habitats Committee approved the *EUR12 Version of the Interpretation Manual of European Union Habitats*, which incorporated the descriptive sheets for priority habitats, similar descriptive sheets for the 36 problematic non-priority habitat types, and the CORINE Biotopes definitions for the remaining non priority habitats. The CORINE definitions were to be considered "a minimal interpretation" as they did not take account of sub-types, regional varieties and/or did not cover all the geographical range of the relevant natural habitat type.

Descriptive sheets were added for the 11 priority natural habitat types attached to Annex I when Austria, Finland and Sweden joined the Union.[21] These were included in the *EUR15*

---

[19] *CORINE Biotopes Manual, Habitats of the European Community* (EUR 12587/3) (Office for Official Publications of the European Communities, 1991).

[20] *Relation between the Directive 92/43/EEC Annex I habitats and the CORINE habitat list 1991* (EUR 12587/3) (Version 1 - Draft, November 1992. CEC-DG XI, Task Force Agency (EEA-TF)).

[21] Accession Act of Austria, Finland and Sweden (OJ L1/1, 1 January 1995, at 135).

Version of the Interpretation Manual of EU Habitats adopted by the Habitats Committee in April 1996.[22] This incorporates further comments for other Annex I natural habitat types, correcting earlier comments and adding newly acquired information. The original CORINE codes are supplemented by the 'Palaearctic codes' based on the 1995 classification of Palaearctic Habitats undertaken on behalf of the Council of Europe.[23] The EUR15 Version which runs to 148 pages must be considered as the definitive *Interpretation Manual of EU Habitats*. However it is expected that revisions of this manual will take place from time to time in order to take account of scientific developments.

3.2.3 Significance of the Interpretation Manual

The *Interpretation Manual of EU Habitats* is of crucial importance to the Member States, the Commission and the Habitats Committee in determining whether a natural habitat type of Community interest is in fact present in a given site. The Manual describes each natural habitat under a number of headings. These include: origin, characteristic flora and fauna species, characteristic abiotic features, associated habitat types, subtypes, and geographical distribution.

3.2.4 Community Interest Criteria for Species

Article 1(g) defines species of Community interest, establishing four categories:

(a) Those which are *endangered*.[24] All priority species fall into this category.[25]

(b) Those which are *vulnerable*, i.e. those species believed likely to become endangered in the near future if causal factors continue to operate.

(c) Those which are *rare*, i.e. those species which are not endangered or vulnerable, but whose small populations and/or restricted geographical areas put them at a greater risk.

---

[22] "Interpretation manual of European Union habitats, version EUR15" adopted by the Habitats Committee on 25 April 1996, European Commission, DGXI.

[23] Devillers, P & Devillers-Terschuren, J, *A classification of Palaearctic habitats* (Council of Europe, 1993).

[24] Except those species whose natural range is marginal in the Community territory (as defined above) and which are not endangered or vulnerable in the western palearctic region.

[25] Article 1(h). See section 3.1.3.

(d) Those which are *endemic*, i.e. those species which require particular attention because they have a very specific habitat and/or the impact of exploitation on their habitat or conservation status would be significant.

3.3 Overview of the Designation Process for *Natura 2000* Sites[26]

3.3.1 Member State and Community Interaction

The designation process for *Natura 2000* sites is a long and complex one. It involves decision-making on the part of both Member States and the Commission. The discretion to be exercised by Member States and the Commission is set out in the Directive, most particularly in Annex III which sets out criteria for selecting sites. Designation is a three stage process.

3.3.2 Preparation of the National Lists of Sites by the Member States

The first stage in the process involves each Member State drawing up a national list of sites and transmitting it to the Commission. The Member State does not have full discretion as to which sites it places on its national list.[27] It must draw up the list based on the relevant scientific information and the standard selection criteria in Annex III (Stage 1) to the Directive.[28] To ensure that the information on each site is standardised, the Commission has designed a *Natura 2000* form which must be completed for each site and transmitted to the Commission with the national list.[29]

The Directive does not mandate any public participation in the preparing of the national list of sites. In implementing the Directive the Irish Regulations have made limited provision for notice of proposals to include sites on the national list and have allowed for objections to be made to such inclusion.[30] This

---

[26] See "In Focus: Steps to the *Natura 2000* Network" *Natura* Issue 1, May 1996, at 2.
[27] See section 3.4.4.
[28] Article 4(1).
[29] See section 3.4.5.
[30] Habitats Regulations, Regulations 4 and 5.

procedure is statutorily limited to those with an interest in land *within* the proposed site.

3.3.3 Selection by the Commission of Sites of Community Importance

The second stage in the process is the selection, from the national lists of sites submitted by the Member States, of sites for adoption by the Commission as sites of Community importance (SCIs).[31] The discretion of the Commission is limited as it must follow the site selection criteria set out in Annex III (Stage 2) of the Directive.

3.3.4 Designation by the Member State of Special Areas of Conservation

The third and final stage in the process is the designation by the Member States of the SCIs as Special Areas of Conservation (SACs). This is the least important stage as its most significant effect is the change of name from SCI to SAC. The term SAC is the one which ultimately applies to sites, and indicates that the relevant site has completed the designation process. In practice, the term is often incorrectly applied to sites which are at an earlier stage of the designation process, e.g. sites on the national list but not yet transmitted to the Commission.

3.4 Preparation of the Candidate List of Sites

3.4.1 Obligation on Member States

The first stage in the site designation process is the drawing up of a national list of sites by the Member State. All lists were to have been submitted to the Commission within three years of notification of the Directive,[32] i.e. on or before 4 June 1995. No Member State met this deadline. As of 30 September 1998, no Member State had submitted a complete list of sites and the relevant information to the Commission.[33] The Commission has taken enforcement actions under Article 169 (renumbered 226) of the EC Treaty against a number of defaulting States.[34]

---

[31] Habitats Directive, Article 4(2).
[32] Habitats Directive, Article 4(1).
[33] "Natura Barometer", *Natura*, Issue 7, September 1998, at 6.
[34] See section 1.5.2.

The defaulting States include Ireland which submitted its first list of 39 sites to the Commission in August 1998.[35] The Irish Regulations refer to our national list of sites as a "candidate list of European sites"[36] (hereinafter referred to as the "candidate list" where convenient). The Minister for Arts, Heritage, the Gaeltacht and the Islands[37] has responsibility for its preparation and transmission to the Commission.

3.4.2 Selection of Sites for the Candidate List

Regulation 3(1) of the Habitats Regulations provides that the Minister shall prepare the candidate list on the basis of the criteria set out in Annex III (Stage 1) to the Directive and relevant scientific information.[38] She is to indicate in respect of each site the natural habitat type(s) in Annex I and/or the species in Annex II, native to the State, which the site hosts. Annex III (Stage 1) sets out criteria for the assessment at national level of the relative importance of sites.

The site assessment criteria for natural habitat types are:[39]
(a) degree of representativity of the natural habitat type on the site,
(b) area of the site covered by the natural habitat type in relation to the total area covered by that natural habitat type within national territory,
(c) degree of conservation of the structure and functions of the natural habitat type concerned and restoration possibilities.

---

[35] *Irish Times*, 7 August 1998.
[36] Regulation 3(1).
[37] Formerly the Minister for Arts, Culture and the Gaeltacht.
[38] This provision is based on Article 4(1) of the Habitats Directive which states "On the basis of the criteria set out in Annex III (Stage 1) and relevant scientific information, each Member State shall propose a list of sites indicating which natural habitat types in Annex I and which species in Annex II that are native to its territory the sites host."
[39] Habitats Directive, Annex III (Stage 1)(A).

The site assessment criteria for species are:[40]
(a) size and density of the population of the species present in relation to the populations present within national territory,
(b) degree of conservation of the features of the habitat which are important for the species concerned and restoration possibilities,
(c) the degree of isolation of the population present on the site in relation to the natural range of the species.

As a final criterion, a *global assessment* of the value of the site for the conservation of the natural habitat type or species concerned must be carried out. There is some uncertainty as to the scope of the word "global" in this context. Annex III (Stage 1) to the Directive is entitled "Assessment at national level of the relative importance of sites." It is questionable whether considering either the conservation status of the natural habitat type or species in other Member States, or the sites submitted by those Member States, would be compatible with "assessment at national level". The meaning of "global" in this context may therefore be limited to cover the territory of the Member State concerned.

Regulation 3(2)(a) provides that, for animal species ranging over wide areas, the sites selected shall correspond to the places within the natural range of such species which present the physical or biological factors essential to their life and reproduction. Regulation 3(2)(b) provides that, for aquatic species which range over wide areas, the Minister shall similarly propose such sites only where there is a clearly identifiable area representing the physical and biological factors essential to their life and reproduction.

3.4.3 *Surveillance*
Surveillance is carried out to acquire the relevant scientific information needed in the preparation of the candidate list of sites. Regulation 7(1) provides that the Minister[41] shall undertake or cause to be undertaken, surveillance of the conservation status of the

---

[40] Habitats Directive, Annex III (Stage 1)(B).
[41] And the Minister for the Marine and Natural Resources in respect of the fish species specified in Part II of the First Schedule, and to the extent (if any) specified therein.

natural habitat types and species of the Community.[42] Particular regard is to be given to priority natural habitat types and priority species. The Minister is to have regard to such surveillance in the adaptation of the candidate list.[43]

The initial candidate list of 207 sites was published by the Minister in March 1997. The list was based on extensive survey work carried out since the 1970s. An Foras Forbartha carried out surveys from the 1970s until the mid-1980s in order to identify important natural areas as a guide for planning authorities. These areas, which had no statutory basis, were termed "Areas of Scientific Interest" (ASIs). In 1987 responsibility was transferred to the National Parks and Wildlife Service (NPWS),[44] which continued the work of listing ASIs, of which there were almost 1,500 by 1989. A major resurvey was carried out by the NPWS from 1992 to 1994 and the areas were reclassified as Natural Heritage Areas (NHAs). At present there is no statutory basis for the NHA designation,[45] but they are nevertheless intended to form the set of sites from which candidate list sites and other conservation designations will be made. The scientific data gathered from this work over the last twenty years formed the basis on which the initial candidate list of sites was drawn up.[46]

3.4.4 Only Scientific Information to be Considered?

Article 4(1) of the Habitats Directive provides that Member States are to propose national lists of sites based on the criteria set out in Annex III (Stage 1) and on relevant scientific information. Regulation 3(1) of the Irish Regulations similarly provides that the Minister is to prepare the candidate list on the basis of these criteria. A critical question which arises in this context is whether or not

---

[42] Regulation 7(2)(a) gives the Minister the power to appoint one or more persons to be an authorised officer for the purposes of undertaking surveillance of the conservation status of the natural habitats and species of Community interest.

[43] Regulation 7 is an especially badly phrased part of the Habitats Regulations. On one reading it appears to state that the Minister shall undertake surveillance only in respect of the fish species specified in Part II of the First Schedule to the Regulations (see Appendix II).

[44] A part of the Office of Public Works (OPW).

[45] The last three years have seen promises by successive Ministers to introduce a Wildlife (Amendment) Act to place NHAs on a statutory footing.

[46] Grist, "Wildlife Legislation – The Rocky Road to Special Areas of Conservation Surveyed" (1997) 4 *IPELJ* 87.

account may be taken of factors other than conservation and scientific factors in selecting sites for designation.

Article 2(3) of the Habitats Directive states that "measures taken" pursuant to the Directive shall take account of economic, social and cultural requirements and regional and local characteristics. The selection of sites is a "measure" taken pursuant to the Directive. It could therefore be argued that Member States, in selecting sites, could take account of the factors listed in Article 2(3). Thus, although not specifically mentioned in Annex III (Stage 1), a case might be made that Member States could consider economic, social and cultural requirements, etc. when designating one site rather than another, or when fixing the boundaries of a site.

However, the jurisprudence on the designation of Special Protection Areas (SPAs) under the Birds Directive suggests the contrary.[47] Article 2 of the Birds Directive is similar in nature to Article 2(3) of the Habitats Directive. It states that Member States, in taking the requisite measures to maintain the population of bird species at a level which corresponds to ecological, scientific and cultural requirements, are to take account of economic and recreational requirements. Article 4 of the Birds Directive specifically requires Member States to classify the most suitable territories in number and size as SPAs for the conservation of Annex I and migratory bird species.

Based on the European Court of Justice judgments in *R v. Secretary of State for the Environment ex parte Royal Society for the Protection of Birds* (Case 44/95) (the Lappel Bank case)[48] and *Commission v. Spain* (Case 355/90) (the Marsimas de Santona case),[49] it is submitted that reliance cannot be placed on Article 2(3) of the Habitats Directive to justify a Member State taking economic, social and cultural requirements, etc. into account in deciding which sites to include in the candidate list or in fixing the boundaries of any particular site. This opinion is supported by the recent case of *WWF-UK Ltd and Royal Society for Protection of*

---

[47] *Commission v. Spain* (Case 355/90) [1993] ECR I-4221; *Regina. v. Secretary of State for the Environment, ex parte R.S.P.B.* (Case 44/95) [1996] ECR I-3805; *Commission v. Netherlands* (Case 3/96), European Court of Justice, 19 May 1998, not yet reported.
[48] [1996] ECR I-3805.
[49] [1993] ECR I-4221.

Birds v. Secretary of State for Scotland.[50] The Scottish Court of Session (Outer House) held that while Member States, in drawing up the boundaries of SPAs, had a discretion as to where boundaries should lie, this discretion could be exercised having regard to scientific criteria only. Moreover, the Court held that the selection of sites and the delineation of boundaries constituted one process and that the discretion to select sites must also be exercised having regard to scientific criteria only.

The philosophy of the Habitats Directive would appear to mandate selection of sites on scientific criteria only while reserving consideration of other factors to the controls stage.[51] There is still some scope for an argument that, particularly in identifying sites (other than priority sites) for protection, Member States have some discretion to take economic, social and cultural requirements, etc. into account.

3.4.5 Natura 2000 Form

To ensure further that the information submitted by the Member States is standardised, the Commission has produced a very detailed *Natura 2000* form which runs to 97 pages and which must be completed for each site. This is another example of how, although the designation process theoretically involves both Member State and Community input in the decision-making, the Annex III criteria limit the level of discretion afforded to a Member State in drawing up its national list of sites. Where conservationists and others contact the Commission claiming that a site omitted from the national list should have been included, the Commission will request them to submit a completed *Natura 2000* form.[52] This enables the Commission to judge the merits of the case by reference to what it considers relevant in determining which sites should be selected.

---

[50] *The Times*, 20 November 1998.
[51] Habitats Directive, Article 6(4). See section 4.1.4.
[52] From discussions with Dr. Catherine O'Connell, Irish Peat Conservation Council.

3.5 Notice

3.5.1 Community Law and the Principles of Natural Justice

The Habitats Directive does not require that notice be given to those with property or other interests in land within a proposed site, nor that they be allowed an opportunity to make objections. This is a matter for the discretion of Member States. However, as discussed above,[53] Community Directives must be transposed into Irish law in the way which best protects Irish constitutional rights, while ensuring that full effect is given to Community Law. In order to accord with the principles of natural justice, it is submitted that notice should be given to those whose property rights in land would be affected by a designation and that they should be given the opportunity to put their case against designation.[54]

Regulation 4 provides that notice of the inclusion of land in the candidate list should be given to certain persons, including those with an interest in the land. Regulation 5 gives those entitled to notice the opportunity to object to the inclusion of land, or to request a review or modification of the candidate list. The Minister is obliged to consider such objections or requests and to decide whether or not to amend the candidate list. This procedure must be exhausted before the Minister may transmit the candidate list to the Commission.[55]

3.5.2 Notice to those with an Interest in the Land

Regulation 4(2)(a) provides that the Minister is required to notify by notice

> every owner and occupier of land mentioned in the candidate list of Europena (*sic*) sites and any holder of a valid prospecting licence or exploration licence duly issued under any enactment which relates to such land of the proposal to include the land in such a list and to transmit the list to the Commission pursuant to the provisions of the Habitats Directive.

---

[53] See section 1.7.3.
[54] See section 4.9.2.
[55] Regulations 4 and 5

Those persons entitled to notice under Regulation 4(2)(a) will hereinafter be termed "those with an interest in the land" where convenient.

Where the address of a person with an interest in the land cannot be found after reasonable inquiry, Regulation 4(2)(b) provides for extensive public notice of the land's inclusion in a candidate list site. Notices and maps showing the site concerned are to be displayed in a conspicuous place in one or more offices of State or local authorities[56] located within, or contiguous to, the site concerned. Where there is no such station or office so located, notices and maps are to be displayed in one or more of such offices within the vicinity of, or closest to, such site. In all such cases, advertisements are to be broadcast on at least one radio station duly broadcasting in the area of the site and to be placed in at least one newspaper circulating in the area.[57] Such radio or newspaper advertisements must request any person affected by the candidate list to contact the Department of Arts, Heritage the Gaeltacht and the Islands.[58]

3.5.3 Contents of the Notice

Under Regulation 4(3) the notification issued by the Minister to those with an interest in the land must, in respect of each site:

(a) be accompanied by an ordance (*sic*) map of appropriate scale in the circumstances, upon which the site is marked so as to identify the land comprising the site and its boundaries;

(b) indicate the operation or activity which the Minister considers would be likely to alter, damage, destroy or interfere with the integrity of the site;

(c) indicate the habitat type, or types, the site hosts or the species the site hosts and for which the site is proposed to be identified as a site of Community importance;

(d) indicate the procedures by which a person may object.

---

[56] Garda Síochána stations, local authority offices, local officers of the Department of Social, Community and Family Affairs, local offices of the Department of Agriculture and Food, offices of Teagasc.

[57] See Scannell, *op. cit.*, at 166-167 for a discussion of what the term "circulating in the area" means in the context of Article 14 the Local Government (Planning and Development) Regulations, 1994 (SI No.86 of 1994).

[58] Regulation 4(2)(b).

3.5.4 Public Notification Adopted in Practice

There is no provision in the Regulations for public notice to be given of the inclusion of land in the candidate list, except where, after reasonable inquiry, the address of a person with an interest in the land cannot be found. However, it appears that in practice the National Parks and Wildlife Service (NPWS) has to date given public notice of the inclusion of land on the candidate list by means of radio and newspaper advertisements.[59]

The decision by the NPWS to provide for more extensive public notice is a sensible one for two reasons. The first is that under the Habitats Regulations restrictions may be imposed on the use of land situated *outside* of a *Natura 2000* site if that use would have an adverse effect on the integrity of a site. Thus, those with an interest in land *outside* of a site may have their property rights restricted as a result of other land's inclusion in a site. They should therefore be entitled to notice of the Minister's proposal in regard to such inclusion and should be afforded the opportunity to make objections,[60] although the possibility that they would appreciate the implications of including land other than their own in the candidate list is remote. The second reason why public notification is sensible is that it encourages public awareness of the designations and public concern and commitment to protecting the sites concerned. It would, however, be preferable if there were statutory authority for this public notice.

It is worth noting that public notice is provided in relation to the designation of refuges for fauna on private land under section 17 of the Wildlife Act, 1976. Under section 17(1) the Minister may publish a notice in *Iris Oifigiúil* of her intention to make an order designating land as a refuge and at least one newspaper circulating in the locality. It would perhaps have been better if the drafters of the Habitats Regulations had included a similar provision, rather than introducing public notice on an extra-statutory ad-hoc basis.

---

[59] Letter from Mr Peadar Caffrey, Assistant Principal Officer NPWS, to authors, 27 July 1998: "An initial list of 207 sites proposed as SAC candidate sites were advertised in the regional and some Dublin papers in March 1997, local radio also carried advertisements at that time. In addition over 10,000 land owners and land users were contacted individually in writing."
[60] See section 4.9.

3.5.5 Notice to Ministers, Statutory Authorities and Planning Authorities

Regulation 4(1) provides that the Minister must cause a copy of the candidate list to be sent to the following: the Minister for the Environment and Local Government, the Minister for Agriculture and Food, the Minister for the Marine and Natural Resources, the Minister for Public Enterprise,[61] the Commissioners of Public Works, the Environmental Protection Agency, and any planning authority within whose functional area the land to which the list relates, or any part of such land, is situated. The Minister is also obliged, where appropriate, to consult with any or all of the above.[62]

3.6 Objections

3.6.1 Submission of Objections

Under Regulation 5(1), persons who are to be served with notice of the land's inclusion in a candidate list site, as well as any other person claiming to be entitled to an interest in the land, are entitled to object. This right to object is an essential aspect of the natural justice requirements mentioned above.[63] Objections must be made within a period of three months from the date of service of the notice. Objections must be made in the manner specified in the notice.[64] Notices issued to date have stated only that objections should be in writing, addressed to the Appeals Section of the National Parks and Wildlife Service (NPWS), be accompanied by a map of the area, and be as informative as possible. They have specifically stated that objections must be on scientific grounds only.

In practice, parties have been allowed to make objections after the three month time limit, the legality of which is questionable. Regulation 5(3) provides that the Minister must consider "any objections received under paragraph (1)". An objection made after the stipulated three month period is not an

---

[61] Formerly, and referred to in the Habitats Regulations as, the Minister for Transport, Energy and Communications.
[62] Regulation 4(1).
[63] See section 4.9.
[64] Regulation 5(1).

objection under paragraph (1) and it is submitted that the Minister is probably not entitled to take it into account.

3.6.2 Requests for Review or Modification of the Candidate List

Under Regulation 5(2) the various Ministers of Government, statutory authorities and planning authorities to whom a copy of the candidate list has been sent may seek a review or modification of the list. Requests for such review or modification must be made within three months of the date the list was *sent* to them. Such Ministers and authorities have no statutory powers to object, although the Minister is obliged to consider their requests for review or modification in the same manner as objections discussed above.

3.6.3 Grounds on which Objections May Be Based

The Habitats Directive requires Member States to draw up their national lists of sites on the basis of criteria in Annex III (Stage 1) and relevant scientific information.[65] It has been argued that it is not permissible for the Minister to consider other factors, e.g. economic, social and cultural requirements, in drawing up the candidate list.[66] Such factors cannot therefore form the basis of objections as it would be contrary to the Directive for the Minister to consider them when deciding whether or not to amend the candidate list. This restriction on the right to object is afforded immunity from constitutional scrutiny by Article 29.4.7 of the Constitution.[67]

Regulation 5(1) itself states that objections can only be made on scientific grounds. This requires the person objecting to show that the Minister's original decision to include the site on the list was flawed in some respect. Objections might be based on the production of additional scientific information which shows that the land does not meet the site selection criteria in Annex III (Stage 1) to the Directive.[68] It is worth noting that Regulation 5(2) which deals with requests for review or modification of the candidate list

---

[65] Article 4(1).
[66] See section 3.4.4.
[67] See section 1.7.
[68] In *WWF-UK. and R.S.P.B. v. Secretary of State for Scotland, supra*, fn 50, the Scottish Court of Session (Outer House) held that reference to economic and recreational activities actually being carried out in the site was permissible where it was part of the process of assessing the site on a scientific basis.

by Ministers of Government, statutory authorities, and planning authorities does not state that such requests must be on scientific grounds.

If Member States were permitted by European Community law to take "economic, social and cultural requirements and regional and local characteristics into account" in selecting candidate list sites, then the Irish Regulations' limitation of objections to scientific grounds might be unconstitutional. Since such limitation would not be required by EC law it would not be immune from constitutional scrutiny. Those with an interest in the affected land would be entitled to object to interference with their right to private property and right to earn a livelihood.[69]

3.6.4 Decision on Objections and Amendment of Candidate List

Under Regulation 5(3) the Minister is obliged to consider any objections received under Regulation 5(1) and/or any requests for review or modification of the candidate list received under Regulation 5(2). She may, having considered these, and having had regard to the site selection criteria set out in Regulation 3,[70] amend the candidate list.[71] It appears that, in practice, objections are first examined by an Appeals Officer in the National Parks and Wildlife Service who then makes a recommendation to the Minister. The Minister must inform all those Ministers of the Government, statutory authorities and planning authorities to whom a copy of the candidate list was sent under Regulation 4(1), and any person on whom notice was served under Regulation 4(2), of her decision regarding objections or requests.[72]

It is probable that in practice most objections submitted by landowners will, if successful, result either in the removal of a site from the candidate list or a reduction in the area of a site. It is submitted that it is not legally permissible for amendment of the

---

[69] See section 1.7.6.

[70] The criteria in Annex III (Stage 1) to the Directive and relevant scientific information.

[71] This could involve either removing a site from the candidate list or reducing the area of a site while retaining it on the candidate list. The Minister has no express power to amend boundaries (as opposed to amending the candidate list) but it is submitted that she has an implied power to do so arising from her obligation to consider objections to the inclusion of land in the candidate list.

[72] Regulation 5(3).

candidate list to result in the addition of new sites to the candidate list or the addition of new land to originally listed sites. The inclusion of new land could adversely affect the interests of landowners. The notice and objections procedure would therefore need to be followed in respect of the additional land.[73]

3.6.5 Appeals Advisory Board

In reaching a decision on objections the Minister is advised by an extra-statutory Appeals Advisory Board for which there is no provision in the Regulations. The concept of such a body originated in early 1997. The Minister, in deciding on objections from landowners against the inclusion of land within sites, would be guided by an independent body made up of the interest groups involved: *viz.* conservationists and land users.[74] As of 30 September 1998, the Board is not yet functioning. It appears that the intention is that the Board will merely advise the Minister in relation to objections, and it will not exercise a decision-making function. The Minister considers herself free to follow or to ignore the Board's advice.[75]

Statutory provision should have been made for the Appeals Advisory Board. Regulation 5(4) provides that the Minister in deciding whether or not to amend the candidate list is to have regard to objections, requests for review or modification, and the criteria in Regulation 3.[76] In the absence of an express discretion to consider further information, it is questionable whether the Minister could take another factor, such as the Board's advice, into account. Furthermore, the Board's present composition suggests that, in practice, matters other than those listed in Annex III (Stage 1) and relevant scientific information could influence its advice and might

---

[73] Regulation 3(3). This is separate from the Minister's power under Regulation 5(4) to amend the candidate list pursuant to objections or requests for review or modification.
[74] As of 30 September 1998, the independent chairman of the Appeals Advisory Board is Mr. Michael Mills, former Ombudsman.
[75] Statement in Irish Wildlife Federation document received by email on 19 August 1998.
[76] The criteria in Annex III (Stage 1) to the Directive and relevant scientific information.

therefore be taken into account by the Minister in making her decision.[77]

3.6.6 Natural Justice Considerations

It might be questioned whether the objections procedure, as currently constituted, accords with administrative law and constitutional requirements of natural justice. The Minister hears objections to her original decision to include the site on the candidate list. In principle, it is preferable that a decision-maker should not hear objections against her own decisions, in particular where constitutional rights are involved.[78] An independent appeals procedure with statutory authority should have been established.

3.6.7 Modification of the Candidate List

Regulation 3(3) gives the Minister a general power to propose modification of the candidate list either having regard to the surveillance carried out pursuant to Regulation 7(1) or where she receives a request that a site be included in the list. It is ambiguous, however, as to whether the Minister may modify the candidate list without going through the notice and objections procedures set out in Regulations 4 and 5. The principles of natural and constitutional justice require that notice be given to those whose property rights in land could be affected by a proposed modification of the candidate list and that they should be given the opportunity to make representations before a final decision is reached.[79] Where the Minister proposes a modification to the candidate list which involves adding or removing sites and/or altering the boundaries of existing sites, such modification could result in the rights of additional persons being affected. It is submitted therefore that express statutory provision should be made so that such persons have an opportunity to make representations with respect to a proposed modification. In the interim Regulation 3(3) should be

---

[77] The Board is composed of representatives of interest groups, viz. farming organisations (IFA, ICMSA), industry (IBEC), conservation organisations, rather than solely persons possessing scientific and biological knowledge.

[78] It is true that the Environmental Protection Agency's powers to hear objections to its own decisions were upheld by the High Court in *Ni hEili v. E.P.A.* [1997] 2 ILRM 458, but the constitutional rights to private property and to earn a livelihood were at issue in that case.

[79] See section 4.9.

interpreted so as to require that notice and an opportunity to object be given.

3.6.8 Informal Appeals

It appears, however, that the Minister considers that the formal notice and objection procedures need not be followed for proposed modifications to the candidate list under Regulation 3(3), at least where such modifications involve the removal of land from the candidate list. The notice issued under Regulation 4(3) to those with an interest in the land refers to the possibility of informally appealing, against the inclusion of land in the candidate list, to the Regional Manager of the National Parks and Wildlife Service. A number of sites have had their boundaries redrawn and have been reduced in area following such informal appeals.[80]

Regulation 5 is substantially undermined by the Minister permitting a system of informal appeals by landowners which does not involve any time limits or procedural rules. While one may welcome the absence of formalities in objections, the informal appeals procedure lacks transparency and is objectionable on that account.

3.7 Sites of Community Importance

3.7.1 Designation of Sites at Community Level

The second stage of the designation process is the selection by the Commission, in agreement with the Minister, of sites from the candidate list for adoption as sites of Community importance (SCIs). This stage was to have been completed within six years of the notification of the Directive (i.e. by 4 June 1998),[81] but due to delays on the part of Member States in submitting their national lists of sites to the Commission, no sites have yet been designated as SCIs. By spring of 1998 more than 6,500 sites had been submitted by Member States, covering over 265,000 km^2 (equivalent to 8% of

---

[80] Since the "formal" objections pursuant to Regulation 5(1) made by those with an interest in the land have yet to be considered by the Minister, it would appear that the alterations to the candidate list made to date are likely to have been made in response to informal appeals.
[81] Article 4(3).

the Community territory) and work is about to "begin in earnest on selecting sites of Community importance".[82]

3.7.2 Examination of Sites by Biogeographical Region

For the purposes of selecting SCIs the land area of the Community is divided up into six biogeographical regions: Alpine, Atlantic, Boreal, Continental, Macronesia and Mediterranean.[83] Each site proposed by the Member States falls into one of these regions. All of Ireland is in the Atlantic region, together with the U.K., the Netherlands and parts of France, Belgium, Spain and Germany.

Examination of the proposed sites is carried out on behalf of the Commission by the European Topic Centre on Nature Conservation (ETC/NC), Paris.[84] The Commission and the ETC/NC organise seminars for each biogeographical region which are attended by representatives of the Member States concerned, independent scientific experts chosen by the ETC/NC and NGO experts appointed by the European Habitat Forum. The purpose of the seminars is to select sites from the national lists submitted by Member States for designation as SCIs. This work is based on the scientific criteria established in Annex III (Stage 2) to the Directive which identifies a series of site attributes which should be considered in the determination of the importance of the proposed sites at the biogeographical region level.

3.7.3 Procedure for Selecting Sites

The Commission has introduced a step by step process for selecting sites for adoption as SCIs. The steps are designed to address all the issues necessary for determining which sites to designate as SCIs. They include:[85]

(a) Checking the Information Received

This involves an analysis of the site information transmitted by the Member States. The ETC/NC examines the *Natura 2000* form for each site to see that they are properly filled in and that the

---

[82] "In Focus: Selecting Sites of Community Importance", *Natura* Issue 6, June 1998, at 2.
[83] These regions are named in the Habitats Directive, Article 1(c)(iii).
[84] See section 1.6.1.
[85] "In Focus: Selecting Sites of Community Importance", Natura Issue 6, June 1998, at 2-3.

information, maps etc. is usable. Any omissions are referred back to the Member States for rectification. This information must be available on all the sites submitted for a given biogeographical region before the process of establishing the list of SCIs can begin.

(b) Establishing a Biogeographic Reference List for each Member State

For each biogeographical region, a definitive list is drawn up by the ETC/NC of the Annex I habitat types and Annex II species which are present in each Member State. This is based on Member State information backed up by independent scientific data, and is subsequently discussed at the biogeographical region seminars. Once finalised the list is submitted to the Habitats Committee for formal adoption.

(c) Analysing the Representation of a Natural Habitat Type or Species

This involves assessing whether or not each natural habitat type and species is sufficiently well represented among the sites proposed by the Member States so as to ensure their maintenance at a favourable conservation status. The analysis is based on known distribution patterns, the ecological and genetic variations and the trends in distribution and abundance of the habitats and species concerned. The Commission relies on the best scientific expertise available, in particular the views of the experts in the biogeographical seminars.

A document is drawn up to record the comments made on the representation of the natural habitat types and species. This document indicates those natural habitat types and/or species for which insufficient sites have been proposed or on which there is insufficient information available to make a proper assessment. This document is then sent to the relevant Member State(s) with a request to provide further sites and information. This stage is not completed until the Commission is satisfied that sufficient progress has been made.

(d) Selection of Sites of Community Importance (SCIs)

This is the most important stage in the selection process for SCIs. The Community importance of a site refers to its contribution to the maintenance or re-establishment at a favourable conservation status of an Annex I natural habitat type or an Annex II species and/or to the coherence of *Natura 2000* as a whole. Annex III (Stage 2) sets out the criteria for the assessment of the Community importance of sites. All sites submitted which contain a priority natural habitat type or priority species are automatically selected as SCIs.[86] For other sites four additional criteria are used in assessing their Community importance:

(a) *uniqueness*: one single site proposed by a Member State for a natural habitat type or species,
(b) *relative value at a national level*: a site having a high national value resulting from its representativity, relative surface area and conservation status,
(c) *diversity*: the number of Annex I natural habitat types and Annex II species present on the site.,
(d) *network coherence*: a site that will ensure the coherence of the *Natura 2000* network, e.g. on a migration route, ecological corridor, continuous ecosystem stretching across one or more internal Community frontiers.

A proposed site may be assessed as being of Community importance, as needing improvement, or as not being sufficiently important to be on the Community list.

A draft list of Community sites is then submitted to the Habitats Committee for approval before being formally proposed to the Commission for formal adoption as part of *Natura* 2000.[87] There is an exception for Member States whose sites hosting one or more priority natural habitat types and priority species represent more than 5% of their national territory. Such Member States may, in agreement with the Commission, request that the criteria listed in Annex III (Stage 2) be applied more flexibly, e.g. that not all sites hosting priority natural habitat types and/or priority species are automatically selected as SCIs.

3.7.4 Candidate List Sites Not Selected as SCIs

Sites placed on the candidate list by the Minister are not automatically selected as SCIs, unless they host a priority natural habitat type or priority species. Although a candidate list site will most frequently be assessed as being of Community importance, it may also be held not be sufficiently important to be an SCI and in

---

[86] Annex III (Stage 2), Article 1.
[87] Article 21

need of improvement. The Irish Regulations do not appear to envisage this possibility that some candidate list sites submitted to the Commission may not be adopted as SCIs. A number of the controls which apply to sites under the Regulations[88] are expressly stated to apply to "sites placed on a list in accordance with Chapter I of Part II of the Regulations". It is questionable whether candidate list sites which are submitted to the Commission but are *not* selected as SCIs remain "sites placed on a list in accordance with Chapter I of Part II of the Regulations". It is submitted that candidate list sites which are adopted as SCIs have moved beyond the candidate list. Conversely, candidate list sites which are rejected as SCIs are not entitled to the protective regime provided under the Habitats Directive.[89]

3.7.5 *Notice of SCI Designation*
Regulation 8 provides that, as soon as practicable after the Minister has received notification from the Commission of the adoption of a candidate list site as an SCI,[90] she must notify those with an interest in land within the site that it has been so adopted and that she proposes to designate it as a Special Area of Conservation (SAC). Some controls on land use are only activated when a site is adopted as an SCI.[91] Whether or not a site has been adopted as an SCI is therefore of some significance to those with an interest in land within the site as such adoption may have further implications for their property and mineral development rights.

Regulation 8 also requires that notice of adoption of a candidate list site as an SCI must be given to various Ministers of Government, statutory authorities and planning authorities.[92] These Ministers, statutory authorities and planning authorities are among the bodies which may be required to impose restrictions on land use

---

[88] See Regulations 14, 17, 18 and 19 and section 4.4.
[89] See section 4.4.1.
[90] Or notice of a decision by the Council that a site has been adopted as an SCI. See section 3.8.
[91] See Regulations 27-32 and sections 4.5-4.6.
[92] The Minister for the Environment and Local Government, the Minister for the Marine and Natural Resources, the Minister for Agriculture and Food, Minister for Public Enterprise, the Commissioners of Public Works, every planning authority within whose functional area the site or any part thereof is situated or whose lands adjoin the site, An Bord Pleanála, and the Environmental Protection Agency.

in SCIs. In order to do so, they must know whether land has been so designated.

3.8 Special Procedure for Sites not on the Candidate List Submitted to the Commission (Article 5 Procedure)

3.8.1 Sites Subject to the Article 5 Procedure

If a site hosting a *priority* natural habitat type or *priority* species does not appear in the candidate list of sites submitted to the Commission, the Commission has the power under Article 5 of the Habitats Directive to initiate bilateral consultation with a view to adding that site to the candidate list. For the Commission to take such action it must consider the site *essential for the maintenance of the priority natural habitat type or the survival of the priority species*. This consideration must be on the basis of relevant and reliable scientific information. It is envisaged that this procedure will be used only in exceptional cases.

3.8.2 Bilateral Consultation

The bilateral consultation between Ireland and Commission is stated to be for the purpose of comparing scientific data. The Commission will present its scientific data indicating that the site concerned hosts a priority natural habitat type and/or priority species and merits being placed on the candidate list. Ireland may also present its data to the effect that the site does not merit inclusion on the candidate list.

Article 5(4) of the Directive provides that, while this bilateral consultation is taking place the site concerned, shall be subject to Article 6(2). This imposes an obligation on the Member State concerned to take appropriate steps to avoid, in respect of those natural habitat types and/or species for which the Commission claims that the site should be designated, the deterioration of natural habitats and habitats of species as well as significant disturbance of species.[93] The Irish Regulations do not properly implement Article 5(4) as they protect sites which are the subject of bilateral consultation from damaging operations or activities, but not from

---

[93] See section 4.1.2.

other damaging actions, e.g. those which require planning permission.[94]

Regulation 6(1) provides that the Minister may agree to the addition of sites to the candidate list where consultation is initiated by the Commission under Article 5.[95] The site is to be treated as added to the list from the date of the agreement.

3.8.3 Council Power to Adopt Site as Site of Community Importance

If after a maximum of six months consultation, the dispute remains unresolved, the Commission *must* forward to the Council a proposal for adoption of the site as a site of Community importance (SCI). The Council must make a decision within three months of such referral, and its decision must be unanimous. Regulation 6(1) recognises that in the absence of the Minister's agreement, the Council may make a decision that the site should be included in the list.[96] The site is to be treated as added from the date of such decision.

3.8.4 Notification and Objection Procedures Must Be Followed

Where consultation is initiated by the Commission in respect of a site, the Minister must follow the notice and consultation procedures detailed in Regulation 4,[97] just as she would if she herself had included the site on the candidate list.[98] She must also consider any objections or requests for review or modification in accordance with Regulation 5(3) before making a decision to include the site in the list "under Regulation 3(1)". It would appear from this that the Minister cannot agree that the site should be added to the national list of sites transmitted to the Commission unless the notice and objection procedures in Regulations 4 and 5 have been exhausted. To do otherwise would be a breach of the principles of natural justice, as the Minister is under no overriding Community law obligation to add the site to the candidate list.

---

[94] See section 4.8.5.
[95] Regulation 6(1).
[96] This is a drafting flaw in Regulation 6(1)(b). Under Article 5 of the Directive the Council does not make a decision to include the site in the candidate list. Rather it makes a decision to adopt the site as an SCI.
[97] See section 3.5.
[98] Regulation 6(2).

3.8.5 Purpose of the Article 5 Procedure

At first sight the Article 5 procedure would appear to be of limited efficacy: it is only applicable to certain sites, and, since it requires a unanimous Council decision to overcome continuing Member State intransigence, it could give rise to some Member State controversy. The procedure will only be initiated where a Member State has failed to submit a site which clearly merits adoption as an SCI. The Member State concerned will already have been informally requested to submit the site during the selection procedure for SCIs. This residual power of the Commission should ensure that Member States designate all priority sites and it gives the Commission an alternative to taking judicial enforcement proceedings.

3.9 Special Areas of Conservation

3.9.1 Final Stage in Designation Process

The third stage in the designation process is the final designation by the Minister of each site of Community importance (SCI) as a Special Area of Conservation (SAC). This is to be done as soon as possible after the adoption of the site by the Commission as an SCI and not later than six years thereafter.[99] Since no SCIs have been adopted by the Commission to date, it is unlikely that there will be any SAC designations in the immediate future.

The key difference between SCIs and SACs is that Article 6(1) of the Directive mandates Member States to establish the necessary conservation measures for SACs but has no application to SCIs.[100] This involves a *positive* obligation on the Member State concerned to manage the site so as to maintain it at a favourable conservation status. Article 6(1) states that the necessary conservation measures may involve management plans, whether specifically designed for the sites or integrated into other development plans,[101] and appropriate statutory,[102] administrative[103]

---

[99] Article 4(4); Regulation 9(1).
[100] Article 6(1). See "In Focus: Protecting *Natura 2000* Sites" *Natura* Issue 2, December 1996, at 2.
[101] An example of such integration is found in Regulation 26(b) which amends the Local Government (Planning and Development) Act, 1963 and requires planning authorities to include development objectives "for the conservation and protection of European sites" in their development plans.

or contractual[104] measures. All the other requirements in Article 6 with respect to the protection of sites apply to SCIs as well as SACs, both under the Directive[105] and under the Regulations.

3.9.2 Priorities in Designation

The six year period allowed to Member States to designate SCIs as SACs is intended "to be used by them to prepare these management or restoration plans for the areas to ensure their favourable conservation status."[106] Regulation 10(1) requires the Minister to establish priorities for the designation of sites as SACs having regard to:
(a) the importance of the sites for the maintenance or restoration at a favourable conservation status of a natural habitat type in Annex I or a species in Annex II to the Directive, or
(b) the coherence of *Natura 2000*, or
(c) the threats of degradation or destruction to which the site is exposed.[107]

Obviously the more important or vulnerable a site is, the greater the priority the Minister should give to its designation as an SAC and to the taking of all appropriate measures to ensure that it remains at a favourable conservation status.

3.9.3 Notice of SAC Designation

Regulation 9(1) requires the Minister to publish, or cause to be published, a copy of every SAC designation in the *Iris Oifigiúil*.[108] There is no statutory provision for notice of the designation to be

---

[102] E.g. declaring a nature reserve under sections 15-16 of the Wildlife Act, 1976
[103] E.g. making finances available to carry out conservation measures, e.g. under REPS. See section 5.4.
[104] E.g. entering into management agreements with the landowners under Section 18 of the Wildlife Act, 1976 and Regulation 12 of the Habitats Regulations
[105] Article 4(5).
[106] "In Focus: Steps to the *Natura 2000* Network" *Natura* Issue 1, May 1996, at 2.
[107] This is based on Article 4(4) of the Habitats Directive which requires Member States to establish priorities for the designation of SACs having regard to similar factors to those stated in Regulation 10(1).
[108] Regulation 9(1).

given to those who have an interest in the land within the SAC,[109] or for a newspaper notice to be made in respect of the designation.

Regulation 11 gives the Minister the power to have notices of the existence of the SAC designation erected and maintained within, on the boundary of, or near any land which is included in an SAC.[110] It is an offence, punishable by a fine of up to £1,000, to interfere with such a notice.[111] The offence of carrying out a notifiable operation or activity without Ministerial consent or reasonable excuse applies not only in respect of owners and occupiers, but also to "users", a category which includes visitors, trespassers and recreational users.[112] Site notices ensure that persons will not be able to claim that they had no notice of the designated site as a "reasonable excuse".

It would have been better to provide for the erection of site notices at an earlier stage in the designation process. A site's status and boundaries are fixed from the date of its adoption as an SCI, so there is no reason why the Regulations could not have provided for the erection of notices at this stage. This would increase awareness of the importance of the site thus deterring people from taking actions which might interfere with its conservation status.

3.9.4 Purpose of the SAC Designation

It might be questioned whether there is any real significance in having the SAC designation in addition to the SCI designation. Member States could have been required to implement the necessary conservation measures referred to in Article 6(1) within 6 years of the adoption of the SCI by the Commission and the term SCI could have been retained for such sites. It is suggested that there are two reasons why the additional designation of SAC was provided for.

---

[109] Owners and occupiers of the land, and holders of prospecting or exploration licences which relate to the land.
[110] Article 17(3) provides for such site notices by stating that Member States may mark areas designated under the Directive by means of Community notices designed for that purpose. Regulation 11 does not state whether or not the site notices erected by the Minister will adopt a Community format.
[111] Regulation 11(2) and 39(a).
[112] Regulation 14.

First, to have Member States make the final designation as SACs accords with the principle of legal certainty. If sites were simply left with a Community designation (i.e. SCI) then their existence might not be enshrined in national law. The extra step of SAC designation affords Member States an opportunity to clarify how designation under the Habitats Directive relates to national conservation and planning law designations. Secondly, although they have no discretion in the matter and are merely renaming sites which the Commission has already adopted as SCIs, the Member States are responsible in the final analysis for the inclusion of land in SACs. This accords with the principle of subsidiarity.[113]

3.10 *Natura 2000* Network – An Evolving Entity

3.10.1 Periodic Review of Natura 2000
The Habitats Directive provides for a large first tranche of sites to be designated as SACs within six years for their adoption as SCIs.[114] Since there are no previously designated sites, this first tranche is necessarily substantial as it must cover all of the Annex I natural habitat types and Annex II species whose maintenance or restoration at a favourable conservation status *Natura 2000* seeks to ensure.

However, the designation of sites is not simply a one-off process which results in an immutable collection of SACs spread across the Community territory. The aim of the *Natura 2000* network is to enable endangered and vulnerable natural habitat types and species to be maintained or restored at a favourable conservation status over the long term. Changes in relation to habitat types and species will be reflected in *Natura 2000*. The impact of the sites already designated must be evaluated. Surveillance is necessary to identify changes and to assess the status of sites already designated. After such surveillance it may be considered that existing sites should be declassified or that additional sites should be designated.

---

[113] See section 1.4.1(b).
[114] This completion date may be ambitious in the light of the delays experienced to date.

3.10.2 Amendments to Annexes I and II

Article 19 of the Directive provides that the Commission may propose amendments to Annexes I-VI to the Directive so as to adapt them to technical and scientific progress.[115] An example of how this may result in changes to *Natura 2000* is when new scientific evidence comes to light showing that a species not previously contained in Annex II has become endangered, vulnerable, rare or endemic. In such circumstances the Commission may propose its inclusion in Annex II. Conversely, a species listed in Annex II may no longer fall into one of the above mentioned categories, and may be removed from Annex II. As a result of this the sites hosting that species might be declassified.

3.10.3 Declassification of sites

The Habitats Directive makes specific provision for the declassification of SACs. Article 9 provides that a site may be considered for declassification where it is "warranted by natural developments" noted as a result of the surveillance provided for in Article 11. It is submitted that human activities which result in deterioration of an SAC could not be said to be natural developments warranting declassification.[116]

It is not clear from Article 9 whether it is for the Member State or the Commission to declassify an SAC. Article 9 states that the Commission shall periodically review the contribution of *Natura 2000* to the achievement of the objectives set out in Articles 2 and 3 and that declassification of SACs may be considered following surveillance and where warranted by natural developments. The discussion of declassification in the context of the Commission reviewing *Natura 2000*'s achievements suggests that the Commission must at least consent to Member State declassification.

Regulation 9(3) permits the Minister, in agreement with the Commission, to declassify an SAC. Before such declassification can take place, the Minister must notify those who were the subject of the original notice of the land's inclusion on the candidate list of

---

[115] Amendments for adapting Annexes I, II, III, V. and VI must be adopted by the Council acting by qualified majority. Amendments for adapting Annex IV must be adopted by the Council acting unanimously.

[116] In such cases measures would have to be taken to restore the site to a favourable conservation status.

sites under Regulation 4(2). She must also notify and, where appropriate, consult with the appropriate Ministers of Government, statutory authorities and planning authorities who are to be notified under Regulation 4(1). Unlike the designation process, however, there is no provision for those with an interest in the land or others to make objections to the Minister's proposal although it is conceivable that such action could affect their property interests. It is suggested that this is a flaw in the Regulations.

Chapter Four

Site Conservation Measures

Controls on Development and Activities

4.1 European Conservation of *Natura 2000* Sites

4.1.1 The Philosophy of the Habitats Directive

As described in the previous chapter, the Habitats Directive[1] seeks to advance nature conservation in the European Community. The conservation objectives of the Directive are sought to be achieved in two ways: site protection and species protection. In Chapter 7, we shall examine the measures which protect species directly. In this chapter, we shall examine how the Directive seeks to achieve conservation by controlling the uses to which *Natura 2000* sites (the designation of which was described in the previous chapter) may be put. Site designation is largely meaningless unless legal measures are taken to protect such sites. It is those legal measures which form the focus of this chapter.

However, it is crucial to appreciate that the Habitats Directive is not based on the premise that all use of land is necessarily incompatible with the conservation of endangered species and habitats. The Preamble to the Directive states that, "the maintenance of such biodiversity may in certain cases require the maintenance, or indeed the *encouragement*, of human activities".[2] In addition, Article 6 of the Directive does not uniformly require the imposition of controls on land use. Such controls may only be imposed where the relevant authority, having carried out an assessment, considers it likely that there will be an adverse effect on the conservation status of the site. However, where the objectives of preserving habitats and of permitting development to continue cannot be reconciled, the Directive requires that development be prohibited, except in certain limited circumstances which will be

---

[1] When read in conjunction with the Birds Directive.
[2] Third Recital to the Preamble, emphasis added.

considered later.[3] Accordingly, although it is important to bear in mind that the Directive is not "anti-development" *per se*, it does mandate controls on land use and it is these controls which form the focus of this chapter.

4.1.2 Explicit Site Protection Requirements of the Habitats Directive

The Habitats Directive focuses on particular sites and subjects those sites to legal controls, mostly detailed in Article 6. In this section we shall describe briefly the scheme of protection envisaged by the Directive and European law generally. Having done that, we shall move to the core of this chapter, namely an examination of the land use controls mandated by the Irish Regulations, interpreted in the light of the Directive.

The Directive specifically deals with four types of site. This has been considered in detail in the previous chapter but needs to be summarised here. First, there are Special Protection Areas (SPAs). These are sites designated under the Birds Directive which now form part of *Natura 2000*. Secondly, there are Special Areas of Conservation (SACs). These are sites which have undergone the full designation process contained in the Directive. Thirdly, there are sites of Community importance (SCIs). These are sites which have been adopted by the Commission and which are awaiting designation by the respective Member States as SACs. Fourthly, there are "Article 5 sites". These are sites, hosting a priority natural habitat type or priority species, which the Commission believes should have been submitted on a Member State's national list for adoption as SCIs. A bilateral consultation process is activated with regard to such sites.[4] Finally, implicit in the Directive is the existence of sites which have not yet been adopted as SCIs. The Irish Regulations specifically deal with such sites, referring to them as sites placed on the "candidate list of European sites",[5] and we shall argue[6] that these sites do have some status in European law despite the fact that they are not specifically mentioned in the Directive.

---

[3] See section 4.1.4.
[4] See section 3.9.
[5] Hereinafter referred to as "candidate list sites", where convenient.
[6] See section 4.1.3.

The scheme of site protection in the Habitats Directive is to be found in Article 6. On its face, Article 6 deals solely with SACs but we shall shortly see that its scope is considerably wider. Article 6(1) places a general obligation on Member States to take proactive conservation measures. Article 6(2) places a slightly more specific obligation on Member States to avoid the deterioration of natural habitats and habitats of species. This obligation in Article 6(2) seems to be further substantiated by Article 6(3)[7] which details a process for assessing plans or projects likely to have a significant effect on a site in view of the site's conservation objectives. Where the assessment reveals that the proposed plan or project will adversely affect the integrity of the site concerned, that plan or project may not be authorised except in circumstances specified in Article 6(4).

It is thus reasonably clear that SACs are subject to each form of protection detailed in Article 6. Article 7 of the Directive provides that designated SPAs shall be subject to the provisions of Articles 6(2), 6(3) and 6(4) of the Directive in place of the obligations which existed under the first sentence of Article 4(4) of the Birds Directive. Similarly, Article 4(5) of the Habitats Directive provides that SCIs shall be subject to the provisions of Articles 6(2), 6(3) and 6(4) of the Directive. Article 5(4) of the Directive provides that Article 5 sites shall be subject to Article 6(2), the obligation to avoid deterioration, during the consultation period.

4.1.3 Implicit Teleological Site Protection Requirement

The Directive itself does not expressly require sites to be protected *before* they have been adopted by the Commission.[8] The scheme, as described earlier,[9] is that the Member State submits a candidate list, the Commission considers it (perhaps suggesting new sites) and agreement is reached. It is normally only when agreement is reached and when the site has been adopted as an SCI by the Commission that the restrictions envisaged by the Directive begin to

---

[7] This view is supported by the fact that, while Article 6(2) refers to "special areas of conservation", Article 6(3) refers simply to "the site", suggesting that it is the site previously mentioned in Article 6(2) which is at issue.
[8] Apart from sites where the Commission has initiated consultation under Article 5.
[9] See section 3.3.

apply.[10] Since the Directive specifically requires protection to be given to one class of sites before agreement has been reached (i.e. priority sites for which the Commission has initiated consultation under Article 5), it might be reasonable to assume that it is not the intention of the Directive to subject any other sites to restrictions before adoption as an SCI occurs. However, such a literal interpretation is generally not considered appropriate where European law is concerned.

However, the Directive itself must be read in the light of Article 130r of the Treaty of Rome which gives the Community competence in environmental matters and under which the Directive was adopted.[11] Two principles of Article 130r are of particular relevance. These are the principle that Community policy on the environment shall aim at a high level of protection and the principle that preventive action should be taken to avoid environmental degradation. All sites submitted to the Commission which host a priority natural habitat type or a priority species will be considered as SCIs.[12] Accordingly, it is submitted that it is certain that the *priority* sites on the candidate list will in the future require the protection envisaged by Article 6(2), 6(3) and 6(4), as SCIs. If the principle of taking preventive action is honoured, it is reasonable to suggest that sites hosting a priority natural habitat type or a priority species should be protected from the moment they are placed on the candidate list as to do otherwise would allow degradation of the sites to occur merely because a formalistic process of designation has not been completed.

The position is different for non priority sites. As noted earlier, in selecting such sites for designation as SCIs, the Commission is performing a different task to that of the Member State in submitting the national list.[13] The designation itself is a very consensual process and there is no certainty that a non-priority site on the national list will eventually be designated as an SCI.[14] In this slightly diluted situation, it is submitted that the principle of

---

[10] Article 4(5).
[11] See sections 1.3 and 1.4.
[12] Annex III (Stage 2) to the Directive. However, it should be noted that it is ultimately the decision of the Habitats Committee as to what constitutes a priority site that is important. See section 3.7.4.
[13] See section 3.7.2.
[14] See section 3.7.4.

preventive action does not apply with such force. Accordingly, it is submitted that the Directive does not require that non-priority sites be protected before they are adopted as SCIs.[15]

4.1.4 Limits to the Protection

Article 6(4) of the Directive specifies certain circumstances in which plans or projects may be authorised, notwithstanding a negative assessment of the implications for the site. This provision is in the nature of a flexibility device, ensuring that nature conservation is not an absolute value by subordinating the maintenance of biodiversity to other specified interests. Article 6(4) should be read as a response to the jurisprudence of the European Court of Justice on the Birds Directive. In *Commission v. Spain* (Case 355/90), the Court spoke of the protective provisions of the Birds Directive as being imperative and not yielding to economic and recreational requirements.[16] Article 6(4) explicitly recognises the importance of social and economic factors and, as such, is a dilution of the level of environmental protection previously afforded by the Birds Directive.[17]

Article 6(4) of the Directive envisages that a plan or project likely to have a significant effect on a site may proceed despite a negative assessment where:

(i) there is no alternative solution, and
(ii) there are imperative reasons of overriding public interest.

Where the site does not host a priority natural habitat type or priority species, such reasons are specifically stated to include social and economic reasons. Where the site hosts a priority natural habitat type or priority species, the reasons must relate to human health, public safety or beneficial consequences of primary importance for the environment or, further to an opinion from the Commission, "other imperative reasons of overriding public interest".[18]

It should be observed that the wording of the Directive imposes no requirement that the Commission agree that the

---

[15] We shall later consider the constitutional implications of this. See section 4.10.2.
[16] [1993] ECR I-4223.
[17] As we noted above, the scheme of restrictions for SPAs under the Birds Directive has been replaced by Articles 6(2), 6(3) and 6(4) of the Habitats Directive.
[18] See section 4.1.4.

suggested reasons are indeed reasons of "overriding public interest". The role of the Commission appears merely consultative.[19] However, if a Member State disagreed with the Commission's opinion and proceeded with the plan or project, it might find such a course of action hard to justify before the European Court of Justice[20] if the Commission were to initiate enforcement proceedings under Article 169. Moreover, the Commission would be unlikely to fund a project where it did not consider that there were imperative reasons of overriding public interest to justify the project's negative impact on a *Natura 2000* site. For these reasons, it is submitted that the Commission's role, although technically procedural, may be of real substance in ensuring a higher level of environmental protection.

4.1.5 Opinions of the Commission

The Commission has to date issued two opinions, both involving motorways, on what it considers to be "imperative reasons of overriding public interest" under Article 6(4).[21] It appears from the opinions that the Commission applied a balancing test weighing the reasons put forward by the German government in favour of motorways[22] against habitat protection reasons.[23] It is not, however, absolutely certain that this was in fact the approach applied by the Commission and one distinguished commentator argues that the Commission's conclusion that the benefits outweighed the costs

---

[19] See Wils, "The Birds Directive 15 Years Later: A Survey of the Case Law and a Comparison with the Habitats Directive" [1994] *Journal of Environmental Law* 219, at 234 (fn 93).

[20] See section 1.6.2.

[21] Opinion on the planned A20 motorway in Germany intersecting the Trebel and Recknitz Valley pursuant to Article 6(4) of Directive 92/43/EEC on the conservation of natural habitats and wild flora and fauna, OJ No. C178/3, 13 July 1995 (hereinafter referred to as "Opinion on the Trebel and Recknitz Valley"); Opinion on the intersection of the Peene Valley by the planned A20 motorway pursuant to Article 6(4) of Directive 92/43/EEC on the conservation of natural habitats and of wild flora and fauna, OJ No. L6/14, 9 January 1996 (hereinafter referred to as "Opinion on the Peene Valley").

[22] The need to build the motorway partly funded by the Communities in a very depressed area of the Community contributing to the construction of the Trans European Network of high quality roads.

[23] The need to protect the priority natural habitat.

was reached in a somewhat simplistic manner.[24] Nevertheless the commentator considered that the balancing test was the best one to use in the circumstances.

It is clear from the Commission's opinions that social and economic factors will be considered by the Commission itself in deciding what constitute "imperative reasons of overriding public interest". In neither case did the Commission engage in a rigorous analysis of whether the expected benefits from the proposed projects outweighed the costs, although this could probably have been assumed in the circumstances of the cases. The Commission emphasised the importance of whether alternatives existed, concluding that there were no viable alternatives in these cases, although it seems that the initial route of one of the motorways (the Peene Valley part) had been changed due to previous Commission pressure. The Commission also emphasised the fact that mitigating and compensatory measures would be taken in order to reduce the negative impact on the habitat. It considered it of importance that the motorway traversing the priority site was to form part of the Trans European Road Network and was to be located in a very disadvantaged area of Eastern Germany where economic development was greatly needed. Thus, the socio-economic considerations were weighty in those two cases and it may also have been important that Community funding was involved for the projects.

The obligation to consult the Commission is thus a novel device for ensuring the protection of priority habitats. It introduces an objective mechanism for deciding when habitat considerations may yield to development which could adversely affect such sites.[25] While the Commission is probably unable to prohibit plans or projects under this provision, its influence will still be felt. It is likely that the Commission's influence will be productive of a greater respect for habitat considerations. However, it must be noted that it is the role of the European Court of Justice to interpret provisions of Community law and it is ultimately that body which

---

[24] Nollkaemper, "Habitat Protection in European Community Law" (1997) 9 *Journal of Environmental Law* 271, at 279.

[25] A decision by a competent authority in a Member State which considered imperative reasons of public interest other than those specified in Article 6(4) would probably be *ultra vires*.

will determine what may be considered imperative reasons of overriding public interest.

4.1.6 A Comparison with the Irish Regulations

The Directive takes as its starting point a particular site and then describes the limits which may be placed on the land uses affecting that site. In contrast, the Regulations focus on types of land use and then proceed to describe both the limits on those uses and the sites to which those limits apply. As such, to attempt a direct comparison between the Directive and the Regulations is to attempt to put square pegs into round holes. The approach which we shall take, therefore, is to describe the entire scheme of protection contained in the Regulations and then to assess whether it meets the requirements of the Directive.

4.2 Introduction to the Irish Regulations

4.2.1 Integrated Habitat Protection

As noted above, while the Directive focuses on sites, the Regulations focus on activities. The Regulations take the two types of activity mentioned in the Directive, "plans" and "projects" and seek to integrate controls on these activities into the existing Irish planning and environmental system. "Plan" is a concept which already exists in Irish law and which is relatively easy to transpose into the Irish Regulations.[26] In contrast, the word "project", which seems to include any use of land, has no direct equivalent in Irish law. In this regard it may be noted that Council Directive 85/337/EEC on the assessment of the effects of certain public and private projects on the environment[27] provides a definition of "project". Article 2 states:

> Project means:
> the execution of construction works or of other installations or schemes, or
> other interventions in the natural surroundings and landscape including those involving the extraction of mineral resources.

---

[26] Although the drafters of the Regulations seem to have encountered some difficulties. See section 4.3.1.
[27] OJ L73/5, 14 March 1997.

Given the similarity of the context in which the concept is used in both directives, it is probable that it is intended to have the same meaning. This meaning seems to encompass all aspects of land use. The Regulations subdivide the land uses covered by the word "project" into the different categories of land use already existing in Irish law, making the necessary amendments to the different statutory schemes to ensure that the Directive is adequately transposed.

In the next section, we shall consider in detail how the word "project" is subdivided. Having done that, we shall consider the different schemes of habitat protection in the Regulations. Before doing that, it is necessary to consider the meaning of some phrases which are used repeatedly in the Regulations. These phrases are generally used to trigger some of the restrictions which apply under the Regulations and an understanding of the phrases is essential to understanding the scheme of restrictions.

4.2.2 "Neither Directly Connected with nor Necessary to the Management of a European Site"[28]

This is the first phrase which may cause some confusion. This phrase is used in many of the paragraphs which trigger the legal restrictions contained in the Regulations and is transposed from the Directive.[29] The effect of this phrase is that the restrictions contained in the Regulations do not apply to activities which are carried out in order to manage a European site or which are authorised by a management agreement for the site. There is no definition of management agreement in the Regulations and it is not clear what the term means. It could be interpreted restrictively to mean a management agreement under section 18 of the Wildlife Act, 1976, of which there are very few, or expansively to mean any formal management agreement, including an agreement made under the Rural Environment Protection Scheme (REPS).[30] It would have been preferable to provide a definition of the term as it is used frequently in the Regulations.

---

[28] This phrase is used in Regulations 15, 17 and 27-32.
[29] The phrase is used in Article 6(3), but obviously does not refer to "European site", as that phrase is an invention of the Irish Regulations. See section 4.2.4.
[30] See section 6.5.3.

4.2.3 "Significant Effect" and "Adverse Effect"[31]

These two phrases are used repeatedly in the Regulations. Where a proposed plan or project is thought likely to have a *significant effect*, an appropriate assessment must be carried out. If that assessment reveals an *adverse effect*, the proposed plan or project may not proceed, except in specified circumstances.[32] This clearly implies that there may be situations where land use would not have an adverse effect and also that some adverse effects may not be significant enough to require the land use to be restricted. This further illustrates the fact that the Regulations cannot be seen as being totally "anti-development". Given that only a likely *significant* effect may trigger an assessment, it is submitted that the plans or projects which will be prohibited will in practice be those causing *adverse* effects which are *significant* (i.e., those causing significant adverse effects). This is of relevance in considering the compensation scheme.[33]

There is no definition of "significant". It may be a mixed question of fact and law which must primarily be judged by the various authorities charged with implementing the Regulations. Since the obligation in Articles 6(2) and 6(3) of the Directive is not to authorise plans or projects which cause significant disturbance of protected species in *Natura 2000* sites and to ensure that there is no adverse effect on the *integrity* of a site, it may be inferred that a disturbance which is not significant and an effect which is not adverse to the *integrity* of a site need not be prohibited. It is probable that the phrase "integrity of the site" in some way correlates with the concept of "maintenance at a favourable conservation status".[34]

4.2.4 "European Site"[35]

An innovation of the Irish Regulations is the use of the phrase "European Site". This is not a designation in the same way as those described in the previous chapter. Instead, it is an umbrella term which includes a number of designations used in the Directive. It is particularly relevant because many of the restrictions in the

---

[31] These phrases are used in Regulations 15-18 and 27-32.
[32] See section 4.1.4.
[33] See section 5.2.3(b).
[34] See section 3.1.4.
[35] This phrase is used in Regulations 27-32.

Regulations only apply to European sites. When we use the phrase "European site" in this book, we use it solely in the sense that it is used in the Regulations. It is a term of art and only has the meaning ascribed to it by the Regulations. Regulation 2 states that three types of site come under the definition of "European site", *viz.*, a site which has been designated by the Member State as a Special Area of Conservation (SAC), a site which has been adopted by the Commission as a site of Community importance (SCI) and a site which has been designated as a Special Protection Area (SPA) under the Birds Directive.

4.2.5 "Environmental Impact Assessment"[36]

Before the Minister, or any other competent authority, can prohibit a proposed "plan or project", she must cause an appropriate assessment to be carried out. In some instances the Regulations stipulate that an Environmental Impact Assessment (EIA) would be appropriate.[37] EIA is a requirement of European and Irish environmental law for certain projects. A developer must submit an Environmental Impact Statement (EIS) with an application for permission to carry out certain projects. This must state the effects of the proposed project on the environment, by reference to a number of specified factors, including the predicted effects of the project on flora and fauna, human beings, soil, water, air, climate and the landscape, and on material assets and the cultural heritage and the interaction between these factors.[38] The competent authority then assesses the environmental impact of the proposed plan or project having regard to the EIS. This assessment becomes a consideration in deciding whether or not to allow the project to proceed.[39]

---

[36] See generally, Scannell, *Environmental and Planning Law*, (Round Hall Press, 1995), chapter 8; Doyle, "Environmental Impact Assessment and Who Assesses What" (1998) 5 *Irish Planning and Environmental Law Journal* 13.

[37] For the restrictions imposed by Regulations 17, 18, 27, 28, 30, 31 and 32, EIA is stated to be an appropriate form of assessment. For the restrictions imposed by Regulations 15 and 29, EIA is not stated to be an appropriate form of assessment. It seems that the original intention was for EIA to be the mandatory form of assessment. See Wils, *loc. cit.*, at 232 (fn 85).

[38] Presumably in this context, the EIS would have to be referenced to the relevant habitat considerations.

[39] With regard to the Regulations, the result of the EIA would seem to be the most important consideration.

4.3 Integration of Habitat Protection into Irish Planning and Environmental Law

4.3.1 The Existing Irish System of Planning and Environmental Controls

Traditionally, planning and environmental law has addressed different aspects of land use with different legislation. The Local Government (Planning and Development) Acts, 1963 to 1993 primarily regulate the development of land, which term includes the carrying out of works and the making of a material change in the use of land.[40] The Air Pollution Act, 1987 regulates the emission of polluting substances into the air, the Local Government (Water Pollution) Acts, 1977-1990 seek to do the same for water while the Waste Management Act, 1996 seeks to prevent and minimise the environmental effects of waste collection, disposal and recovery. The Environmental Protection Agency Act, 1992 introduces a system of integrated pollution control for the more polluting industries and developments and aims to prevent or minimise all potentially polluting emissions to the various environmental media (air, water, soil) from specified activities, mostly industries.[41] In addition to these environmental statutes many other statutes, such as the Dumping at Sea Act, 1996 and the Foreshore Acts, 1933-1992 regulate either particular activities or activities in particular areas.

The Habitats Regulations attempt to make the necessary amendments to certain specified statutes to ensure that the regulatory system in those statutes will be used to achieve habitat protection. In addition, they create a new regulatory framework whereby certain operations or activities which were previously unregulated, or inadequately regulated, may be controlled. The new regulatory framework therefore deals with certain land uses which were not already subject to some form of regulatory control. One of the more significant of these activities is farming which, although not normally subject to planning control, could clearly have a significant impact on the preservation of natural habitats.

The Regulations, therefore, effectively divide the phrase used in the Directive, "project", into various categories, subjecting each category of activity to its own scheme of regulation. This approach

---

[40] Local Government (Planning and Development) Act, 1963, section 3.
[41] The Act also regulates the release of genetically modified organisms into the environment.

is problematic in one respect. Article 6(3) of the Directive requires that an appropriate assessment be carried out where a plan or project, "either individually or in combination with other plans or projects" is likely to have a significant effect on the site. The result of the Regulations' subdivision of the phrase "plan or project" is that only the cumulative effects of *one* category of activity may be considered. So, for example, if the appropriate authority considers that a proposed "operation or activity" when combined with a proposed "development" is likely to have a significant effect on the site, there is no authority in the Regulations for an appropriate assessment to be undertaken. For example, if a landowner applied to the Minister for permission to spray fertiliser (an operation or activity) and also to a planning authority for planning permission to quarry (development), neither the Minister nor the planning authority would be authorised, under Irish law, to consider the cumulative effect of the fertiliser spraying and the quarry development in deciding whether to seek an assessment of the proposed project. This amounts to a failure to implement the Directive properly.

While the Regulations have subjected all forms of project, subject to the reservations expressed in the previous paragraph, to regulatory control so as to preserve habitats, they have not been as diligent in integrating habitat considerations into the making of plans. Apart from requirements placed on planning authorities in Regulation 26 to incorporate objectives for the conservation and protection of European sites in their development plans, the Regulations do not require any other statutory authority to alter or adapt statutory plans in order to achieve the objectives of the Directive or to assess the implications of those plans for the conservation objectives of *Natura 2000* sites.[42] Many Ministers and local authorities adopt statutory environmental management plans. This omission is a failure to implement the Directive properly, especially Article 6(3) of the Directive which expressly requires that *plans* and projects be subjected to an appropriate assessment of their implications for *Natura 2000* sites. It is submitted that it would have been appropriate, for example, to require that objectives for the conservation and protection of European sites be incorporated into

---

[42] See Regulation 13.

special amenity area orders,[43] orders made under Chapter II of Part II of the Wildlife Act, 1976, water quality management plans[44] and air quality management plans,[45] waste management plans,[46] and other plans and policies adopted under statutory authority. It is also submitted that requirements to incorporate such objectives and to require assessment of the conservation implications should have been mandated for all non-statutory plans, and perhaps certain policies, dealing with the provision of infrastructure or proposed developments adopted by public authorities as these could also be classified as plans which might have a significant effect on *Natura 2000* sites.

With these reservations in mind, we shall examine the way in which the Regulations have integrated into Irish law the land use controls mandated by the Directive.

4.3.2 *The Structure of the Regulations*
Regulation 2 defines a number of important terms used in the Regulations. The most important of these is the definition of "operation or activity" which means any use of-

(a) land (including the foreshore and the seabed out to the exclusive fishery limits of the State), and
(b) water covering such land,
  other than-
   (i) development which is not exempted development within the meaning of the Local Government (Planning and Development) Acts, 1963 to 1993, or
   (ii) development by a local authority, or
   (iii) an operation or activity which requires consent or other authorisation, pursuant to any enactment set out in Part I or II of the Second Schedule.

---

[43] Local Government (Planning and Development) Act, 1963, section 46 as amended by Local Government (Planning and Development) Act, 1976, section 40.
[44] Local Government (Water Pollution) Act, 1977, section 15 as amended by Local Government (Water Pollution) Amendment Act, 1990, section 11.
[45] Air Pollution Act, 1987, section 46.
[46] Waste Management Act, 1996, section 22.

Site Conservation Measures 103

This definition operates by taking the all-encompassing concept, "any use of land ... and water" and then excluding categories of activity which are regulated under other statutes. The first exclusion (i) excludes "unexempted" development from the definition of operation or activity, because planning permission is already required for all such development of land under the jurisdiction of planning authorities.[47] Most development by local authorities[48] is also classified as exempted development[49] but not *all* such development: hence the second exclusion (ii) classifies local authority development separately and excludes *all* such development from the definition of operation or activity.[50] This is a hugely significant exclusion as it is likely that much of the development which could take place in *Natura 2000* sites would be carried out by local authorities. The final exclusion (iii) refers to three relatively discrete categories of activity. First, certain activities for which an environmental authorisation under a statute specified in Part II of the Second Schedule to the Regulations is required, e.g. certain discharges of pollutants to air or water, waste collection, recovery or disposal and the carrying on of an activity subject to integrated pollution control.[51] Secondly, land use which requires Ministerial authorisation (in some form) under a statute specified in Part I of the Second Schedule, e.g. land reclamation, dumping at sea, discharges to waters, development on the foreshore, mining or petroleum activities.[52] Thirdly, land use which a Minister in her own capacity wishes to carry out under a statute specified in Part I of the Second Schedule e.g. land reclamation or drainage, fisheries development and harbour development.[53] An "operation or activity" is therefore defined as any use of land or water other than those which are already subject to the legislation referred to above. It is

---

[47] Regulation 27 amends the planning system to ensure that habitat considerations are taken into account when a decision on a planning application or appeal is made. See section 4.5.

[48] Local Authority is defined broadly by Regulation 2 so as to include the council of a county, the corporation of a county or other borough, the council of any urban district, a sanitary authority, a planning authority and a road authority.

[49] Local Government (Planning and Development) Act, 1963, section 4. See Scannell, *op. cit.*, at 151-154.

[50] Such development is controlled by Regulations 29 and 30.

[51] These activities are controlled by Regulation 32.

[52] These activities are controlled by Regulation 31.

[53] These activities are also controlled by Regulation 31.

worth noting that any activities which require a ministerial consent under a statute other than those contained in Part I of the Second Schedule[54] fall within the definition of "operation or activity" and must be regulated according to that scheme.[55]

It is necessary to draw particular attention to the third exclusion, as it amounts to the paradoxical statement that "an operation or activity which requires consent or other authorisation" is not an "operation or activity". The only way to resolve this seeming contradiction is to treat "operation or activity" as a legal term of art which does not encompass operations or activities which require a consent or other authorisation under the legislation specified in the Second Schedule to the Regulations. Nevertheless, the fact that the Regulations use the phrase "operation or activity" in two such different ways is to be regretted. To avoid confusion, we shall hereinafter refer to "operations or activities which require a consent or other authorisation" simply as licensable activities, where convenient.

This chapter will deal with controls over development and activities which could affect protected habitats under the following categories:

(i) Controls placed on the carrying out of "operations or activities" as defined in Regulation 2.

(ii) Controls applicable when a person is required to obtain some sort of authorisation for "unexempted development", for licensable emissions of air and water pollutants and for activities governed by the statutes specified in the Second Schedule. The similarities between these three types of activity require that they be examined together. These are essentially, though not exclusively, private sector activities.

(iii) The system which applies to development and activities by Government Ministers under statutes specified in Part I of the Second Schedule and to land uses and activities carried out by local authorities. Again, the similarities between these two types of land use control enables them to be treated together. These are usually public sector activities.

---

[54] See, for example, Regulation 119 of the Local Government (Planning and Development) Regulations, 1994 and the Air Navigation and Transport Act, 1936.

[55] Regulations 14-18. See section 4.4 generally.

(iv) Proactive conservation measures, mandated by Article 6(1) of the Directive.

4.4 Control of Operations or Activities

4.4.1 The Requirement to Obtain Consent

Under Regulation 4 the Minister must notify owners and occupiers of land mentioned in the candidate list of European sites and holders of prospecting or exploration licences which relate to such land that their lands or interests are affected by the proposed designation of the site.[56] The notice must specify the operation or activity which the Minister considers likely "to alter, damage, destroy or interfere with the integrity of the site." Regulation 14 provides that it shall be an offence to carry out, cause to be carried out or continue to carry out, without reasonable excuse, an operation or activity mentioned in the notice, unless a number of conditions are met. The conditions are that the operation or activity be carried out by the owner, occupier or user of the land,[57] one of whom must have notified the Minister in writing of the proposal to carry out the operation or activity, and that either the Minister's written consent is obtained or the operation or activity is carried out in accordance with the terms of a management agreement provided under Regulation 12.

A number of points may be noted. First, this obligation applies with regard to sites on the candidate list and to SACs.[58] It is not explicitly stated to apply to SCIs. As Article 4(5) of the Habitats Directive requires that SCIs be subject to Articles 6(2), 6(3) and 6(4) of the Directive, this omission amounts to a failure to transpose adequately the terms of the Directive. The obligation is also not stated to apply to SPAs. As Article 7 of the Directive requires that the scheme of protection under the Birds Directive be replaced by that contained in Articles 6(2), 6(3) and 6(4) of the Habitats Directive, this also amounts to a failure to implement the Directive properly.[59]

---

[56] See section 3.5.
[57] It seems clear that any person carrying out, causing to carry out or continuing to carry out an operation or activity on land constitutes a "user of the land".
[58] See section 3.7.4.
[59] It could be argued that the power of the Minister, under Regulations 17 and 18, to seek a court order prohibiting an operation or activity which adversely affects

Secondly, regardless of whether or not the operation or activity is in accordance with the terms of a *management agreement in accordance with section 18 of the Wildlife Act, 1976*,[60] the owner, occupier or user must apply for the Minister's consent. However, where the operation or activity is in accordance with the terms of the management agreement, there is no need to obtain the Minister's consent, merely an obligation to notify the Minister of the proposal. This causes no problems with regard to management agreements which were concluded after the Regulations came into force as such agreements would presumably take habitat considerations into account. However, it is at least possible that a management agreement pre-dating the Habitats Regulations would not have dealt with all matters in the manner required by the Directive. Accordingly, the exclusion of operations or activities, which are carried in accordance with the terms of such an agreement, from the need to obtain ministerial consent may amount to a failure to transpose the Directive adequately.

Thirdly, the reference in Regulation 14(1) to "continue to carry out ... an operation or activity ..." would seem to entail that operations or activities which were carried out prior to the coming into force of the Regulations are also the subject of the consent requirement. However, by virtue of Regulations 14(2)(b), the carrying out of operations or activities, which have already obtained the consent of the Minister, is not an offence. Accordingly, the phrase "continue to carry out" does not seem to refer to operations or activities which have already received consent.

Regulation 14 may, on its face, require that consent for the carrying out of an operation or activity be obtained, even where the Commission has not adopted the site because it does not consider it to be an SCI. However, it is submitted that, where the Commission has refused to adopt a site as one of Community importance, there is

---

European site (the definition of which includes SPAs and SCIs) fills the lacuna in Regulation 14. However, the powers in Regulations 17 and 18 are enforcement powers and are not regulatory in nature: we would accordingly submit that it would not be practically feasible to use this power as a substitute for the type of protection provided in Regulation 14 and envisaged by the Directive.

[60] Regulation 14(2)(b). This phrase seems narrower than "neither directly connected with nor necessary for the management of" (discussed in section 4.2.2) and it thus appears that consent would be required for an operation or activity carried out under any other kind of management agreement.

no longer any clear legislative authority in European law for imposing any restrictions. Any attempt by the Minister to require compliance with the consent procedure in these circumstances would probably be *ultra vires* and unconstitutional because it would not be a power exercised "for the purposes of giving effect to the Directive".[61]

4.4.2 The Minister's Decision

Regulations 15 and 16 detail the process which the Minister must follow in deciding whether to give her consent to an application for permission to carry out an operation or activity. Where she considers that the proposed operation or activity is likely to have a significant effect on the site, either alone or in combination with other operations or activities,[62] she must cause an assessment to be made of the implications for the site in view of the site's conservation objectives.[63] She must, where she considers it appropriate, obtain the opinion of the general public[64] and may only give consent for the operation or activity where she has ascertained that it will not adversely affect the integrity of the site.[65] However, where the Minister is satisfied that, notwithstanding a negative assessment[66] and in the absence of an alternative solution,[67] the operation or activity must be carried out for "imperative reasons of overriding public interest" including those of a social or economic nature, consent may be given. Where the site concerned hosts a priority natural habitat type or a priority species, the reasons of overriding public interest are less extensive and must relate to

---

[61] There is however a legal presumption that a Minister will not exercise a delegated power in an unconstitutional manner. Accordingly, a constitutional action cannot be brought against the theoretical existence of the power, only against the actual exercise of the power. See *East Donegal Co-op v. Attorney General* [1970] IR 317; (1970) 104 ILTR 81.

[62] As we observed earlier, the Minister may not consider the cumulative effect of allowing an operation or activity and a development. See section 4.3.1.

[63] Regulation 15 does not state that an environmental impact assessment (EIA) shall be an appropriate form of assessment. However, given that Regulations which implement Community law are to be interpreted schematically, *per* Murphy J in *Lawlor v. Minister for Agriculture* [1990] 1 IR 356, it is probable that an EIA would be considered an appropriate form of assessment.

[64] Regulation 16(1). This is necessitated by Article 6(3) of the Directive.

[65] Regulation 16(1).

[66] Regulations 16(2)(a), Article 6(4) of the Directive.

[67] Regulation 16(2)(b), Article 6(4) of the Directive.

human health, public safety or beneficial consequences of primary importance for the environment or other reasons which the European Communities (*sic*) consider to be of overriding importance.[68] Where consent is given, despite a negative assessment of the impact, the Minister must ensure that the necessary compensatory[69] measures are taken to ensure the coherence of *Natura 2000*.[70]

The Minister has no power to give a conditional consent under this Regulation. Why this should be is incomprehensible as in many cases conditional consents may achieve the objectives of the Directive and simultaneously protect the applicant's property rights.[71] All other competent authorities charged by the Regulations with protecting *Natura 2000* sites under other legislation may grant conditional authorisations.

4.4.3 Duty to Give Reasons

Regulation 16(3) provides that the Minister must give reasons for any *refusal* to give consent. However, there is no duty contained in the Regulations to give reasons for *granting* consent. The Minister's reasons might be available under the Freedom of Information Act, 1997 or the European Communities Act, 1972 (Access to Information on the Environment) Regulations, 1998[72] but it is submitted that they should be made available contemporaneously with the Minister's consent and incorporated into it.

---

[68] Regulation 16(5). This process was discussed earlier, see section 5.1.4. The reference to "European Communities" should be read as a reference to "European Commission". Also, the wording of Regulation 16(5) wrongly suggests that the Commission must consent to the proposed operation or activity: this wrongly transposes the provisions of Article 6(4), although it may be acceptable, from the perspective of European Community law, as constituting merely a higher level of environmental protection. However, principles of Irish constitutional law may be relevant in this regard. See section 1.7.6.

[69] It is not clear what "necessary compensatory measures" means, although some guidance as to the Commission's interpretation may perhaps be derived from Opinion on Trebel and Recknitz Valley and from Opinion on Peene Valley.

[70] Regulation 16(6).

[71] In practice, the National Parks and Wildlife Service seems to have taken the approach of defining each "operation or activity" very narrowly, meaning that there may not always be a need to impose conditions on the consent. This may have implications for the provision of compensation, which we shall discuss in section 5.2.3.

[72] SI No 125 of 1998.

There is an obligation on any public authority which grants an authorisation involving an EIA after 14 March 1999 to inform the public of the "main reasons and considerations on which the decision is based."[73] As an EIA is often deemed to be an appropriate assessment for the purposes of the Regulations, this new Community law obligation may necessitate an amendment of the Regulations in the near future.

4.4.4 Appeals against the Minister's decision

Regulation 16(4) provides that the owner, occupier or user of the land has 30 days after the day on which the decision to refuse consent is given to serve notice of appeal on the Minister. The appeal will be determined by an arbitrator who must be a barrister or solicitor of at least 7 years standing, appointed by the Minister specifically to hear the appeal in question. If the arbitrator determines that consent should have been given by the Minister under Regulation 16(4), consent must be given.[74] Regulation 16(4)(b) refers to a consent given by the Minister under paragraph 4. However, under paragraph 4 the Minister has no power to give consent. Presumably Regulation 16(4)(b) is a misprint and means to refer to the Minster's consent under Regulation 16(2).

An important point must be made about the arbitrator. It is undesirable and possibly unconstitutional that the arbitrator is appointed by the Minister. Arbitrators should be appointed by a neutral person in order to ensure openness, fairness and impartiality. This is recognised in practice as most contracts which provide for arbitration require an agreed arbitrator or an arbitrator nominated by a person who is not party to the dispute.

The effect of Regulation 16(4)(a)(i) is that the owner, occupier or user of the land has no right to appeal against a refusal where the site hosts a priority natural habitat type or a priority species.[75] It is difficult to understand why this should be so. The fact

---

[73] Council Directive 97/11/EC of 3 March 1997 amending Directive 85/337/EEC on the assessment of the effects of certain public and private projects on the environment. OJ L73/5, 14 March 1997.

[74] Regulation 16(4)(b).

[75] It is one of the most regrettable features of the Regulations (and indeed the Directive) that they do not make important points, such as this drastic limitation of the right of appeal, openly but instead rely on obtuse references to other parts of the Regulations.

that it is justifiable in order to implement the Directive does not necessarily defend it from a claim that the procedural rights of those whose property interests or procedural rights have been diminished or have been violated.[76]

4.4.5 Enforcement
(a) Operations or Activities on Sites

Regulation 17(3) *obliges* the Minister to apply to court to prohibit the *continuance* of an operation or activity when:

(i) an operation or activity is being carried out or may be carried out on a site on the Candidate list, an Article 5 site[77] or a European site, and

(ii) that operation or activity either alone or in combination with other operations or activities[78] is considered likely to have a significant effect on the site, and

(iii) she has carried out an appropriate assessment of the implications for the site in view of its conservation objectives,[79] and

(iv) she, having regard to the appropriate assessment, considers that the operation or activity will adversely affect the integrity of the site concerned.

Regulation 17 allows the Minister to apply to court to prohibit an operation or activity to which she has already consented, a point which may be problematic. It is curious that the power given to the Minister in Regulation 17(3) is merely to apply for an order to prohibit the *continuance* of an operation of activity.[80] This implies that an operation or activity must actually have commenced before the Minister may apply for an order.[81] The appropriate court is the

---

[76] See section 4.9.

[77] See section 4.1.2.

[78] But not in conjunction with development or licensable activities. See section 4.3.1.

[79] Regulation 17(2) provides that EIA is here considered to be an appropriate form of assessment.

[80] This is despite the fact that Regulation 17(1) refers to an "operation or activity which is being carried out *or which may be carried out*". (Emphasis added.)

[81] It is possible that the drafters of the Regulations saw Regulations 17 and 18 as corollaries of the revocation provisions which exist for permissions, licences and other authorisations. However, the effect of Regulations 17 and 18 is somewhat

Circuit Court within whose area the lands or part of the lands lie or the High Court.[82] The Court's powers include a power to make whatever interim and interlocutory orders it considers appropriate, having regard to the prescribed criteria for determining whether consent may be granted.[83]

(b) Operations or Activities Outside Sites

Regulation 18 places a similar obligation on the Minister when an operation or activity is being carried out, or is proposed to be carried out, on any land which is *not within* the sites specified in Regulation 17, but which is likely to have an adverse effect on the integrity of such a site. Again, the Minister's obligation, subsequent to an assessment in the same way as described with regard to Regulation 17, is to apply for an order to prohibit the *continuance* of the operation or activity. The obligation on the Minister under Regulation 18 to take action, where appropriate, to prohibit activities *outside* designated sites means that a person could have severe restrictions placed on her use of land without having had any opportunity to be consulted over the land designation which preceded the imposition of these restrictions. This raises significant constitutional and administrative law problems which will be discussed later.[84]

Regulations 17 and 18 theoretically make it possible for the Minister to seek to restrain activity which is taking place on a site which is on the candidate list despite the fact that the Commission has chosen not to adopt the site as an SCI. Where the Commission does not adopt the site, it could strongly be argued that there is no clear legislative basis in European law for this potential restriction of property rights. Accordingly, the imposition of such a restriction would exceed what is permissible by delegated legislation, rendering any restriction *ultra vires* and unconstitutional.[85]

---

more far reaching. Section 27 of the Local Government (Planning and Development) Act, 1976 was amended to deal with an analogous situation.
[82] Regulation 17(5).
[83] Regulation 17(4). See also Article 6(4) of the Directive.
[84] See sections 4.9 and 4.10.
[85] See section 1.7.6.

(c) Power to Require Restoration of a Site

Regulation 19 provides that where an operation or activity has been carried out on a site on the Candidate list, an Article 5 site[86] or a European site,[87] and this is "in contravention of the conditions of Chapter III of this Part", the Minister may direct the owner, occupier or user of the land or the person who carried out the operation or activity to restore the land within a specified period in accordance with the direction. If the required restoration is not carried out within the specified period or within such further period as the Minster may allow, the Minister may take whatever action she considers necessary including the authorisation of another person to take the required steps. She may recover any expenses reasonably incurred as costs from the person to whom the direction was made.

Regulation 19(1)(c) provides that a person who fails to comply with a direction under *subparagraph (a)* shall be guilty of an offence. However, there is no subparagraph (a) in Regulation 19. Consequently, it is submitted that persons who fail to comply with a direction will not be guilty of an offence. Legislation imposing criminal penalties is strictly interpreted and it is very unlikely that a court would excuse this mistake in the Regulations and allow the offence to be successfully prosecuted.[88]

It is unclear what the expression "in contravention of the *conditions* in Chapter III of this Part" means. This expression would make perfect sense if the Minister was allowed to give a conditional consent but the Minister is not empowered to do this. It may refer to the conditions in Regulation 14(2) concerning the application for consent or it may refer to the conditions in Regulation 15 and 16 which must exist before an operation or activity is authorised (i.e. no adverse effect).

Regulations 17, 18 and 19 may not be used to enforce the Habitats Regulations against other Ministers, or persons acting under Ministerial, local authority, EPA authorisations or under planning permissions.[89] While the review provisions with regard to permissions, licences and other authorisations may be corollaries of Regulations 17 and 18, there does not seem to be any corollary of

---

[86] See section 4.1.2.
[87] SCI, SAC, SPA.
[88] *State (Murphy) v. Johnston* [1983] IR 235.
[89] See sections 4.5 and 4.6.

Regulation 19. Therefore, it seems that restorative measures in respect, for example, of damaging development is not authorised by the Regulations. This may be a failure to implement the Directive properly.

4.5 Control of Land Uses Subject to Planning Permission, and of Licensable Activities

4.5.1 The Existing Systems

Planning permission is required for any development on, in or under land unless it is exempted from the requirement to obtain planning permission.[90] Unauthorised development (i.e. development without the required permission or development carried out in breach of planning permission) is an offence.[91] A similar regime has been imposed on many other uses of the environment. Thus, for example, the unauthorised release of polluting matter into water is also an offence.[92] In deciding whether to grant an authorisation, whether it be in the form of a licence or permission, the appropriate authority must consider a number of matters prescribed by legislation and must comply with basic principles of constitutional and administrative law. The methodology of the Regulations is to integrate habitat considerations into the making of these decisions. Regulation 27 deals with the alterations to the planning code. These alterations are then replicated for other authorising/licensing provisions. We shall therefore use Regulation 27 as our paradigm. We shall make only brief references to Regulations 31 and 32 which essentially prescribe the same procedures for Ministers, local authorities, An Bord Pleanála and the EPA when dealing with applications for various authorisations.

4.5.2 Integration of Habitat Considerations into the Planning System

Planning and development matters are dealt with under Part IV of the Regulations. Regulation 27 concerns the integration of habitat

---

[90] Local Government (Planning and Development) Act, 1963, sections 4 and 24. See Scannell, *op. cit.*, chapter 6; Galligan, *Irish Planning Law and Procedure* (Round Hall Sweet and Maxwell, 1997), chapter 5.
[91] Section 24 of the Local Government (Planning and Development) Act, 1963.
[92] Section 3 of the Local Government (Water Pollution) Act, 1977.

considerations into the planning system. Of crucial importance is that these considerations are only relevant in respect of European sites. The definition of European site[93] embraces SCIs, SACs and SPAs. Candidate list sites and Article 5 sites are not European sites. Accordingly, there is no clear legislative basis *in Irish law* for a planning authority or An Bord Pleanála to consider the conservation or protection of habitats on a candidate list site or an Article 5 site unless objectives for such a site are contained in a development plan. Any decision on a planning permission for such a site which did consider such matters could, under Irish law, be *ultra vires* and open to challenge. There may be a legal basis in Community law, however, for considering the conservation and protection of these sites, or at least those of them which contain priority natural habitat types or priority species. There may be an implied power to consider the effects of a proposed development on candidate List sites as part of a planning authority's obligation to have regard to the policies of Government Ministers[94] or An Bord Pleanála's obligation to keep itself informed of the policies of certain specified public authorities whose functions have or may have a bearing on the proper planning and development of the areas concerned.[95]

4.5.3 Decision on Planning Applications

Regulation 27 provides that in deciding on a planning application, where the proposed development is neither directly connected with nor necessary to the management of a European site but is likely to have a significant effect on that European site, either individually or in combination with other developments,[96] the planning authority (or An Bord Pleanála) must ensure that an appropriate assessment of the implications for the site in view of the site's conservation objectives is undertaken. An EIA is stated to be an appropriate assessment.[97] Planning permission may only be granted where it is ascertained that the proposed development will not adversely affect the *integrity* of the European site concerned.[98] Regulation 27(4) authorises the imposition of conditions and restrictions on any

---

[93] See section 4.2.4.
[94] Local Government Act, 1991, section 7(1)(e).
[95] Local Government (Planning and Development) Act, 1976, section 5.
[96] Regulation 27(1).
[97] Regulation 27(2).
[98] Regulation 27(3).

planning permission granted. This is a recognition that the manner in which it is proposed to carry out the development, as well as the conditions or restrictions which could be imposed on the development, might meet concerns about the implications of the proposed development for the integrity of the site.

If "imperative reasons of overriding public interest" exist, the planning authority or An Bord Pleanála may, having ascertained that there is no alternative solution, grant permission notwithstanding a negative assessment of the implications of the proposed development for the European site in question.[99] As outlined above,[100] where the site in question hosts a priority natural habitat type or priority species, the "overriding reasons" cannot be of a merely socio-economic nature, unless the Commission is consulted.[101] If a planning authority or An Bord Pleanála wishes to obtain the opinion of the Commission as to what might qualify as other "imperative reasons of overriding public interest", it must refer the matter to the Minister for the Environment who in turn will contact the Commission. A decision cannot be made before the Commission's opinion has been communicated to the planning authority or An Bord Pleanála.[102]

4.5.4 Authorisations under the Second Schedule

Regulation 31 deals with certain authorisations by Government Ministers[103] (as well as with development and activities carried out

---

[99] Regulation 27(5).

[100] See section 4.1.4.

[101] The reasons must relate to human health, public safety, or beneficial consequences of primary importance for the environment. See Regulation 27(6). For a discussion of the Commission's opinions on what may be overriding reasons, see section 4.1.4.

[102] Regulation 27(7) and 27(8). The statutory time limits for deciding on an application or appeal will not run during the period of consultation with the Commission. Regulation 27(9) and 27(10).

[103] Under the enactments set out in the Part I of the Second Schedule. It is worth noting that the Harbours Act, 1946 was repealed a number of months *before* the Regulations came into force yet is still listed in the Second Schedule. However, Regulation 2(4) provides that, except where the context requires otherwise, "a reference to any enactment shall be construed as a reference to that enactment as amended or adopted by any subsequent enactment including these Regulations." It is suggested therefore that the curious reference to the Harbours Act, 1946 should be read as a reference to the Harbours Act, 1996.

by Ministers in their own capacities)[104] under legislation specified in Part I of the Second Schedule and provides that the same alterations should be made to those systems of authorisation as are made by Regulation 27 to the planning system. Thus the impact of a proposed activity, to which the legislation applies, on a European site must be considered. Similarly, Regulation 32 deals with the licensing activities of local authorities, An Bord Pleanála and the Environmental Protection Agency under legislation specified in Part II of the Second Schedule.[105] The potential impact of the proposed activity on a European site is deemed by Regulation 32 to be a relevant factor in deciding whether or not to grant licences or authorisations under the specified legislation.

It should be noted that the restrictions in Regulations 31 and 32 apply to any development or activity, for which a consent or other authorisation is required under legislation specified in the Second Schedule and which "adversely affects" a European site, regardless of whether that development or activity is actually proposed to be carried on within a European site or outside a European site. Accordingly, a landowner may have restrictions placed on her use of land without any prior notice or consultation, as the Regulations require that only persons with an interest in sites proposed for designation be notified.[106] This raises significant constitutional and administrative law problems.[107]

4.5.5 *Review of Existing Planning Permissions*

Regulation 27(11) establishes a procedure whereby a planning permission granted for development *within* a European site immediately before the coming into force of the Regulations can be reviewed. The Regulations were made on 26 February 1997. If the Minister considers that such development *within* a European site

---

[104] For a discussion of Ministers regulating their own development, see section 4.6.4.

[105] They are the Air Pollution Act, 1987, the Environmental Protection Agency Act, 1992, the Local Government Water Pollution (Amendment) Act, 1990 (*sic*), the Waste Management Act, 1996 and the Water Pollution (Amendment) Act, 1977 (*sic*). As the EPA is now responsible for the majority of pollution licences, it is the most significant authority covered by Regulation 32.

[106] Regulation 4(2). See section 3.5.

[107] See sections 4.9 and 4.10.

would have a significant adverse effect on the ecological features[108] of that site, she may request the planning authority or An Bord Pleanála to review the decision in accordance with the provisions of Regulation 27. The planning authority or An Bord Pleanála must affirm, modify or revoke such permission depending on the results of the review.

It should be noted that the Regulations do not expressly amend planning legislation in order to integrate the power to review a planning permission under Regulation 27(11) into the power to revoke or modify planning permissions in section 30 of the Local Government (Planning and Development) Act, 1963, as amended. It is suggested that Regulation 27(11) in the first instance empowers the Minister to ask for a review. The review is to be done "in accordance with the provisions of this Regulation". It is suggested that this means that the assessment procedure, contained in Regulation 27(1), should be followed as if an application were made for planning permission. Depending on the results of the review, the planning authority or An Bord Pleanála must affirm, modify or revoke the planning permission.

However, it could be argued that Regulation 27(11) operates merely by providing another ground on which planning authorities may exercise their powers of review under section 30 of the Local Government (Planning and Development) Act, 1963, as amended.[109] The appeal of this argument is that section 30 imposes a number of sensible limits on the power to revoke or modify. For instance, it provides that, where the development consists of works, a revocation or modification may not affect works which have already commenced or, in the case of works which have been commenced but which, consequent on the making of a variation in a development plan, will contravene such plan, before the works have been completed.[110] Where the development consists of a change of

---

[108] It is unclear why a different phrase is used here to that used when considering the grant of a planning permission in the first instance. It may be that "ecological features of the site" has a wider meaning than "integrity of the site", but it is submitted that the different terminology can only lead to confusion. It should be noted that "integrity of the site" is the phrase used in Article 6(3) of the Directive.
[109] Local Government (Planning and Development) Act, 1976, Section 39(i).
[110] Local Government (Planning and Development) Act, 1963, Section 30(5)(a). However, revocation or modification of permission for the carrying out of works shall not affect so much of the works as has been previously carried out.

use, section 30 provides that a permission cannot be revoked or modified once that change of use has taken place.[111] Section 30 also provides for a compensation mechanism for those whose lands have been rendered incapable of reasonably beneficial use in their existing state as a result of the review or revocation.

It would clearly be desirable for the review provision in Regulation 27(11) to be subject to such limits. However, a counter argument is that, while Regulation 27(11) applies both to planning authorities and to An Bord Pleanála, section 30 applies only to planning authorities. An Bord Pleanála has no power to review or modify planning permissions under section 30. It therefore seems unlikely that Regulation 27(11) could be viewed as an implicit amendment, or extension, of section 30. Accordingly, it is suggested that the power to revoke or modify in Regulation 27(11) is subject to no limitations, other than those inherent in the provision itself, and that no compensation provisions apply in respect of the power. Both of these points may be constitutionally problematic.

The Minister's direction to review only applies in relation to European sites. Therefore, as regards sites designated under the Habitats Directive, the review procedure can only be activated when the Commission has adopted the site as an SCI and not when the site has been placed on the candidate list. It should also be noted that planning permissions granted after the coming into force of the Regulations are not subject to any review provisions. It seems strange that there should be a period of time between 26 February 1997 and the adoption of the site as an SCI, in which unexempted development on that site may never be subjected to habitat considerations.[112] This is particularly curious when it is recalled that *Natura 2000* is a continuous process: some sites may not be adopted as SCIs for many years, even decades. Indeed, no sites have, at the date of writing, been adopted as SCIs, so this temporal lacuna is currently operative. It is suggested that the Regulations should be amended to provide that the review provision should operate in respect of licences, consents and other authorisations granted before

---

[111] Local Government (Planning and Development) Act, 1963, section 30(5)(b).
[112] That is, planning permissions granted before 26 February 1997 may be reviewed, planning permissions granted after the adoption of the site as an SCI must take into account habitat considerations, but for planning permissions granted between those two points in time, habitat considerations do not apply. This temporal lacuna may offer a window of opportunity to a canny developer.

a site has been adopted as an SCI. This would avoid the possibility of such a grave lacuna opening up in the scheme of habitat protection.[113]

4.5.6 Reviews of Existing Ministerial Authorisations

Regulation 15(2) attempts to achieve something similar with regard to licences, approvals, consents, or other authorisations granted or issued pursuant to any of the enactments set out in the Second Schedule (hereinafter referred to simply as "authorisations").[114] Regulation 15(2) provides that the Minister may request the review of existing *Ministerial* authorisations[115] where an operation or activity has been undertaken, or is proposed to be undertaken, and which is considered by the Minister to be likely to have a significant adverse effect on the ecological features of the site. In this case, however, protection is provided not for "European sites" but rather for "sites proposed for designation as a[n SAC]". This phrase does not encompass sites which have actually been designated as SACs or as SPAs, although it does seem to encompass candidate list sites. Given that SACs will have been subject to a number of years of protection under the Habitats Regulations before they are designated, their omission from the review procedure in Regulation 15(2) may not be problematic. However, it is submitted that the failure to establish a review provision with regard to licensable activities being carried on within an SPA amounts to a failure to transpose adequately the requirements of Article 7 of the Directive.

Regulation 15(2) refers to "any of the enactments set out in the Second Schedule." These enactments include the Air Pollution Act, 1987, the Environmental Protection Agency Act, 1992, the Local Government Water Pollution (Amendment) Act, 1990 (*sic*), the Waste Management Act, 1996 and the Water Pollution

---

[113] Indeed if the courts were to accept that the limitations on review, contained in section 30, apply to reviews under Regulation 27(11), it may become completely ineffective.

[114] It is a point of some curiosity that, while the issuing of licences is dealt with under the planning and development part of the Regulations, the review of such licences is dealt with under the operation or activity part of the Regulations. This leads to anomalies which we shall detail later.

[115] The exact phrase used is that the Minister "may request the relevant Minister of the government responsible for granting or issuing the licence, approval, consent or other authorisation" to review it.

(Amendment) Act, 1977.[116] Licences under these Acts are not granted by Ministers; they are in fact granted by local authorities, An Bord Pleanála and the EPA. Yet Regulation 15(2) empowers the Minister to ask only "the *Minister* responsible for issuing the licence ..." to review it, in light of the implications for the site in view of the site's conservation objectives. This is a serious defect in the Regulations. The result is that licences issued by statutory bodies, such as the EPA, An Bord Pleanála and local authorities, are not properly covered by Regulation 15(2).[117]

It should also be noted that, when considering an application for a licence or any other authorisation granted or issued under any of the legislation specified in the Second Schedule, the protection of habitats becomes a consideration only when an application is made with respect to a *European site*. One might wonder why an attempt was made to confer a power to *revoke or modify* a licence for a candidate list site, on the basis of protection of habitats, when there is no statutory authority to *refuse* a licence, on the basis of protection of habitats, for such a site when an application is made.[118] This anomaly is probably the direct result of locating the provisions concerning the review of licences in Part II of the Regulations while locating the issuing of licences in Part IV. We shall later consider whether it is permissible for Part II provisions in general to apply to sites before they have been adopted as SCIs.[119]

A further anomaly arises from Regulation 15(2). The power to review only applies to where the licence or other authorisation was granted before the coming into force of the Regulations. Therefore, if an authorisation was granted *after* the Regulations came into force, there is no statutory authority for the Minister to require that the authorisation be reviewed. It seems curious that there should be a period, between 26 February 1997 and the

---

[116] There is no such Act. It is possible that the drafters of the Regulations intended to refer to the Local Government (Water Pollution) Act, 1977.
[117] It is probable that Community law would oblige a competent national authority to strain the language of Regulation 15(2) so as to enable the review of licences issued by statutory authorities, but this does not excuse the Irish failure to implement the Directive properly in this regard.
[118] Thus, if a landowner had her licence for an activity affecting a candidate list site revoked, she would merely have to reapply for a new licence as the competent authority would then have no statutory authority to consider the preservation of habitats.
[119] See section 4.10.2.

appearance of the site on the candidate list, in which licensable activities on that site may never be subjected to habitat considerations. This is particularly curious when it is recalled that *Natura 2000* is a continuous process. Some sites may not be put on the candidate list for many years, even decades. It is suggested that the Regulations should be amended to provide that the review provision should operate in respect of licences, consents and other authorisations granted before a site has been placed on the candidate list. This would avoid the possibility of such a grave temporal lacuna opening up in the scheme of habitat protection.

In contrast with the position with respect to the revocation and modification of planning permissions, provision is specifically made in Regulation 20(1)(b) for the payment of compensation for revoking or modifying Ministerial authorisations.

4.6 Public Authority Land Use

4.6.1 Four Systems of Control

In planning law generally, public authority development and activities may be divided into four categories:
(i) Local authority development which is exempted completely from planning control or subjected only to self-regulation under Part X of the Local Government (Planning and Development) Regulations, 1994, as amended.[120]
(ii) Development (mostly local authority development which is subjected to some level of external regulation, often in the form of Ministerial certification.
(iii) Development and activities by Ministers in their official capacities which are regulated (usually self-regulated) according to particular statutes.
(iv) Public authority development which is subject to the full rigour of planning requirements.

The approach of the Regulations again is to integrate habitat considerations into the existing regulatory scheme. Given that the

---

[120] See Part X of the Local Government (Planning and Development) Regulations, 1994, SI No. 86 of 1994, as amended by SI Nos. 69 of 95, 121 and 161 of 97, and 124 of 98. This deals with the majority of local authority development.

Habitats Regulations themselves introduce a new regulatory scheme (for operations or activities), there are now five schemes which may be applicable to public authority land use. We shall examine each of these in turn.

4.6.2 Self Regulation of Local Authority Development

Regulation 29 provides that, in carrying out development to which Part X of the Local Government (Planning and Development) Regulations, 1994, as amended, applies, a local authority is bound to consider the effect of the development on a European site. Where the local authority considers that the development is likely to have a significant effect on the site, either individually or in combination with other developments, it must ensure that an appropriate assessment[121] of the implications for the site in view of the site's conservation objectives is undertaken. The local authority may proceed with the proposed development only after having ascertained that it will not adversely affect the integrity of the site concerned,[122] taking into account the manner in which it is proposed to carry out the development and also the conditions or restrictions which could be imposed on the development. The development may be permitted despite a negative assessment of its effects where the local authority is satisfied that there are no alternative solutions and where there are "imperative reasons of overriding public interest".[123]

4.6.3 Independent Regulation of Local Authority Development

For certain local authority and road authority development, sections 50 and 51 of the Roads Act, 1993 and Regulation 123 of the Local Government (Planning and Development) Regulations, 1994 require that the road authority or local authority must, having submitted an EIS to the Minister for the Environment, obtain a certificate from the Minister before proceeding with the development. Regulations 28 and 30 provide that, where such development is proposed to be carried out and is likely, either individually or in combination with other developments, to have a significant effect on a European site,

---

[121] Regulation 29 does not state that an EIA is an appropriate form of assessment although, for the reasons given above, an EIA should be considered to be appropriate.
[122] Regulation 29(2).
[123] Regulation 29(4). See also section 4.1.4.

the Minister must cause an appropriate assessment to be done.[124] The Minister cannot certify the development where it would have an adverse effect on the site, unless there are no alternative solutions and there are imperative reasons of overriding public interest, those reasons being judged by the same criteria as for all other projects.[125] This external regulation is potentially a more effective means of ensuring that the objectives of the Directive are met than the self-regulation described in the previous section.

4.6.4 Self Regulation of Ministers' Development and Activities

Regulation 31 deals both with Ministers authorising in some way the activity of others[126] and with Ministers carrying out activity in their capacities as Ministers, under legislation specified in Part I of the Second Schedule. It is the latter that concerns us here. The process operates in exactly the same way as described in the previous section: there must be an assessment[127] and the activity may only proceed where it is ascertained that it will not adversely affect the integrity of the European site. Where there is a negative assessment, the same provisions, as described above,[128] regarding the absence of alternative solutions and permitting the activity for imperative reasons of overriding public interest apply.

4.6.5 Public Authority Development and Activities Subject to Full External Control

If development carried out by Ministers (State development) is subject to the general requirement to obtain planning permission, it will be subject to Regulation 27. Habitat considerations will thus be taken into account by planning authorities and An Bord Pleanála in the process of dealing with the planning application as described above.[129] However, a good deal of State development is exempt from planning control either under the Local Government (Planning and Development) Regulations, 1994[130] or because it takes place outside the functional area of local authorities which generally ends

---

[124] EIA is stated to be appropriate. See Regulations 28(2) and 30(2).
[125] See section 4.1.4.
[126] See section 4.5.4.
[127] EIA is stated to be appropriate. See Regulation 31(2).
[128] See section 4.1.4.
[129] See section 4.5.
[130] Especially Regulation 156. See Scannell, *op. cit.*, at 159-163.

at the foreshore.[131] Such development, provided that it is not regulated under a Statute specified in the second schedule, would therefore come within the definition of "operation or activity" in Regulation 2 and would thus be subject to the scheme of restrictions in Regulations 14-18. Therefore, two different regimes of external regulation may apply to public authority development: i.e. those schemes contained in Regulation 27 and in Regulations 14-18.

4.6.6 Review of Decisions to Allow or Undertake Public Authority Projects

There is no provision for reviewing, revoking or modifying certificates granted by the Minister for the Environment for local authority developments subjected to environmental impact assessment procedures[132] or approvals granted under the Roads Act, 1993, or for reviewing decisions by local authorities to carry out developments under Part X of the Local Government (Planning and Development) Regulations, 1994 to 1997. There is also no power to review, revoke or modify a decision by a Government Minister to carry out an operation or activity under a Statute specified in Part I of the Second Schedule.[133] This further illustrates the fact that public sector activity is subjected to less stringent regulation than private sector activity.

4.7 Proactive Conservation Measures

As noted earlier,[134] Member States are obliged under Article 6(1) of the Directive to take proactive conservation measures with regard to SACs only. This obligation is transposed into Regulation 13 which imposes a number of obligations on the Minister when a site has eventually been designated as an SAC under Regulation 9. She must establish the appropriate conservation measures: these can include,

---

[131] It is this category of activity which is controlled by Regulation 31.
[132] See Scannell, *op. cit.*, at 300-302.
[133] Regulation 31, which deals with Ministerial authorisations, covers both activities which require an authorisation and activities undertaken by a Minister under a Statute specified in Part I of the Second Schedule. In contrast, Regulation 15(2) merely covers the review, revocation or modification of authorisations and does not cover the situation where the Minister is undertaking activities under one of the specified statutes.
[134] See section 3.9.2.

if necessary, management plans, either specifically designed for the sites or integrated into appropriate plans,[135] as well as administrative or contractual measures which correspond to the ecological requirements of Annex I habitat types and Annex II species.[136] Article 6(2), which applies to SACs, SCIs and SPAs, imposes a general obligation on Member States to avoid the deterioration of natural habitats. This obligation is transposed into Regulation 13(3) with the difference that it is imposed on the Minister and only relates to SACs. She must also take appropriate steps to avoid the deterioration of natural habitats and the habitats of species as well as the disturbance of species for which the sites have been designated, insofar as such disturbance could be significant in relation to the objectives of the Directive.[137] It must be questioned whether such word-for-word transposition is acceptable. Merely restating a Community law obligation as an Irish law obligation on the Minister does not contribute to the achievement of the aims of the Directive.[138]

It can be seen that there are real differences between a site which is merely an SCI and one which has been designated as an SAC. The Minister has *positive* obligations to ensure the protection of species and habitats in SACs and must be proactive in so doing. Prior to designation as an SAC, the objectives of the Directive are to be achieved simply by relying on the legal measures discussed above[139] which are intended to prevent persons acting in a way which adversely affects the site.

Regulation 12 empowers the Minister to enter into a management agreement in accordance with section 18 of the Wildlife Act, 1976 in respect of a European site or land adjacent to such a site or any part of it.

While the Minister herself has the power under Regulation 13 to establish conservation measures in SACs, this power does not arise until the site has been designated as an SAC under Regulation 9 which could be anytime up to six years from the date a site is adopted by the Commission.[140] In many instances, this may be too

---

[135] Regulation 13(1).
[136] Regulation 13(2).
[137] Regulation 13(3).
[138] See section 1.7.2.
[139] See sections 5.4 to 5.6.
[140] Regulation 9(1).

late. In addition, Regulation 13 only empowers the Minister to establish conservation measures in respect of SACs, not in respect of areas outside of SACs on which there might be activities which might affect SACs.

4.8 Inadequate Implementation of the Directive

4.8.1 Structure of the Analysis

In the preceding sections, we have highlighted specific failures to transpose the provisions of the Directive properly. We must now turn to the crucially important question of whether the integrated protection scheme in the Irish Regulations adequately transposes the site protection requirements of the Directive. This section is a summary of what has already been discussed, with the difference that we are now examining the issue from the perspective of European Community law, not Irish law. We shall not repeat every submission we have made regarding inadequate implementation of the Directive. Instead, the focus of this section is to identify whether, broadly speaking, each site gets the level or protection required by the Directive. We shall also discuss some of the more important general failures to transpose the Directive properly, before suggesting the approach of Community law to such failures.

4.8.2 Irish Protection of SACs

As noted earlier, SACs are subject to the restrictions contained in Articles 6(1), 6(2) and 6(3) of the Habitats Directive. Article 6(1) protection is transposed into Regulation 13 in a manner which is substantially acceptable, although some reservations were expressed concerning the review of existing management agreements which may not adequately incorporate habitat considerations.[141] The Article 6(2) obligation to avoid deterioration of SACs is met jointly by the court order provisions of Regulations 17 and 18, and by the provisions of Regulation 14-16 and 26-32. The Article 6(3) obligation, which in our view is a substantiation of Article 6(2), is adequately transposed with regards to SACs. They are specifically protected from adverse operations or activities[142] and they come

---

[141] See section 5.4.1.
[142] Regulations 14-16.

within the definition of European site,[143] and are therefore subject to the provisions of Regulation 26-32.[144]

4.8.3 Irish Protection of SPAs

As noted earlier, Article 7 of the Directive provides that SPAs should be subjected to the provisions of Articles 6(2), 6(3) and 6(4). SPAs fall within the definition of European site[145] and are thus protected from all activities and development which are the subject of licences, authorisations or permissions.[146] However, Regulations 14-16 as drafted do not provide that SPAs should be protected from operations or activities. While a Minister may apply to court under Regulations 17 and 18 for an order of prohibition[147] with regard to operations or activities being carried out in, or affecting, an SPA, it is submitted that this is not an adequate level of protection. It certainly is not sufficient to subject SPAs to the appropriate assessment requirements of Article 6(3). This amounts to inadequate transposition of the Directive.

4.8.4 Irish Protection of SCIs

The situation with regard to SCIs is the same as that for SPAs, in that Article 4(5) of the Directive states that the obligations contained in Article 6(2), 6(3) and 6(4) apply to such sites. SCIs come within the definition of European site, and so are covered by Regulations 17, 18 and 26-32. However, as with SPAs, SCIs are not subjected to the consent procedure for operations or activities contained in Regulations 14-16. For the same reasons as outlined in the previous paragraph, it is suggested that the provisions of Regulations 17 and 18 are not sufficient to remedy this defect. It thus amounts to inadequate transposition of the Directive.

4.8.5 Irish Protection of Article 5 Sites

Article 5(4) of the Directive imposes the Article 6(2) obligation on Member States with respect to Article 5 sites. In our view, the Article 6(2) obligation is substantiated by Article 6(3): The provisions of Article 6(2) would thus be sufficiently transposed if

---

[143] Regulation 2.
[144] Regulations 27-32.
[145] Regulation 2. See section 4.2.4.
[146] Regulations 27-32.
[147] Regulations 17 and 18.

Article 5 sites were subjected to all the general land use controls in the Regulations. However, only Regulations 17(1)(b), 18(1)(b) and 19(1)(ii) deal with Article 5 sites. Regulation 17(1)(b) obliges the Minister to apply to court to prohibit an operation or activity which might adversely affect the integrity of an Article 5 site.[148] Regulation 18(1)(b) provides likewise with respect to operations or activities which take place on land which is not within an Article 5 site but which might adversely affect such a site.[149] Regulation 19(1)(i) provides for the taking of restoration measures where an operation or activity has been carried out on such a site.[150] It is suggested that these means of protection, which leave the onus on the Minister to take action, would amount to acceptable transposition of the obligation under Article 6(2) if they applied to all forms of land use. This is not the case.

Regulations 17, 18 and 19 deal only with the prohibition of operations or activities: other land uses are not covered. Accordingly, the Regulations provide that Article 5 sites may be protected from "operations or activities" where the Minister takes action, but cannot be protected from development under planning legislation,[151] from local authority development[152] or from activities which are subject to the authorisations specified in the Second Schedule to the Regulations. These are clearly failures to transpose Article 5(4) adequately.

4.8.6 Irish Protection of Candidate List Sites

We argued earlier that sites on the candidate list hosting a priority natural habitat or a priority species required, on a teleological interpretation of European law, protection from any plans or projects which may have an adverse effect on them. An examination of the Regulations reveals that such sites are only protected from operations or activities[153] and not from the land uses dealt with in

---

[148] See section 4.4.5(a).
[149] See section 4.4.5(b).
[150] See section 4.4.5(c).
[151] Because Regulation 17 only applies to an "operation or activity" and not to, for example, development which requires planning permission which is controlled here by Regulation 27. See section 4.5.
[152] Regulations 28, 29 and 30. See section 4.6.
[153] Regulations 14-19. See section 4.4.

Regulations 27-32. It is suggested that this amounts to a failure to transpose the Directive adequately.

4.8.7 Irish Protection of Sites Generally

As described earlier,[154] the Regulations do not adequately transpose the requirements of the Directive in regard to all plans likely to have a significant effect on habitat sites. Development plans are the only plans specifically mentioned in the Regulations[155] and, even there, there is no provision for assessment of their implications for a site in the manner prescribed in Article 6(3). It is submitted that this amounts to a failure to transpose the requirements of the Directive adequately. As was also described earlier,[156] there is no properly phrased provision in the Irish Regulations which allows for the review of existing planning permissions or of existing environmental authorisations issued by statutory authorities: it is submitted that this amounts to a failure to implement the Directive properly.

4.8.8 The Doctrines of Direct and Indirect Effect

It was suggested earlier[157] that it is possible that the provisions of the Directive may be directly effective. This view is derived from the fact that, in *Commission v. Spain* (Case 355/90),[158] the Court of Justice held that the site protection requirements of Article 4 of the Birds Directive applied independently of whether sites were actually designated. Thus, where it was clear that a site should be designated, restrictions on activities should apply.[159] However, it is not clear whether this amounted to the direct effect of designations within the Member State or merely to the imposition of a duty on the Member State to take the necessary measures to preserve the integrity of sites which should have been designated but were not. It could be argued that the Article 5 procedure, and the more consensual process of site designation contained in the Habitats Regulations generally, means that the doctrine of direct effect does not apply.

---

[154] See section 4.3.1.
[155] See Regulation 26.
[156] See section 4.5.5 and 4.5.6.
[157] See section 1.7.4.
[158] [1993] ECR I-4223.
[159] See casenote in 1993 *European Environmental Law Review* 269, at 273.

If one accepts the view that the doctrine of direct effect applies, it is probable that the restrictions detailed in Article 6 could be applied directly to designated sites where the Regulations have not provided for the level of protection required by the Directive. This may be of particular application to the Article 6(2) obligation, the wording of which is similar to that of Article 4(4) of the Birds Directive, considered in *Commission v. Spain*.

If the doctrine of direct effect were held not to apply, the doctrine of indirect effect might then be of relevance. This doctrine, as discussed earlier, obliges competent national authorities to interpret national legislation so as to meet the requirements of a Directive which has not been properly implemented. It is possible that this doctrine could be applied so as to remedy some of the deficiencies in the Irish scheme of protection. However, it cannot be overemphasised that neither the doctrine of direct effect nor the doctrine of indirect effect absolve Ireland of its failure to transpose the Directive properly. It is suggested that in the interests of legal certainty, if nothing else, the Regulations should be amended to ensure that the Directive is properly transposed.

4.9 Public Participation and the Requirements of Administrative Law

4.9.1 Basic Principles

"There has never been any doubt that the rules of natural justice apply to State interference with property rights."[160] Property rights are also protected under Community law[161] and under the European Convention of Human Rights.[162] Consequently, the rules of natural justice must be respected in administrative decision making in general. They apply with even more force when a constitutionally protected right is involved. It should also be noted that the rules of natural justice have, in Ireland, been placed on a constitutional basis and are often referred to as the "rules of natural and constitutional

---

[160] Hogan and Morgan, *Administrative Law in Ireland* (3rd ed., Round Hall Sweet and Maxwell, 1998), at 598.
[161] See, for example *Hauer v. Land Rheinland-Pfalz* (Case 44/79) [1979] ECR 3727; [1980] 3 CMLR 42 and *Nold v. Commission* (Case 41/73) [1974] ECR 49; [1974] 2 CMLR 338.
[162] Article 6.

justice".[163] The rule of natural justice which is relevant in the present context is the rule of *audi alteram partem* (hear both sides). This requires that, before a decision is made, a person whose rights are affected is entitled to an opportunity to be heard. This involves giving that person notice of the proposed decision and requiring the public authority to listen to her representations.

For present purposes, the restrictions on land use may be divided into two categories: those which apply to designated land under the Regulations and those which apply to undesignated land.[164] With regard to the former, persons with property rights are usually given notice of the proposed designation, the consequences of which may include land use restrictions[165] and an opportunity to object.[166] In contrast, where the land is undesignated, there is no statutory requirement to give notice and no right to object is provided for under the Regulations. It will be remembered that restrictions may be imposed under Regulation 18 where the Minister is obliged in certain circumstances to apply to court to prohibit an operation or activity from taking place on land which is not within a designated site. Also, under Part IV of the Regulations, restrictions on permitted development and authorised activities apply where the proposed development or activity[167] has an adverse effect on a European site, regardless of whether or not it takes place within a European site. Those with property interests in undesignated land may have been given neither notice of the proposed designation and its implications for their interests, nor an opportunity to object. The question which arises is whether a decision to restrict land use on undesignated land is invalid because of a failure to comply with the rules of natural and constitutional justice.

---

[163] Hogan and Morgan, *op. cit.*, at 510. See, for instance, *State (Gleeson) v. Minister for Defence* [1976] IR 280.
[164] What the land is designated as is irrelevant for present purposes. The relevant point is that designation of land under the Regulations is accompanied by notice.
[165] Regulation 4(2).
[166] Regulation 5.
[167] See section 4.5.

4.9.2 Compliance of the Habitats Regulations with Administrative Law

It was submitted earlier,[168] that there was functional unity between a land use plan or other environmental management plan and the subsequent restrictions imposed by reference to those plans. The land use restrictions imposed under the Regulations are imposed by reference to the original designation.[169] Accordingly, we would suggest that a procedural defect at the designation stage is amplified at the restriction stage (in the form of an actual restriction on the land use of the unnotified party) and that it is open to an aggrieved person to challenge the restriction by reference to defective procedures[170] in the designation process.

In the case of *TV3 v. Independent Radio and Television Commission*,[171] a case which involved a form of property right, the High Court held that a clear warning should have been given to the applicant that an adverse decision was envisaged. From this it could be argued that notice should be given to those affected by a habitat designation, regardless of whether or not it is their land which is actually designated. This view may be reinforced by reference to the planning case of *Keogh v. Galway County Council*[172] in which the applicants successfully argued that they should be given notice in the development plan of a proposal which might affect them although the designation in the plan was not one which affected their lands. In *McPharthalain v. Commissioners of Public Works*,[173] it was held that notice should have been given of the designation of a site as one of scientific interest.[174]

---

[168] See section 2.5.3.
[169] A landowner who did not have the opportunity to object to a designation, for instance on the basis that it was not scientifically required, could find herself prejudiced when a restriction is imposed on the land on the basis of scientific arguments which she has never been able to challenge.
[170] Defective in the sense that notice was not given to a person who would be affected by the decision.
[171] [1994] 2 IR 439. In this case a franchise would have been withdrawn if information required by the Commission was not furnished on the promised day.
[172] [1995] 1 ILRM 141. However, it should be noted that this case was decided on the basis of an interpretation of the planning code. Also, Carney J seemed to place some emphasis on the fact that the information provided by the respondent, in the development plan, was actually misleading.
[173] [1992] 1 IR 111 (HC); [1994] 3 IR 353 (SC).
[174] Although this case supports a notice requirement, it is limited to notifying the owner of the actual designated site. However, a broader reading of the case

It is submitted that, in so far as it is practicable to do so, specific notice should be given of proposed designations to all whose rights might be affected, i.e. not just to the owners of, or those with interests in, the actual sites proposed for designation.[175] Accordingly, it is suggested that the Regulations do not fully comply with the requirements of natural justice. It is also suggested that landowners and others with interests in land affected should have their representations considered before a decision is made.

It is possible that the requirements of administrative law in this regard might come into conflict with the duty to give effect to Community law. However, procedural rights do form part of the general principles of the European Community, in the light of which the Directive must be read.[176] It is possible that the European Court of Justice would interpret the Directive in a way which respected the principle of *audi alteram partem*. If the Court's interpretation were to coincide with Irish constitutional requirements, a conflict between the two legal orders would be avoided.

4.9.3 A Policy Argument in Favour of Wider Public Participation

The environment is a shared resource and the principle of shared responsibility in European environmental policy requires that all co-operate in its protection.[177] A policy of ensuring widespread public participation in environmental decision-making is enshrined in most statutes dealing with the environment.

In *Attorney General (McGarry) v. Sligo County Council*,[178] McCarthy J described the development plan as a contract between three parties: the developer, the local authority and the general public. This notion of the environmental contract with three

---

would suggest that the reason for the notice requirement is that the applicant's interests might have been adversely affected, a rationale which applies equally to designated and undesignated land.

[175] Even if a court did not accept that specific notice should be given, it would seem that general notice is a minimal requirement. The Regulations do not provide for general notice, although it seems that the National Parks and Wildlife Service (NPWS) has given some general notice. It is unclear whether this would be considered adequate by a court.

[176] See *Al-Jubail Fertilizer Co. and Saudi Arabian Fertilizer Co. v. Council* (Case 49/88) [1991] ECR I-3187; [1991] 3 CMLR 377. This case concerned the right to a fair hearing.

[177] See section 1.4.1(b).

[178] [1991] 1 IR 99; [1989] ILRM 768.

interested parties is one which runs throughout the case law. In a number of recent cases, concluding with *Lancefort v. An Bord Pleanála*,[179] some judges have emphasised the importance of balance in environmental law, particularly the importance of balance between the three parties to this environmental contract. It must be questioned whether balance can be achieved in a system where only those with an identified property interest in the matter are given rights to make representations. It is submitted that greater rights for public participation in the process by which sites are designated should be provided for in the regulations.

4.10 The Constitutionality of the Restrictions

4.10.1 Relationship with Administrative Law

The administrative law requirements discussed in the previous section could be characterised as procedural constitutional law.[180] The Regulations pose two related questions. First, are the particular decisions to impose restrictions on property rights correctly taken? This is the procedural question which was considered in the previous section. Secondly, is the substance of the restriction imposed compatible with the constitutional requirements? This is the substantive issue of constitutional law and respect for private property and rights to earn a livelihood. It may appear artificial to separate the two questions, but it is submitted that this is necessary if the discrete issues are to remain clear.

4.10.2 Is Species Protection a Legitimate State Activity?

As noted above,[181] any restriction of property rights must serve a legitimate State interest. Those parts of the Regulations which are *necessary* to implement the Directive cannot be successfully challenged on constitutional grounds.[182] However, in line with the test outlined earlier, it must be questioned whether the Directive has been implemented in as constitutional a manner as possible.

---

[179] [1998] 2 ILRM 401.
[180] Indeed its authority is now deemed to derive from Article 40.3 of the Constitution in which inheres a right to fair procedures. See *East Donegal Co-op v. Attorney General* [1970] IR 317; (1970) 104 ILTR 81.
[181] See section 2.3.
[182] See section 1.7.6.

It is submitted that the Regulations go beyond what was *necessitated* by the Directive in some respects. While they generally purport to follow the scheme of protection laid down in the Directive, they also impose restrictions on sites which the Directive and Community law generally do not require to be protected.[183]

It was submitted above,[184] that the Regulations fail to implement the Directive properly to the extent that they do not fully protect *priority* sites before they are designated by the Commission.[185] The converse of this is that there is no authority in Community law for restricting plans or projects on non-priority sites before they have been adopted by the Commission.[186] Accordingly, applying the test outlined earlier,[187] the Regulations have not fulfilled the obligation on the State to implement the Directive in as constitutional a manner as possible because they provide for the delimitation of property rights by Ministerial order in a situation where European law does not require such a delimitation.

This conclusion is bolstered by reference to the arbitrariness of the scheme of restrictions. Operations and activities, some of which may be relatively small scale, may be prohibited in circumstances where there are no powers to prohibit large-scale development permitted under planning legislation on the basis of habitat protection.[188] Licences may be revoked for a particular site because of habitat considerations, despite the fact that such considerations would not justify a refusal of an application for the same licence on the same site. Licences and permissions which were in existence before the Regulations came into force may be revoked, while licences or permissions which were issued after the Regulations came into force but before the designation of the relevant sites may not be revoked.[189] Perhaps most damning of all, because the phrase "operation or activity" is partly defined by reference to who is carrying it out,[190] restrictions on land use under

---

[183] See section 1.7.3.
[184] See section 4.8.
[185] Such sites are protected only from operations or activities. See section 4.8.6.
[186] Such restrictions are imposed by Regulations 14-19. See section 4.4.
[187] See section 1.7.2.
[188] See 4.5.6.
[189] See section 4.5.5 and 4.5.6.
[190] According to Regulation 2, read in conjunction with Regulation 31, neither development carried out by a local authority nor development or activities carried out by a Government Minister, under certain specified legislation, can constitute

the Habitats Regulations depend as much on the identity of the person who proposes to carry out a project as on the effect that the project will have on the protected habitat site.[191] For these reasons, it is suggested that the restrictions which apply to non-priority sites before they are designated may be unconstitutional.

4.10.3 The Payment of Compensation

It was submitted above[192] that a requirement that compensation be paid could be constitutionally necessary even where a restriction of a property right is constitutionally permissible. This is because the requirement of compensation does not depend on the validity of the reasons for restricting a property right but rather on the *effect* which that restriction has on the individual concerned: is she being asked individually to pay a disproportionate cost of achieving a general public good? This is something which could quite possibly happen under the Regulations. While it is acceptable for the State to seek to implement Community directives and to protect natural habitat types and species, this is not a kind of public good which a private individual should be obliged to pay for if the cost of so doing is disproportionate. The provision of compensation would not undermine the obligation to give full effect to Community law, a point illustrated by the fact that the Regulations envisage that compensation will be paid in some circumstances. The adequacy of the compensation scheme will be discussed further in the next Chapter.

4.11 Enforcement

4.11.1 Criminal Liability

Regulation 14(3) provides that it is an offence to carry out a specified operation or activity without the consent of the Minister,

---

an "operation or activity." The restrictions of activities by such bodies only apply to European sites.

[191] It is without doubt sometimes legitimate to distinguish between private sector and public sector activity. However, where the purpose of the restriction is the protection of natural habitats, the distinction between public and private sector surely becomes irrelevant. It is thus difficult to appreciate why local authority and Ministerial development is not subjected to the same regulatory regime as that applicable to the private sector.

[192] See section 2.4.

unless it is carried out in accordance with a management agreement. There is no definition of what constitutes a management agreement. Regulation 39 provides that a person convicted of such an offence is liable on summary conviction to a fine not exceeding £1,500 and/or to 6 months imprisonment. The fact that the offence is to be tried summarily means that the prosecution can be brought by any member of the public acting as a common informer as well as by the Minister.

Where a body corporate commits an offence, Regulation 38 provides that a director, manager, secretary or other officer of that body corporate will also be deemed guilty of the offence if it can be proven that the offence was committed with the consent or connivance of, or attributable to any neglect of that person. This facility to impose personal liability on company directors and senior management has been a standard feature of environmental statutes for a number of years.[193]

4.11.2 Restoration of Land in a European Site Following Damage

Although its marginal note refers to a "European site", Regulation 19 itself states that the power to require restoration of a damaged site also arises in respect of Article 5 sites and in respect of candidate list sites. The Minister may issue a direction in writing requiring that action to restore the site be taken within a given time frame. Subparagraph (c) of Regulation 19(1) provides that "[a]ny person who fails to comply with a direction under subparagraph (a) shall be guilty of an offence". There is no subparagraph (a). Since penal statutes must be strictly construed,[194] it is therefore submitted that this offence could not be successfully prosecuted.

If the directed action is not taken within the specified period, the Minister may take such action as she considers necessary including authorising of a person to enter the land and to take the directed action. The Minister may recover in a competent court any expenses reasonably incurred as a simple contract debt. Regulation 19(3) provides that any person, who by act or omission impedes or obstructs a person so authorised from entering on land for the

---

[193] See, for example, section 11(2) of the Air Pollution Act, 1987. However, only recently has the EPA, or any other enforcement authority, been prepared to prosecute the director of a company and the facility remains little used.
[194] *State (Murphy) v. Johnston* [1983] IR 235.

purposes of taking the directed action, shall be guilty of an offence. The provisions of Regulations 38 and 39, described above, also apply to this offence.

4.11.3 Powers of Enforcement under Planning Law

It is not within the scope of this text to engage in an exhaustive analysis of the enforcement powers available under legislation other than the Habitats Regulations. Specialist texts should be consulted.[195] It is worth noting, however, that legislation listed in Part II of the Second Schedule and planning legislation is enforceable by any member of the public. Possibilities for public enforcement of environmental legislation administered by Ministers are less extensive.

---

[195] See Scannell, *op. cit.*, at 252-257, 353-61, 437-43, 538-539 and Galligan, *op. cit.*, chapter 11.

Chapter 5

The Payment of Compensation

An Uneasy Compromise

5.1 Introduction

At common law, the owner of land was entitled to use and develop her land as she wished, provided that she did not interfere with the rights of others. The introduction of controls over land use represents a delimitation of private property rights which is considered constitutionally permissible provided that the controls are imposed for the common good and that the restrictions are in accordance with the principles of social justice.[1] Controls over land use are also permissible if they are *necessitated* by the obligation to give effect to EC law.[2] This does not mean that EC law itself is insensitive to private property rights. The European Court of Justice has recognised that private property rights are fundamental rights which must be respected in EC law.[3] The European Convention of Human Rights also provides for the protection of private property rights; and the provisions of this Convention, as well as its

---

[1] See section 2.4. This is generally interpreted to mean that if, the justice of the case calls for the payment of compensation, provision must be made for so doing. So in *Central Dublin Development Association v. Attorney General* (1975) 109 ILTR 109, Kenny J stated that when Article 43 is invoked the issues in each case are: "... whether the legislation has been passed with a view to reconciling the exercise of property rights with the exigencies of the common good, whether the Oireachtas may reasonably hold that view and *whether the restriction would be unjust without the payment of compensation* ".(Emphasis added.)

[2] In *Lawlor v. Minister for Agriculture* [1990] 1 IR 356, Murphy J referred to principles in EC and Irish law which require "that the means taken to achieve legislative aims must bear a reasonable correspondence or proportionality with the intended objective".

[3] See, for example, *Hauer v. Land Rheinland-Pfalz* (Case 44/79) [1979] ECR 3727; [1980] 3 CMLR 42 and *Nold v. Commission (*Case 41/73) [1974] ECR 49; [1974] 2 CMLR 338. See also Hogan and Whyte, Kelly, *The Irish Constitution*, (3rd ed., Butterworths, 1994), at 284-292.

jurisprudence, are considered relevant by the European Court of Justice when it is deciding on matters concerning fundamental rights. In some circumstances, restrictions will not be constitutional unless compensation is payable to those whose rights are restricted.[4] It is for this reason that the Habitats Regulations provide for the payment of compensation in some circumstances where property rights are restricted for the purposes of giving effect to the Directive. Provision for the payment of compensation ensures that an individual is not required to bear the cost of achieving a general public good when this is the sort of cost which should be borne by the community at large.

Restrictions of private sector land use under the Habitats Regulations can broadly be classified into three categories:
(i) Restrictions which apply to "operations or activities".[5]
(ii) Restrictions imposed through planning legislation.[6]
(iii) Restrictions on operations and activities which are imposed under legislation which could broadly be classified as legislation enacted to prevent or control environmental pollution or degradation.[7]

The Local Government (Planning and Development) Act, 1990 provides for the payment of compensation for restrictions on property rights imposed through planning legislation. This compensation scheme is described in detail in other works.[8] No compensation is payable where restrictions are imposed in order to prevent or control environmental pollution or degradation because it is considered that the Constitution does not require that a person be compensated for restricting the emission of pollutants or for other environmentally damaging activities. In this Chapter, we shall consider the compensation payable for (i) restrictions placed on the carrying out of operations or activities and (ii) restrictions placed on

---

[4] See section 2.4.
[5] See section 4.4.
[6] See section 4.5.
[7] See section 4.5. This legislation is specified in the Second Schedule to the Regulations.
[8] See Scannell, *Environmental and Planning Law* (Round Hall Press, 1995), at 240-251; Galligan, *Irish Planning and Procedure Law* (Round Hall Sweet and Maxwell, 1997), chapter 12.

development and licensable activities.[9] We shall then consider the impact of the REPS scheme in this regard.

5.2 Compensation Payable for Refusal of Consent to the Carrying out of Operations or Activities

5.2.1 Definition of Operation or Activity[10]

As described above, an operation or activity as defined in Regulation 2 of the Habitats Regulations has a specific meaning which excludes (i) what might be termed exempted development in planning legislation, (ii) *all* development by local authorities and (iii) operations or activities for which a consent or other authorisation is required under certain specified legislation,[11] mostly legislation to control either environmental pollution or activities which could detrimentally affect the environment.

5.2.2 The General Scheme of Compensation

Regulation 20 establishes a scheme to compensate certain persons where consent to carry out an operation or activity has been refused. A claim for compensation must be made not later than six months from the date of issue of the Minister's decision under Regulation 16[12] or from the date of "the modification or revocation of the lease or licence to which paragraph (1)(b) relates."[13] It may be difficult to ascertain the precise "date of issue of a decision". The usual and well tested practice in environmental legislation is to refer to the date on which the decision is *made*. In the absence of any guidance on the matter, the date of the decision should be regarded as the date of issue.

As a general rule, compensation is payable where the Minister refuses consent for an operation or activity. However, this

---

[9] Activities to which the legislation specified in the Second Schedule applies.
[10] See section 4.3.2.
[11] Second Schedule to the Regulations.
[12] It should be noted that Regulation 16(1) does not *expressly* give the Minister power to refuse consent. Such a power must be *implied* from the provisions of Regulation 16(1), 16(3), 16(4) and elsewhere.
[13] Regulation 20(4) refers to a lease or licence "to which paragraph (1)(b) relates". This paragraph 1(b) in turn refers to a lease or licence in Regulation 15(2). However, Regulation 15(2) does not refer to leases, but only to a licence, approval, consent or other authorisation.

is subject to a number of exceptions described in the following paragraphs. It could be observed that the extent of the exceptions is such that they are more significant than the general right of compensation itself.

5.2.3 Circumstances in Which Compensation is Not Payable
(a) Regulation 20(5)
Regulation 20(5) provides that compensation is not payable if:
(i) the Minister is in negotiation with the land owner or occupier, as the case may be, for the purchase by agreement of the land, or
(ii) the Minister is in negotiation with the land owner or occupier, as the case may be, for the establishment of a management agreement under section 18 of the Wildlife Act, 1976, or
(iii) compulsory purchase of the lands is in train.

There is no provision in the Regulations in respect of the unsuccessful conclusion of these processes. As noted above, there is a six-month limit within which the owner or occupier must apply for compensation. It is quite conceivable that this time period could be exceeded by the negotiations, possibly leaving the owner or occupier with no right to compensation for the restriction on land use. At common law, a Minister would probably be estopped from enforcing a time limit in these circumstances. However, since the six-month limit is a statutory rule, it is suggested that justice and equity requires an amendment of the Regulations to provide for a suspension of the six month period while the Minister is negotiating or while the compulsory proceedings are in progress. Until provision is made to do this, a landowner should be advised to apply for compensation within the six month period, regardless of whether or not the Minister is negotiating or entering into a management agreement or compulsory purchase proceedings are in train.

(b) Regulation 20(6)
The exceptions which Regulation 20(6) makes to the availability of compensation are much more significant. It provides that compensation will not be payable where the proposed operation or activity would "significantly adversely affect":

(i) one or more specific natural habitat types in Annex I to the Habitats Directive, or

(ii) one or more species or the habitats of these species in Annex II to the Habitats Directive, or
(iii) one or more species of bird or their habitat or other habitat specified in Article 4 of the Birds Directive.

This obtuse provision, instead of referring to species and habitats in the Regulations, refers back to the Habitats and Birds Directives and provides that compensation is not payable if an operation or activity would significantly adversely affect *any* natural habitat type in Annex I (not just priority habitats) or any species of Community interest or the habitats of those species in Annex II to the Habitats Directive.

Since, as a general rule, Regulation 16(1) only permits the Minister to give consent to an operation and activity on land in an SAC or a site on the candidate list[14] if she has ascertained that it will not "adversely affect the integrity of the site", the scope of this exemption is unclear. There is a difference between "adversely" affecting and *"significantly* adversely affecting".[15] There may also be a difference between adversely affecting the *integrity of the site* and significantly adversely affecting *a habitat type*, or the habitat of an Annex II species, although the two will overlap in many instances. It is possible however that a designated site could be larger than a habitat. Clearly therefore, the Minister in giving reasons for a decision to refuse consent under Regulation 16(3) should distinguish between operations or activities which adversely affect the integrity of an SAC or a site on the candidate list and those operations or activities which significantly adversely affect the habitats and species specified in (i), (ii) and (iii) above.[16]

There is one circumstance where compensation will be payable for refusing consent even though an operation or activity will significantly adversely affect the habitats and species specified in (i), (ii) and (iii) above. This is where:

---

[14] Regulation 14 does not explicitly subject SPAs and SCIs to this obligation to obtain consent. See section 4.4.1. However, see section 4.8.7 for arguments concerning the doctrines of direct and indirect effect in this regard.
[15] However, as we noted in the previous chapter, see section 4.2.3, restrictions will generally only be imposed where there is a significant adverse effect, making this provision in Regulation 20 meaningless.
[16] This confusion could have been easily avoided by using the same terminology in Regulation 20 as in Regulations 14-16.

> [T]he refusal of consent or revocation of a lease or licence results in the discontinuance of the use to which the land has been put by the person concerned in the period of 5 years immediately preceding such refusal, modification, or revocation or in the curtailment of such use of land.

It should be noted that the five year use is personalised to the "person concerned", presumably the applicant for compensation. Consequently, if an applicant has, for example, bought, inherited or otherwise acquired the land shortly *before* the Minister's decision but has not, for some reason, entered into occupation of it, or has it put to some use on her behalf, she will not be entitled to compensation as she personally has not used the land "in the period of 5 years immediately preceding such refusal".

Indeed, it is submitted that Regulation 20(6) requires that the land must have been put to one use for the duration of the five years. This interpretation is necessitated by the fact that Regulation 20(6) refers to "*the* use to which the land has been put *by the person concerned* in the period of 5 years immediately preceding such refusal".[17] If the reference were to "*a* use to which the land had been put", it would suffice for the purposes of claiming compensation to show that the land had *some* use in the previous five years. However, such is not the case and the applicant must perform the difficult task of demonstrating that the land has been "put to" one ascertainable use in the previous five years by herself. This could militate against a developer or landowner who had built up a landbank for future development or expansion or to provide a *cordon sanitaire* around a development to minimise claims against herself for nuisances but who has let the land lie fallow pending future uses.

It is not clear whether an applicant (or in the case of a company or club, the company or the club itself) must personally have put the land to the use, or whether it would be sufficient for somebody to use it as an agent or employee of the person concerned. It is submitted that it would be sufficient if an applicant's agent or employee had used the land in the five year period but it would require some stretching of the words of the

---

[17] Emphasis added.

section to allow an applicant to claim compensation for a restriction on a use which had been carried out by a person who had, for instance, rented land from her or had been allowed to use it for no consideration.

It is also unclear what would constitute a "use" for the purposes of the Regulations or how generally the concept of *the use* would be drawn. For instance, would farming be considered as one use, or would tillage farming be considered a different use to livestock farming? Since the provision of compensation may be a constitutional requirement,[18] it is suggested that Regulation 20(6) should be interpreted in a manner which most favours the applicant for compensation. Such an approach would necessitate a broad definition of use.

(c) Regulations 17 and 18
Compensation is not payable where the Minister has successfully applied to court under Regulations 17 or 18 to prohibit an operation or activity on land where the operation or activity is liable to have an adverse effect on a candidate list site, a European site or an Article 5 site.[19] It is difficult to see why compensation should not be available for this type of land use restriction when it is available, in theory at least, for a restriction imposed by way of a refusal of consent under Regulation 16(1) to carry out an operation or activity on the same sites.[20] We shall return to this issue when we consider whether the compensation scheme meets the minimal constitutional requirements.[21]

5.2.4 Who May Claim Compensation?
Regulation 20(1)(a) provides that compensation may be payable "to the owner or occupier or user as the case may be". A strict interpretation of this phrase would suggest that compensation may

---
[18] See *Central Dublin Development Association v. Attorney General* (1975) 109 ILTR 69, discussed in section 2.4.1.
[19] See section 4.4.5.
[20] It would thus seem to be in the financial interests of the Minister not to specify more than one operation or activity in the original notice, as she would have to apply to court to prohibit any operation or activity which is not specified in the original notice. Where she applies to court, she will not have to pay compensation to the landowner, whereas she would have to pay compensation if she were refusing consent for a notified operation or activity.
[21] See section 5.2.6.

only be paid to *one* of those three persons in any particular case. The reference to the interest in land to "which *he or she*" (not "they") is entitled supports this interpretation. It is quite possible that an occupier *and* owner *and* user of the land could each have an interest in the land which had been diminished as a result of the restriction. An example would be where the owner of land leased it to a particular person who allows it to be used for a particular period by a community or recreational group.[22] In such circumstances, it seems strange that only one of the persons with an interest in the land should be allowed to claim compensation.

5.2.5 The Measure of Compensation

Regulation 20(1) provides that the compensation paid should be "an amount equal to the loss suffered by the owner, occupier or user by the depreciation of an interest in the land to which he or she is entitled". Regulation 20(2)(a) further states that the amount shall be determined by reference to the "difference between the antecedent and subsequent value of the land or of an interest in the land consequent on the refusal of consent". Regulation 20(2)(a) states that any amount which the landowner receives is to be offset by the value of any amounts received under the REPS scheme, described below,[23] and that any amounts which the proposed operation or activity would have received in the form of grant aid from a Minister or Statutory Authority, if consent had been given under *Chapter II* of Part II of the Regulations, will not be taken into account in assessing the difference between the antecedent and subsequent value of the land. There does not appear to be any situation where consent could be given under Chapter II of Part II of the Regulations. Consequently, this last provision is meaningless.

Regulation 20(3) provides that, in the absence of agreement, the amount of compensation shall be determined by arbitration, under the Acquisition of Land (Assessment of Compensation) Act, 1919, and sections 69-83 of the Lands Clauses Consolidation Act, 1845, in all respects as if the claims arose in relation to compulsory acquisition of land. Finally, Regulation 20(8) provides that compensation can be paid either by way of a single payment or an

---

[22] For example, a gun club or a local development association for fund-raising activities.
[23] See section 5.4.

annual sum. It may only be paid to a person having, or claiming to be entitled to, an interest in or over the land in question. This does not seem to coincide with Regulation 20(1)(a) which provides that compensation may be payable "to the owner or occupier or user as the case may be".[24]

5.2.6 Constitutionality

In Chapter 2 which deals with the constitutional guarantee of private property, reference was made to the fact that compensation is frequently necessary in order to ensure the constitutionality of a restriction of property rights.[25] In Chapters 2 and 4, it was suggested that the restriction of operations or activities on non-priority sites *before* their adoption as SCIs by the Commission may be unconstitutional because it does not benefit from the constitutional immunity given to measures necessitated by the obligations of Community membership provided in Article 29.4.7 of the Constitution. While accepting that the restrictions which apply to uses of such sites *after* they are designated as SCIs are constitutional,[26] it was argued that, even in this instance, compensation should still be payable where one person is required to bear a disproportionate burden and where the restrictions are of little direct benefit to that person. It is suggested that the effective sterilisation of land which is possible under the Regulations may be tantamount to an outright appropriation of property for which compensation could be constitutionally required.[27]

The question which is considered here is whether the compensation scheme in the Regulations in respect of a refusal for the carrying out of an operation or activity is adequate. In this regard, the land use restrictions which are relevant are those which flow from the consent procedure in Regulations 14-16 and those

---

[24] See section 5.2.4.
[25] See section 2.4.
[26] This would apply especially if the sites were priority sites. See however, Article 8 of the Directive which permits Member States to postpone action in certain circumstances. See section 7.2.
[27] See section 2.4.3. See *Lucas v. South Carolina Coastal Commission,* 120 S Ct (1 Ed 2d) 798 (1992) where the US Supreme Court held that where a State adopts a regulation that deprives landowners of all economically beneficial use of their property, it may resist compensation only if the taking can be justified by the necessity to abate nuisances, as defined by the common law or statute. Lucas was denied a permit to build for recreational and coastal protection reasons.

which can be imposed on designated sites under Regulation 17. It was submitted that the restrictions which can be imposed under Regulation 18 on operations or activities *outside* designated sites are invalid because they fail to observe the guarantee of fair procedures inherent in Article 40.3 of the Constitution.[28] However, if an Irish court were to hold that European Community law required a restriction imposed under Regulation 18 to be upheld, it is then arguable that compensation should be payable. Thus, the comments which are made in the following sections could equally apply to restrictions imposed under Regulation 18.

5.2.7 An Arbitrary Compensation Scheme

The proportionality test, as stated in *Daly v. Revenue Commissioners*,[29] requires that restrictions of property rights serve a legitimate aim and be neither disproportionate nor arbitrary. It is submitted that, because the constitutionality of the restriction depends on the provision of adequate compensation, an arbitrary compensation scheme amounts to an arbitrary delimitation of property rights. The compensation scheme in Regulation 20, apart from being carelessly drafted, is arbitrary in certain respects. The provision excluding compensation for uses of land which have not taken place in the previous 5 years is capable, on its face, of imposing great injustice. It is probably inspired by a similar provision in section 12 of the Local Government (Planning and Development) Act, 1990 under which compensation can usually be denied where planning permission is refused for development which would materially contravene a development objective in a development plan for the use solely or primarily (as may be indicated in the development plan) of particular areas for particular purposes unless the objective for the specified use applied to the land at any time within the five years immediately prior to the date a planning application was made and the development would not have materially contravened that objective. However, this five year exception does not operate where a person takes land with notice of the development objective.[30]

---

[28] See section 4.9.2.
[29] [1995] 3 IR 1.
[30] Local Government (Planning and Development) Act, 1990, Third Schedule, paras. 11-14.

This statutory provision is an example of the protection of legitimate investment-backed expectations by the Oireachtas. But there is a difference between zoning provisions in a development plan and designations under the Habitats Regulations. The former are adopted after the planning authority has published notice of the making of the draft plan, has invited representations, has considered and heard objections to the draft plan (at a public hearing when requested) and expressly notified owners and occupiers where provisions relating to a public right of way or a proposed listing of their buildings relate to their lands. The procedures by which *Natura 2000* sites are designated are considerably less protective of constitutional rights.[31]

Regulation 20 provides for compensation only for restricting the use of designated land by a particular person carried out in the five year period before the Minister refused consent for an operation or activity (or modified an authorisation),[32] not before the designation.[33] Even if land were continuously owned or occupied by one person in the preceding five years, she might not have known that it was important to carry out *some* use (let alone, one identifiable use) on the land in order to establish an entitlement to compensation rights. The five year period does not make allowances for the fact that much habitat land, by nature and accidents of ownership, is the kind of land which is sporadically used or expressly purchased and maintained as a reserve for future development.

Furthermore, Regulation 20 is inconsistent with other compensation schemes: whether or not compensation is payable in respect of the restriction of property rights seems to depend largely on the legislation under which a restriction is imposed and the claim for compensation made. Therefore, a person who is refused consent to carry out an "operation or activity" which could significantly adversely affect the habitat of a priority species is not entitled to claim compensation. However, compensation would usually be payable if the same person was refused *planning permission* to carry out a major development on the same site.[34] Indeed, it would almost certainly be payable where the permission was refused for

---

[31] See section 3.5.
[32] See section 5.3.7.
[33] Authorisation used as a generic term here.
[34] See section 5.3.2.

development outside the site.[35] Finally, compensation may not be claimed where a person is prohibited by a court order under Regulation 17 or 18 from carrying out an operation or activity which adversely affects sites on the candidate list, European sites or Article 5 sites.

5.2.8 Minister's Power to Award Compensation "where it would not be just and reasonable to refuse it"
Regulation 20(7) empowers the Minister, where she has refused consent to an operation or activity (or where another Minister has revoked or modified a licence or lease pursuant to legislation specified in the Second Schedule),[36] to make an order declaring that it would not be just and reasonable to exclude compensation under Regulation 20(6). She may make such an order of her own initiative. While this may alleviate some of the hardship caused by the anomalies of the compensation scheme, it is suggested that it amounts to little more than an *ex gratia* scheme of compensation. In *E.S.B. v. Gormley*,[37] the Supreme Court held that a statutory compensation scheme was required where property rights were infringed: a mere *ex gratia* scheme would not suffice.[38] This Ministerial power is tantamount to an administration of justice by a Minister. This is a function constitutionally reserved to the courts.[39] It is particularly invidious in that it provides a protection, and a tactical advantage, to the State which may rely on the fact that the vast majority of property owners will accept that compensation is not payable because Regulation 20(6) so provides. If a doughty person challenges a refusal of compensation, the Minister may make an order under Regulation 20(7) to render moot any litigation challenging decisions under the Regulations, even on the steps of the courthouse. This provision would be more acceptable if the Minister were required to make a decision on whether or not it is

---

[35] *Ibid.*
[36] See section 5.3.7.
[37] [1985] IR 219.
[38] Although the "just and reasonable" exception is here placed on a proper legislative basis, and as such differs from *Gormley* where there was no statutory basis, the effect of the two schemes is the same. A Public Authority is given an absolute and unreviewable discretion whether to grant compensation. It is submitted that this was the real mischief present in *Gormley* and that this mischief is replicated in the Regulations.
[39] *Constitution of Ireland*, Article 34.1.

just and reasonable to pay compensation at the time a consent to carry on an operation or activity is refused, or within a short time thereafter.

Finally, Regulation 20(7) does not apply where an operation or activity is prohibited by court order. Accordingly, it is submitted that Regulation 20(7) is not sufficient to remedy the defects in the compensation scheme.[40]

5.2.9 Community Law and Compensation

There is nothing in the Directive, or in Community law generally, which militates against providing for the payment of compensation in appropriate cases.[41] Indeed, the Preamble to the Directive expressly recognises that the adoption of measures intended to promote the conservation of priority natural habitats and priority species of Community interest may "impose an excessive financial burden" on certain Member States. It also states that the "polluter pays principle can have only limited application in the special case of nature conservation". With these considerations in mind, the Community provided for co-financing to alleviate the Member States' burden of implementing the Directive in so far as priority species and habitats are concerned.[42] It is submitted that this is an implicit recognition by the Community that there are circumstances where persons ought to be compensated for interferences with their fundamental rights when they are asked to pay a disproportionate part of the burden of habitat and species protection.[43] But co-financing, in so far as it is used to mitigate interferences with private property rights, consists largely of measures to compensate farmers,[44] and not others who may have had restrictions placed on the exercise of their property rights It may be surmised that farmers have their own specific compensation scheme because they alone

---

[40] It should be noted that a similar provision exists in section 14 of the Local Government (Planning and Development) Act, 1990. However, as far as can be determined, it has only once been used by the Minister for the Environment. This provision should at least require the Minister to make a decision on whether or not it is just and reasonable within a given time frame.
[41] See section 7.2.
[42] See section 7.2.
[43] See discussion of constitutional requirement of compensation generally, section 2.4.
[44] Most notably the Rural Environment Protection Scheme (REPS). See section 5.4.

have the political and organisational skills to defend their property rights.

It is submitted that the State's obligation, under the *Meagher* test as outlined earlier,[45] is to make Regulations which accord with the constitutional obligations to provide compensation for disproportionate interferences with fundamental constitutional rights. A proper compensation scheme, and/or some more imaginative ways of achieving the objectives of the Directive, could ensure that the requirements of Community law and fundamental rights guaranteed in the Constitution are more harmoniously met.

5.3 Compensation Provisions Relating to Planning Permissions and Licensable Activities

5.3.1 Habitat Protection in Planning Legislation

As described earlier, the protection of habitats from unexempted development is achieved through the integration of habitat considerations into planning and environmental legislation.[46] Under planning legislation as amended by the Habitats Regulations, the powers granted to planning authorities are less extensive than those vested in the Minister for Arts, Culture, the Gaeltacht and the Islands under the Habitats Regulations because only European sites (SACs, SCIs, and SPAs) are protected under planning legislation. Sites on the candidate list are not explicitly protected.[47]

5.3.2 Compensation Under the Planning Acts

In a similar manner to the Regulations, the Local Government (Planning and Development) Act, 1990 grants a general right to compensation where planning permission is refused or granted subject to onerous conditions, and then subjects this general right to exceptions.[48] Compensation will not be granted for the refusal of permission for certain types of development, for the imposition of

---

[45] See section 1.7.3.
[46] See section 4.5.
[47] But see section 4.8.7.
[48] Section 11 grants the right to compensation while section 12 refers to the schedules which state the types of circumstance in which compensation may be refused. See generally Scannell, *op. cit.*, at 240-251; Galligan, *op. cit.*, at 313-337.

certain types of condition and where permission is refused for certain reasons.[49]

It is possible that a planning authority could rely on some of the reasons in the Schedules to the 1990 Act to deny compensation for refusing permission for development which could adversely affect a European site. For instance, it is permissible to deny compensation if permission is refused for any development which consists of, or includes, the making of any material change in the use of any structures or other land.[50] Or compensation might not be payable if a reason, or one of the reasons, for refusing planning permission was that a development would materially contravene "a development objective indicated in the development plan for the use solely or primarily (as may be indicated in the development plan) of particular areas for particular purposes (whether residential, commercial, industrial agricultural or otherwise)".[51] Compensation could be refused if planning permission was granted subject to any condition relating to the preservation of amenities of places and features of natural beauty or interest or the preservation and protection of trees, shrubs, plants and flowers, or the filling of land.[52] But none of the above possibilities clearly and specifically addresses the position where a proposed development is likely to affect adversely a European site. The courts require that the reasons given for refusals of planning permission be expressed "as closely as possible" to the wording of statutory reasons for excluding compensation if compensation is to be successfully excluded.[53] It is therefore submitted that, since the protection of a European site is not a specified ground for denying compensation under the 1990 Act, a refusal of planning permission on the ground that a project would adversely affect such a site, would not be a refusal for a reason which excludes the payment of compensation.

---

[49] Local Government (Planning and Development) Act, 1990, section 12.
[50] *Ibid.*, Second Schedule, para. 1.
[51] *Ibid.*, Third Schedule, para. 11.
[52] *Ibid.*, Fourth Schedule, paras. 18, 19, 27.
[53] See for instance, *XJS Investments Ltd. v. Dun Laoghaire Corporation* [1986] IR 750; *Dublin County Council v. Eighty-Five Developments Ltd.* [1993] 2 IR 392; *J Wood & Co. Ltd. v. Wicklow County Council* [1995] 1 ILRM 151.

5.3.3 Development Objectives

However, as noted in the preceding paragraph, one of the stated reasons for refusal in the Local Government (Planning and Development) Act, 1990, whereby compensation need not be paid, is where permission is refused on the grounds that the proposed development would contravene a development objective specified in the development plan.[54] The land would have to be specifically designated *solely or primarily* as a European site in the plan for this non compensatable reason to apply. Regulation 26 amends the Local Government (Planning and Development) Act, 1963 by inserting the following paragraph in sections 19(2)(a) and (2)(b) of the 1963 Act:

> for the conservation and protection of European Sites in the area to which the development plan relates.

Regulation 26 also amends section 19 by empowering local authorities to indicate in development plans objectives for the:

> protection of features of the landscape which are of major importance for wild fauna and flora in accordance with the Habitats Directive.

Accordingly, *if* a provision for the protection of a European site were inserted into the development plan and if the site was designated for use solely or primarily as a European site, the conservation and protection of European sites would become a development objective in the plan. It is suggested, however, that persons whose property rights could be affected should be given specific notice of any such proposed designation in the interests of ensuring the constitutionality of the designation.[55] If a reason, or one of the reasons, for refusing planning permission was that a development would materially contravene a development objective to conserve and protect a European site, compensation could be legally denied.[56] This may act as a strong financial incentive to local

---

[54] Local Government (Planning and Development) Act, 1990, Third Schedule, para. 11.
[55] See section 4.9.
[56] By way of exception, section 12 of the Act provides that, where the development plan is altered, five years must elapse before compensation can be

authorities to integrate requirements relating to European sites into new development plans or to renew existing plans so as to take these considerations into account.

5.3.4 Not Just and Reasonable to Deny Compensation

Section 14 of the 1990 Act empowers the Minister of the Environment to order compensation where it would not be just and reasonable to deny it. This is a close parallel of the power in Regulation 20(7)[57] discussed above, and the same comments apply. It is worth noting that this power has very rarely been exercised.

5.3.5 An Alternative View

In a circular letter,[58] "Friends of the Irish Environment" have argued strongly that compensation should not be paid where planning permission is refused on the basis of habitat considerations. Their argument is put forward on three fronts. First, they maintain that, if it is against the law to grant permissions, there can be no possible basis for paying compensation. Secondly, they maintain that the Planning Acts have been superseded by the Regulations: as the Regulations deal explicitly with compensation in some circumstances they should be taken to have excluded it in all other circumstances. Thirdly, they seem to suggest that refusal of compensation is a measure necessitated by Community law.

This argument is flawed on each ground. First, it is well established that compensation may be a constitutional requirement where private property rights are restricted by law.[59] Secondly, the Planning Acts have not been superseded by the Regulations. It is abundantly clear from Part IV of the Regulations that the protection of habitats from development is achieved by the integration of

---

refusable, unless a person has bought the land since the new plan came into force as she then would notice of the restriction and could not claim that investment-backed expectations had been frustrated. Despite this five-year saver, it may still be the case that a person is unjustly denied compensation, for the same reasons as set out above with regard to refusal of consent under Regulations 14-18. (See section 5.2.3.) Indeed, in this case it is possible that the longer the person has owned the land the more likely she is to be denied compensation. This causes constitutional problems in the same way as outlined above.

[57] See section 5.2.8.
[58] Friends of the Irish Environment Circular Letter No. 1, 30 November 1997. The full text of the letter can be read at http://www.anu.ie/wirl/friends/circ1.htm.
[59] See section 2.4.

habitat considerations into the existing planning code. It is thus not the case that Regulation 20 implicitly repeals sections 11 and 12 of the Local Government (Planning and Development) Act, 1990. Thirdly, refusal of compensation is not *necessitated* by Community law.[60] The Habitats Directive does not exclude the possibility of compensation being payable; indeed it impliedly recognises that it will be paid by providing in Article 8 for Community co-financing of "measures essential for the maintenance or re-establishment of priority sites and habitats of priority species as well as the *total costs of those measures*".[61] It is submitted that the obligation on the State, under the *Meagher* test, is to implement the Directive in as constitutional a way as possible, thus giving effect to the constitutional requirement of compensation.[62]

5.3.6 Planning Permission Revoked or Modified

In Chapter 4 we noted that planning permission could be revoked or modified in certain circumstances.[63] Section 17 of the Local Government (Planning and Development) Act, 1990 provides that compensation is payable for expenditure in carrying out works rendered abortive by a revocation or modification under the 1963 Act. It is also payable when a permission has been revoked or modified by the imposition of conditions on the same basis as if a permission were refused or granted subject to certain conditions. However, no provision is made for the payment of compensation where planning permission is revoked or modified as a result of the Minister's request to a planning authority or An Bord Pleanála, under Regulation 27(11), to review an existing planning permission.[64]

---

[60] As already noted, the Directive recognises that the polluter pays principle will have only a limited application to conservation law, and Article 8 provides for a scheme of co-financing which can be used to finance the provision of compensation. See section 7.2.
[61] See section 7.2.
[62] As the Constitution is not necessarily incompatible with the provisions of Community law on this point, the Constitutional requirements must be met.
[63] See section 4.5.5.
[64] Unless, that is, one holds the view that the power in Regulation 27(11) is merely an additional reason for exercising the power in section 30. See section 4.5.5.

5.3.7 Compensation for Modification, Revocation or Refusal to Issue an Environmental Licence

There are no provisions generally providing compensation when a licence, consent or other authorisation under legislation specified in the Second Schedule to the Regulations is refused. However, as noted earlier,[65] one of the curious aspects of the Regulations is that they deal with the issuing of Ministerial consents, licences, etc. in the planning and development section (Part IV) while they deal with the modification and review of licences under the operation or activity section (Part II). Regulation 15(2) provides that the Minister for Arts, Culture, the Gaeltacht and the Islands may request any other Minister who has granted or issued any "licence, approval, consent or other authorisation" granted or issued pursuant to any of the enactments in the Second Schedule to the Regulations to assess the implications for a site on the candidate list or for an SAC and in the light of the assessment to affirm, modify or revoke any of the above. As noted above,[66] Ministers do not grant any kind of authorisations under some of the legislation in the Second Schedule and it is likely that Regulation 15 is defective.

A possible corollary of (or justification for) this quirk in the legislative drafting, is that the Regulations do provide a scheme of compensation for instances where such a licence or other authorisation is revoked or modified. Regulation 20(1)(b) provides that where a *Minister* modifies or revokes a *lease or a licence* by virtue of Regulation 15(2), the *lessee or licensee* is entitled to compensation on more or less the same conditions as if consent were refused for an operation or activity.[67] No provision is made for the recipients of the other types of authorisations mentioned in Regulation 15(2) to receive compensation and the said Regulation 15(2) does not expressly refer to leases at all. There does not appear to be any provision made for compensation where air, water, waste or IPC licences are revoked or modified as these licences are not granted by *Ministers*.[68]

---

[65] See section 4.5.5.
[66] See section 4.5.5.
[67] See section 5.2.
[68] However, if one reads Regulation 15(2) to give effect to European Community law obligations, thus allowing the Minister to ask a statutory authority to review a licence, it is strongly arguable that one should take a similarly broad view of Regulation 20(1)(b) and allow compensation to be claimed for a revocation or

5.4 The Rural Environment Protection Scheme

5.4.1 Introduction

As noted earlier, plans or projects which are directly connected with or necessary to the management of a site are not subject to land use controls. The preference of both the European Commission and the State is to achieve the protection of habitats by agreement with landowners instead of by resorting to legal regulation. Accordingly, the various schemes operated in this regard are important. These involve compensating the landowner, usually a farmer, for refraining from using his land in a particular way. The most significant of these schemes is the Rural Environment Protection Scheme[69] (hereinafter referred to as "REPS" where convenient), an administrative scheme established by the Department of Agriculture, Food and Forestry in implementation of Regulation 2078/92/EEC.[70]

The primary aim of Regulation 2078/92/EEC is to provide an aid scheme for farmers to encourage the introduction of farming practices and production methods which reflect the increasing concern for the conservation of wildlife habitats and endangered species of flora and fauna and the protection of the landscape. Its secondary aim is to bring about a diversification of agricultural income and a reduction in agricultural production. This dichotomy of aims has resulted in differing perceptions of REPS. It has been alleged that the Government views it as primarily a farm income supplement with an environmental label. In contrast, conservationists expected it to be "an environmental Scheme with an added socio-economic benefit."[71]

---

modification made on foot of such a review. This does not excuse Ireland's inadequate implementation of the Directive in this respect.

[69] See *Cap Reform Information Series: Rural Environment Protection Scheme* (Department of Agriculture, Food and Forestry, April 1997).

[70] Council Regulation 2078/92/EEC of 30 June 1992 on agricultural production methods compatible with the requirements of the protection of the environment and the maintenance of the countryside, OJ L215/85, 30 July 1992 amended by Commission Regulation 2772/95/EEC, OJ L288/35, 1 December 1995, Commission Regulation 746/96/EEC, OJ L102/19, 25 April 1996 and Commission Regulation 1962/96/EEC, OJ L259/7, 12 October 1996.

[71] Hickie, *Evaluation of Environmental Designations in Ireland* (2nd ed., Heritage Council, 1997), at 87.

In order to be eligible to join REPS, an applicant must be farming at least three hectares. Certain land, e.g. the dwelling house and its curtilage, public roads, lake areas, commercial forestry or set aside land, cannot be considered in determining the area of the land for the purposes of the Scheme. This land must either be owned by the farmer, or be leased to him for at least five years since participants must remain in the scheme for at least that period. Farmers who comply with the scheme conditions qualify for a basic annual payment per hectare, up to a maximum of 40 hectares, for a period of five years.[72] At present, there are 33,000 farmers in the scheme.

5.5.2 Agri-Environment Plans

The most important aspect of REPS is the agri-environment plan. This contains information on the farm and how the farmer proposes to undertake the various measures required by REPS over the five year period. The plan must be submitted on a 12 page application form produced by the Department of Agriculture, Food and Forestry.[73] A 25" map of the land identifying the main features on the farm must also be submitted together with other supplementary materials. Only REPS planning agencies approved by the Department may draw up the plan.[74] The list of such planning agencies, which includes Teagasc and private agencies, has been criticised on the grounds that the agencies are composed chiefly of farm planners and agricultural scientists who may have no previous experience of conservation management.[75] Applications are examined by Department inspectors and submitted for final approval. The absence of qualified ecologists from the approval process has been criticised. Therefore, it must be questioned whether the approval process and, in turn, the agri-environment

---

[72] Farmers with land area in excess of 40 hectares must implement REPS measures on all their lands.
[73] Referred to as the REPS I form.
[74] A list of approved REPS planning agencies is available from the Department of Agriculture, Food and Forestry.
[75] Hickie, *op. cit.*, at 86.

plans themselves, place sufficient emphasis on the ecological aspect of the Scheme, particularly in relation to *Natura 2000* sites.[76]

There are twelve compulsory measures with which the farmer must comply under the Scheme. These include the retention of wildlife habitats, the protection and maintenance of waterbodies, the adoption of a grassland management plan, the adoption of a waste management, liming and fertilisation plan, and the cessation of the use of herbicides, pesticides and fertilisers in and around hedgerows, ponds and streams. The farmer must keep farm and environmental records and carry out any other environmentally-friendly activity which the Minister for Agriculture, Food and Forestry may prescribe. In addition, there are seven supplementary measures, any or all of which the farmer may decide to undertake and in respect of which there is an additional payment. However, where the farmer participates in more than one supplementary measure, she will not receive an additional payment for each measure. Instead, she will be paid the highest additional amount.[77]

Irish SPAs and proposed SACs are drawn from a list of Natural Heritage Areas (NHAs) drawn up by the National Parks and Wildlife Service (NPWS).[78] A farmer with land which falls within an area identified as an NHA must undertake a supplementary measure for the preservation of that area, in accordance with conditions specified by the NPWS, should she wish to participate in REPS. Such farmers are entitled to an additional payment per hectare up to a maximum of 40 hectares. In addition, further payments may be made if a farmer is obliged to reduce her livestock numbers to meet the NPWS conditions. Any condition imposed by the NPWS relating to the conservation of the habitats or species for which a site is identified, in effect, forms part of the agri-environment plan for the site. This gives REPS agri-environment

---

[76] This conclusion is supported by the fact that the Scheme is administered by the Department of Agriculture, Food and Forestry and not the National Parks and Wildlife Service.
[77] A detailed 75 page handbook entitled *Rural Environment Protection Scheme: Agri-Environmental Specifications* has been published by the Department of Agriculture, Food and Forestry. It covers each step of the application process for joining the Scheme and details how the compulsory and supplementary measures should be undertaken.
[78] See section 3.4.3.

plans a potentially wide sphere of operation allowing them to function as comprehensive management plans.

Regulation 2078/92/EEC does not require land forming part of REPS to be monitored in any way and, to date, no system has been put in place to monitor whether the goals of agri-environment plans are being fulfilled in practice. The Department of Agriculture, Food and Forestry is said to be considering some form of monitoring for REPS following pressure from conservationists and the European Commission.[79] A system of monitoring and surveillance of natural habitats and flora and fauna is required under the terms of the Regulations and the Directive.[80]

5.5.3 REPS and the Habitats Regulations

Regulation 20(2)(a) of the Habitats Regulations provides that the amount of any funding received under REPS shall be offset against the amount of compensation, if any, payable under Regulation 20 for a refusal of consent for the carrying out of operations or activities. In practice, where land lies within an SPA or a proposed SAC, the farmer is offered the opportunity to join REPS as an alternative to receiving compensation under Regulation 20.[81] Landowners with land in SPAs or proposed SACs who enter REPS, or who are already participating in REPS, will receive an extra payment per acre in addition to the basic REPS payment and the NHA supplement.[82] While the normal REPS payment is paid by the Department of Agriculture, Food and Forestry this top-up payment is paid by the Department of Arts, Heritage, the Gaeltacht and the Islands. While a landowner is not entitled to normal REPS payments for more than 40 hectares of land, she is entitled to the top-up payment in respect of the additional land.[83]

Chapter 4 examined the controls which may be imposed on land designated under the Habitats Regulations. One of the most significant restrictions is that which relates to operations and

---

[79] Hickie, *op. cit.*, at 86.
[80] Habitats Regulations, Regulation 7 and Habitats Directive, Article 11.
[81] These two alternative compensation packages are set out in a press release from the Department of Arts, Culture and the Gaeltacht, 26 February 1997.
[82] Whether or not all of such land is within the designated site.
[83] The number of hectares for which the top-up payment is paid includes hectares not within a designated site where the total area of all the land is less than 40 hectares.

activities. Regulation 14(1) provides that a landowner, served with notice under Regulation 4(2), must give the Minister written notice of a proposal to carry out an operation or activity of a type specified in the notice.[84] It appears that consent to a proposal for operations or activities directly connected with or necessary to the management of a site should be granted by the Minister as a matter of course because the Regulations require only operations or activities "*neither* directly connected with nor necessary to the management of the site",[85] but likely to have a significant effect thereon, to be subject to assessment.[86]

Neither the Regulations nor the Directive elaborate on what is meant by "neither directly connected with nor necessary to the management of the site."[87] It could be argued that a narrow interpretation should be adopted so that only operations or activities which have as their objective the maintenance or improvement of the conservation status of the site are permitted to escape assessment. However, it is suggested a preferable view is that anything carried out under a management plan for the site falls within the ambit of the term "neither directly connected with nor necessary to the management of the site" and is therefore exempt from assessment. A management plan is the product of negotiations between landowners and the NPWS. The NPWS will have considered the plan's implications for the conservation status of the site and are most unlikely to have agreed to it if any of its provisions are likely to produce effects adverse to the maintenance of a site at a favourable conservation status.

The NPWS and the Minister have taken the view that, where land forming part of a designated site is in REPS, anything dealt with in the REPS agri-environment plan is "directly connected with or necessary to the management of the site", and that there is consequently no need to subject the proposed operation or activity to assessment by the Minister. Indeed, the Ministerial notice sent to landowners indicating notifiable operations and activities states:

> Where a landowner has a current approved plan under the Rural Environment Protection Scheme or any scheme which

---

[84] See section 5.4.1.
[85] Emphasis added.
[86] Regulation 15(1).
[87] Habitats Directive, Article 6(3).

the Minister considers to be equivalent s/he need only notify the Minister of activities not covered in the plan.

This extract does not accord with the terms of the Regulations. The Regulations require the landowner to give written notice to the Minister of all proposals to carry out notified operations or activities,[88] whether or not they are considered to be "directly connected with or necessary to the management of the site", i.e. covered by an agri-environment plan under REPS. However, the notice implies that it is for the *person who proposes to carry out an operation or activity* to decide whether that operation or activity falls within the terms of the agri-environment plan and therefore whether she is under an obligation to notify the Minister of her proposal. In such a system of "self-assessment", landowners will tend to look at the plan with their own interests in mind. More importantly, they may well not have the expertise to compare properly the provisions of the plan with the details of notifiable operations and activities in order to determine whether the operation or activity is covered by the plan. This system is particularly regrettable in the absence of an effective system of REPS monitoring. It is arguably contrary to the provisions of the Directive.

Regulation 20(6) of the Habitats Regulations provides that compensation will not be payable in respect of a refusal of consent to, or the modification or revocation of a lease or licence in respect of, an operation or activity which would significantly adversely affect a natural habitat type or species specified in the Habitats Directive or the Birds Directive unless such refusal, modification or revocation results in the discontinuance of a use to which the land was put by the person concerned within a five year period immediately preceding the refusal, modification or revocation. This means that if a farmer, who participated in REPS for five years, decides to leave the Scheme, she will discover that the operations or activities which she had carried on before joining REPS must be notified to the Minister. If she is refused consent to carry out those operations or activities, because the operations or activities would significantly adversely affect a natural habitat type or species, a claim for compensation under Regulation 20 will fail because the

---

[88] Regulation 14(1-2).

operation or activity had not been carried out within the immediately preceding five year period.[89] In these circumstances, a farmer may have little alternative to continued participation in REPS.

The use of REPS agri-environment plans as management plans for the purposes of the Habitats Regulations is a sensible one. The Deputy Director General of DG XI has stated, in the context of the accession of Central and Eastern European countries to the Habitats Directive, that "[a]gri-environmental measures, if properly designed and quickly put in place, should significantly contribute to preserving valuable semi-natural habitats."[90] From the Irish exchequer's point of view the use of REPS, with its Community funding,[91] to protect designated sites would appear to be a cost effective approach.

---

[89] This is of particular concern given the potential similarity in practice between "significant adverse effect on the ecological features of the site" (Regulation 15(2)(a)), "adversely affect the integrity of the site" (Regulation 16(1)) and "significantly adversely affect" (Regulation 20(6)). See section 5.2.3.
[90] Garvey, *Natura* 2000, Issue 6 (June 1998), at 1.
[91] See section 7.3.2(d).

Chapter 6

Species Conservation Measures:

Protecting Specimens as well as Sites

6.1 Introduction

6.1.1 Background to Protection of Species Measures

A variety of legal mechanisms are used for the conservation of species.[1] One such mechanism is the designation of key sites. Controls are imposed on human activities which have negative or potentially negative impacts on species within the site. The establishment of Special Areas of Conservation (SACs) and the creation of the *Natura 2000* network under the Habitats Directive is an example of this "site protection" mechanism. Another mechanism used in conservation of species is affording legal protection to individual members of wild flora and fauna species. In the case of fauna species such protection can involve prohibitions on the hunting, killing or capture of animals. In the case of flora species protection usually takes the form of prohibitions on damaging or removing individual plants. Unlike "site protection" measures, these "protection of species" prohibitions are generally universal in geographical scope. This results in a greater number of individual members of species being subject to protection, but the larger area also makes enforcement more difficult.

The "site designation" aspect of the Habitats Directive, i.e. the designation of Special Areas of Conservation, etc., has to date been the focus of most attention in Ireland. The fact that Articles 12 to 16 of the Directive, entitled "Protection of species", require Member States to introduce a system of protection for individual members of certain flora and fauna species appears to have been ignored. This lack of interest is partly due to the fact that, unlike site designation on privately owned land, a system of protection for

---

[1] See Bell and Ball, *Environmental Law*, (4th ed., Blackstone Press, 1997), at 490-493.

individual members of certain flora and fauna species was already well-established in Irish law under the Wildlife Act, 1976 and previous legislation.[2] More cynically, it might be argued that the manner in which the obligations imposed by Articles 12 to 16 of the Habitats Directive are dealt with in the Irish Regulations has resulted in many of the *protection of species* protections not yet having effect in Irish law. In regard to several obligations the Regulations merely state that the Minister shall take the requisite measures without providing any framework within which they are to be taken, and it seems that to date no such measures have in fact been taken.

The fact that the "protection of species" aspect of the Directive has attracted relatively little attention should not be taken as indicating either that it is irrelevant in the Irish context or that it goes no further than the pre-existing provisions of the Wildlife Act, 1976. It will be shown that, in respect of certain species, the level of protection required by the Directive is higher than mandated by the Wildlife Act. In addition, the exceptions to, and derogations from, protection measures permitted under the Directive are narrower than under the Wildlife Act.

This chapter will look at the *protection of species* measures mandated by the Directive and how they have been implemented in Irish law. This section looks first at the main requirements of the Directive and the species which are subject to its protection. It examines the manner in which these requirements have been implemented by the Habitats Regulations, often by amendment of provisions of the Wildlife Act, 1976. Some of the general concepts involved are then discussed. The remaining sections focus on protection of flora species, protection of fauna species, the prohibition on indiscriminate means of capture and killing of fauna species, and the State's power to derogate from the *protection of species* Articles of the Directive.

6.1.2 The Protection of Species Obligations of Habitats Directive
There are two categories of species which are subject to the *protection of species* provisions of the Habitats Directive:

---

[2] Flora: section 21 and the Flora (Protection) Order, 1987, SI No. 274 of 1987. Fauna (excluding wild birds): section 23.

(a) *Annex IV species:* These are wild flora and fauna species for which Member States are obliged to establish a *system of strict protection*. The Annex IV species native to Ireland are set out in Part I of the First Schedule to the Habitats Regulations.[3]

(b) *Annex V species:* These are wild flora and fauna species which are not considered to be in need of strict protection but which may require measures to ensure that the taking of their specimens does not jeopardise their maintenance at a favourable conservation status.[4] The Annex V species native to Ireland are set out in Part II of the First Schedule to the Habitats Regulations.[5]

The system of strict protection required for Annex IV species is outlined in Articles 12 (animal species) and 13 (plant species) of the Directive. It comprises two main aspects: first, a prohibition on deliberate destruction or interference with members of the species; secondly, a prohibition on the keeping, transport and sale or exchange of members of the species. Article 14 provides for Member States to take measures to ensure that the taking of Annex V species is compatible with their maintenance at a favourable conservation status and gives a non-exhaustive list of possible measures. Article 15 applies to both Annex IV and Annex V wild fauna species and requires Member States to prohibit certain indiscriminate means of capture and killing of such species, in particular those listed in Annex VI to the Directive. Article 16 permits Member States to derogate on certain specified grounds from some or all of the *protection of species* obligations contained in Articles 12 to 15.

6.1.3 Habitats Regulations and Wildlife Act, 1976

Part III of the Habitats Regulations, entitled PROTECTION OF FLORA AND FAUNA, purports to give effect in Irish law to the requirements of Articles 12-16 of the Habitats Directive. It does this by amending sections of the Wildlife Act, 1976,[6] and by introducing new self-

---

[3] See Appendix II.
[4] See section 3.1.4.
[5] See Appendix II.
[6] The amended sections of the Wildlife Act usually only apply in respect of Annex IV and/or Annex V species, with the original sections (which usually

contained provisions. The Regulations appear to assume that certain sections of the Wildlife Act, 1976, and/or other pre-existing legislation, already fully implement certain requirements of the Directive. An assumption which is not well founded.

Chapter III of Part II of the Wildlife Act provides for the protection of three categories of species: wild birds, wild fauna (excluding wild birds) and wild flora. The Birds Directive includes *protection of species* measures applicable to all species of wild birds in the European territory of the Community. These provisions are similar (but not identical) to those in the Habitats Directive. Since the measures on wild birds in the Wildlife Act, 1976 relate to the Birds Directive they will not be discussed here. The discussion will be confined to the protection of flora and wild fauna (excluding wild birds).

6.1.4 "Specimen"

Protection of species measures give legal protection to individual members of species. The definition of individual members of species is important as it determines the scope of the protection. The Habitats Directive uses the term "specimen" to refer to individual members of species and Article 1(m) defines it as meaning:

> any animal or plant, whether alive or dead, of the species listed in Annex IV and Annex V, any part or derivative thereof, as well as any other goods which appear, from an accompanying document, the packaging or a mark or label, or from any other circumstances, to be parts or derivatives of animals or plants of those species.

This wide-ranging definition is adopted in the Irish Regulations.[7] The term was previously used, but not defined, in the Wildlife Act, 1976. The Directive's definition of "specimen" depends in part on the definitions of "animal" and "plant", but does not define them.

---

involve a lower level of protection) continuing to apply where all other species are concerned.

[7] Regulation 2(2) provides that a word or expression that is used in the Regulations and is also used in the Habitats Directive shall, unless the contrary intention is expressed, have in these Regulations the meaning it has in the Habitats Directive.

This may cause some uncertainty in relation to organisms such as fungi and lichens which cannot easily be classified as "plants".[8]

The meaning of "specimen" for the purposes of the Habitats Directive is further extended in regard to Annex IV species. Paragraph 3 of Article 12 provides that the aspects of the system of strict protection referred to in paragraphs 1(a), 1(b) and 2 shall apply to "all stages of life" of Annex IV(a) animal species. Similarly, paragraph 2 of Article 13 provides that the aspect of the system of strict protection referred to in paragraph 1 shall apply to "all stages of the biological cycle" of Annex IV(b) plant species. So, Article 13(2) would, for example, apply the prohibitions in Article 13 to seeds and spores.

6.2 Protection of Wild Flora

6.2.1 General Scheme of Protection: Wildlife Act, 1976

Section 21 of the Wildlife Act, 1976 provides for the protection of specimens of wild flora species. The Act itself does not contain a list of protected flora species. Section 21(1) gives the Minister the power to make an order (termed a flora protection order) declaring a particular species, or particular species, protected. This protection can either extend throughout the State or be limited to a particular area or areas.[9] The most recent such order is the Flora Protection Order, 1987[10] which lists 68 species of flora for protection throughout the State. Section 21(2) provides that a copy of each such order must be sent to An Bord Pleanála and to any planning authority in whose area the order applies.

---

[8] In the Irish context, however, the Wildlife Act, 1976 defines "flora" to include, *inter alia*, fungi and lichens.
[9] Where the Minister proposes to make an order declaring a species protected in a particular area or areas (as opposed to generally throughout the State), she must first consult with any planning authority in whose area or any part of such area, the proposed order would, if made, apply.
[10] SI No. 274 of 1987.

6.2.2 Definition of Flora

"Flora" is defined in section 2 of the Wildlife Act as:

> all plants (both aquatic and terrestrial) which occur in the wild (whether within or outside the State) and are not trees, shrubs or other plants being grown in the course of agriculture or horticulture and includes in particular lichens, mosses, liverworts, fungi, algae and vascular plants, namely flowering plants, ferns and fern-allied plants and any community of such plants.[11]

6.2.3 Prohibited Actions

Where a species of flora is declared protected under a flora protection order, section 21(3) of the Wildlife Act provides that a person shall not save under and in accordance with a licence granted by the Minister under the section:

(a) cut, pick, uproot or otherwise take any specimen of that species, or the flowers, roots or other part of such specimen,
(b) purchase, sell or be in possession of any such specimen or the flowers, roots or other parts thereof,
(c) wilfully alter, damage, destroy or interfere with the habitat or environment of the species.

The Minister has a general power under section 21(5) of the Wildlife Act to licence a person to cut, pick, uproot or otherwise take specimens of a specified species of protected flora or to alter or interfere with the habitat or environment of such specimens. The purposes for which the licence is granted must be specified in the licence and may include scientific or educational purposes.

Section 21(4) provides that a person who contravenes section 21(3) shall be guilty of an offence. It is widely considered that this offence is minor in scope but it is not. It has a very extensive potential which has been much underestimated. It includes physically interfering with protected flora, engaging in commercial activities involving protected flora, merely being in possession of

---

[11] Section 21(9) states that for the purposes of section 21 "plant" includes a tree or shrub.

them and carrying out any development, operation or activity which would have a deleterious effect on the habitat or environment of a protected species.

The maximum penalty on summary conviction for an offence under section 21(4) is £50 for the first offence, £100 for the second offence, and £200 for the third and subsequent offences.[12] Where the Minister is satisfied that a particular species of flora or fauna is in danger of extinction throughout the State or in a particular area of the State, he may make regulations under section 74(4) declaring the species to be one to which section 74(3) relates.[13] This has the effect of increasing the penalty for offences under section 21(4) to maximums of £250 for a summary conviction, and £500 for a conviction on indictment.

6.2.4 The Habitats Regulations - Strict Protection of Annex IV(b) Flora Species

The Habitats Regulations provide for the protection only of such flora species as are listed in Annex IV(b) and Annex V(b) to the Directive. There are no known Annex IV(b) flora species native to Ireland. The Habitats Regulations do not therefore provide for any system of strict protection specifically for such species. Regulation 21 amends section 21 of the Wildlife Act, 1976 and extends its provisions to Annex V(b) flora species native to Ireland. The result of this amendment is that a system of strict protection is established in respect of Annex V(b) species although the Directive does not strictly require this.

6.2.5 Measures in Respect of Annex V(b) Flora Species

Under the Directive, Annex V species are not subjected to the strict protection requirements required for Annex IV species. However, Article 14(1) requires a Member State if it deems it necessary after surveillance to take measures to ensure that the taking in the wild and exploitation of Annex V species is compatible with their maintenance at a favourable conservation status. The Annex V(b) flora species native to Ireland are listed in Part II of the First Schedule to the Regulations.[14]

---

[12] Section 74(1).
[13] Section 74(3) prescribes criminal offences and penalties for contravening certain provisions of the Act.
[14] See Appendix II.

Regulation 24(1) of the Habitats Regulations implements Article 14(1) by providing that the Minister may, having regard to the surveillance provided for in Regulation 7(1), by direction take measures in respect of the Annex V(b) flora species listed in Part II of the First Schedule to ensure that the taking in the wild of such specimens of wild flora, as well as their exploitation, is compatible with their being maintained at a favourable conservation status. A non-exhaustive list of possible directions is given in Regulation 24(2). This is substantially the same as the list in Article 14(2) of the Habitats Directive except that it omits directions relating to sale, breeding or artificial propagation, and to assessment of the effects of measures adopted.

Ministerial directions under Regulation 24(1) must be published in the *Iris Oifigiúil*. Under Regulation 24(5)(a) it is an offence to fail to comply with such direction. Regulations 24(5)(b) provides that it is a defence for the defendant to show that he or she was not aware of the direction at the relevant time and that he or she could not reasonably be expected to have known of it at that time. This is one of those exceptional cases where ignorance of the law is a defence.

6.2.6 Application of Amended Section 21 of the Wildlife Act

The Habitats Directive does not require that any measures be taken in respect of Annex V(b) flora species above and beyond those provided for in Regulation 24(1) of the Habitats Regulations. Member States need only take such measures where they deem it necessary, and they have a discretion as to what these measures may be.

Regulation 21 of the Habitats Regulations, however, provides for additional protection for the Annex V(b) flora species listed in Part II of the First Schedule, over and above that provided in the Wildlife Act, 1976. This is achieved by applying an amended version of section 21(3) of the Wildlife Act to those species. Under section 21(3), as amended by Regulation 21, it is provided that a person shall not:

 (a) cut, pick, collect, uproot or otherwise take, *injure, damage, or destroy* any specimen to which the section applies or the flowers, roots, seeds, spores or other part of such specimen,

(b) purchase, sell, *keep for sale, transport for sale or exchange, offer for sale or exchange* or be in possession of any such specimen *whether alive or dead* or the flowers, roots, *seeds, spores* or other part thereof,

(c) wilfully alter, damage, destroy or interfere with the habitat or environment of any species of flora to which an order under this section for the time being applies.[15]

A person who contravenes section 21(3) is guilty of an offence.[16]

The amended section 21(3) only applies to those Annex V(b) species listed in Part II of the First Schedule to the Regulations and not to flora species specified under flora protection orders or indeed any other flora. The original, i.e. unamended, section 21(3) continues to apply to those flora species listed under flora protection orders which are not Annex V(b) species. The amended section 21(3) is more specific than the original and is wider in a number of respects. It specifically prohibits any taking, injuring, damaging or destruction of any specimen. The original section 21(3) only prohibited the taking of specimens. "Taking" might not include damage or injury, which are specifically prohibited under the amended section 21(3). The amended section also prohibits the keeping for sale, transport for sale or exchange and offering for sale or exchange of specimens. These were not specifically prohibited under the original section which referred only to purchasing, selling and being in possession of specimens. The amended section also specifies that the prohibition on purchase, sale, keeping for sale, etc. of specimens applies to dead as well as live specimens, and that the prohibitions apply to the seeds and spores of the specimen.[17]

6.2.7 Amended Section 21 as a Possible System of Strict Protection for Annex IV(b) Flora Species?

It has been noted above that there are no identified Annex IV(b) flora species native to Ireland. The Habitats Regulations do not therefore institute the system of strict protection for Annex IV(b) flora species set out in Article 13 of the Directive. It is possible, however, that revision of the Annexes IV and V to the Directive

---

[15] Amendments in italics.
[16] Section 21(4).
[17] See section 6.1.4.

under Article 19 could result in the identification of some Irish Annex IV(b) flora species. In that event, section 21(3), as amended for the purposes of the species in Part II of the First Schedule to the Habitats Regulations (i.e. those Annex V(b) flora species native to Ireland) would meet the requirement for a system of strict protection for flora species, if new flora added to Annex IV(b) were listed in Part II of the First Schedule to the Regulations.

It could be argued that the amended section 21(3) is in fact stricter than the system of strict protection set out in Article 13 of the Directive. Article 13(1)(a) requires the prohibition of the "*deliberate* picking, collecting...", while 21(3)(a) creates an offence of strict liability, one for which no mental element is required. *Any* cutting, picking, collecting etc., even if not done deliberately (e.g. accidentally or negligently) will result in the person being guilty of an offence. On the other hand, section 21(5) permits the Minister to licence the prohibited acts for such purposes as he specifies. Consequently the Minister has power under section 21 to permit the picking, collecting, etc. in circumstances which are much wider than envisaged under Article 13, derogation from which is only permitted in limited circumstances where the conditions listed in Article 16 are satisfied.

6.3 Protection of Wild Fauna

6.3.1 *General Scheme of Protection: Wildlife Act, 1976*
Section 23 of the Wildlife Act provides for the protection of certain of animals of certain species of wild fauna. These animals are termed "protected wild animals"[18] Section 23(1) provides that the section applies to any animal which is of a species of fauna specified in the Fifth Schedule to the Act. The Minister may, after consultation with the Minister for Agriculture and Food, extend the protection to other species of fauna by regulations specifying that animals of that species shall be animals to which section 23 applies.[19] The Minister for the Marine and Natural Resources must consent where such regulations relate to any species of fish or aquatic invertebrate.[20] The Minister also had the power to make

---
[18] Section 23(4).
[19] Section 23(2)(a).
[20] Section 23(3)(a).

regulations delisting any of the species in the Fifth Schedule.[21] Again, the Minister must first consult with the Minister for Agriculture and Food, and the consent of the Minister for the Marine and Natural Resources must be obtained if the animal to be delisted is a species of fish or aquatic invertebrate.[22]

6.3.2 Definition of Fauna
Fauna is defined in section 2 of the Wildlife Act as meaning:

> all wild animals (both aquatic and terrestrial) and includes in particular wild birds, wild mammals, reptiles, non-aquatic invertebrate animals and amphibians, and all such wild animals' eggs and young, but in relation to fish or aquatic invertebrate animals (or their eggs or spawn or brood or young) only includes fish and such aquatic invertebrate animals which are of a species specified in regulations under section 23 of the Act which are for the time being in force.

6.3.3 Prohibited Actions
Section 23(5) provides that it is an offence for a person to:

(a) hunt a protected wild animal which is not an exempted wild mammal otherwise than under and in accordance with a permission or licence granted by the Minister under the Act

(b) hunt an exempted wild mammal otherwise than
  (i) under and in accordance with such a permission or a licence granted by the Minister under the Act other than section 29
  (ii) under and in accordance with a licence granted by the Minister under section 29 of the Act and (also) on a day, or during a period of days, specified in a relevant order under section 25 of the Act.

(c) injure a protected wild animal otherwise than while hunting it,
  (i) in case the protected wild animal is not an exempted wild mammal, under and in accordance with such a

---

[21] Section 23(2)(b).
[22] Section 23(3)(b).

permission or a licence granted by the Minister under the Act
  (ii) in case the protected wild animal is an exempted wild mammal, either,
    (A) under and in accordance with such a permission or a licence granted by the Minister under the Act other than section 29, or
    (B) in the manner and on a day, or during a period of days, mentioned in subparagraph (ii) of paragraph (b),
(d) wilfully interfere with or destroy the breeding place of any protected wild animal.

Section 23(7) provides for certain cases where what would otherwise be an offence under section 23(5) will be deemed not to be so. It provides that it shall not be an offence:

(a) while engaged in agriculture, fishing or forestry, or in zoology or in any other scientific pursuit, unintentionally to injure or kill a protected wild animal, or
(b) while so engaged to interfere with or destroy the breeding place of such an animal, or
(c) while constructing a road or while carrying on any archaeological operation, building operation or work of engineering construction, or while constructing or carrying on such other operation or work as may be prescribed, to kill or injure such an animal or to destroy or injure the breeding place of such an animal, or
(d) to capture an injured or disabled protected wild animal for the purpose of killing it humanely or with the intention of tending it and of later releasing it later, or
(e) to kill humanely a protected wild animal which is either injured in the manner described in paragraph (a) or captured in the manner describe in paragraph (d) or so to kill a protected wild animal injured in the circumstances described in paragraph (c).

The Minister has the power under section 23(6) of the Act to licence any person to capture or humanely kill at any time a protected wild animal of a species specified in the licence. Such a licence may be granted for such educational, scientific *or other purpose* as is specified in the licence,

6.3.4 Strict Protection of Annex IV(a) Fauna Species

Regulation 23(1), implementing Article 12(1) of the Habitats Directive, provides that the Minister shall take the requisite measures to establish a system of strict protection for the species of fauna set out in Part I of the First Schedule (i.e. those Annex IV fauna species native to Ireland). This system is composed of three aspects:

(i) Prohibition of :
   (a) all forms of deliberate capture or killing of specimens of the species in the wild,
   (b) the deliberate disturbance of the species particularly during the period of breeding, rearing, hibernation and migration,
   (c) the deliberate destruction or taking of the eggs of the species from the wild,
   (d) the deterioration or destruction of breeding sites or resting places of those species.

(ii) Prohibition on the keeping, transport and sale or exchange, and offering for sale or exchange, of specimens taken from the wild (except those legally taken prior to the implementation of the Directive).

(iii) Establishment of a system to monitor incidental capture and killing of the species and in the light of information gathered, take further research or conservation measures to ensure that such incidental capture or killing does not have a significant negative impact on the species.

6.3.5 Prohibition of Deliberate Capture or Killing of Specimens

Under Regulation 23(2) it is a criminal offence to:

(a) deliberately capture or kill any specimen of the species listed in Part I of the First Schedule, or
(b) deliberately disturb these species particularly during the period of breeding, rearing, hibernation and migration, or

(c) deliberately take or destroy the eggs of the species from the wild, or

(d) damage or destroy a breeding site or resting place of an animal of the species.

This regulation implements Article 12(1) of the Directive. A person guilty of an offence under the regulation is liable on summary conviction to a fine of up to £1,500 and / or 6 months imprisonment.
There would appear to be two different types of offence created by Regulation 23(2). The first type is created by subparagraphs (a) to (c) where the word "deliberately" is used in defining the offence. The second type is that in subparagraph (d), of damaging or destroying a breeding site or resting place. Here the word "deliberately" is omitted from the definition of the offence. The type of offence created by Regulation 23(2) is one which would be described as regulatory in nature, and which would generally be considered as an offence of strict liability, i.e. not requiring a *mens rea* or mental element. The omission of "deliberately" while it is included in the other three subparagraphs indicates that anyone who damages or destroys a breeding site is guilty of an offence, even there was no intention to damage or if it were done negligently or accidentally.
The distinction between the two types of offence illustrates the policy behind the Habitats Directive of placing greater emphasis on protecting *habitats* of species rather than the species itself. The main component of the Directive involves site protection measures, e.g. the establishment of Special Areas of Conservation and the *Natura 2000* network. Even where *protection of species* measures (as opposed to site protection measures) are concerned greater emphasis is placed on protecting breeding sites and resting places than on individual specimens. A person who damages the breeding site or resting place of a listed species is strictly liable, whereas if he had killed a specimen of the species he would be liable only if he had *deliberately* done so.

6.3.6 Prohibition on Keeping, Transport, Sale, etc. of Specimens

Regulation 22 implements the prohibition in Article 12(2) on keeping, transport, sale etc. of specimens by inserting a new section 45(1) into the Wildlife Act, 1976. The new section 45(1) applies only to those species listed in Part I of the First Schedule to the

Habitats Regulations (i.e. those Annex IV(a) fauna species which are native to Ireland). It provides that:

[a] person who is not a licensed wildlife dealer shall not keep for sale, sell, transport for the purpose of sale or exchange, offer for sale or exchange, purchase for resale or exchange or engage in taxidermy in respect of fauna, at any stage of life, set out in Part I of the First Schedule to the Habitats Regulations.

The new section 45(1) fails to property implement Article 12(2) of the Directive in two respects. First, Article 12(2) appears to require Member States to prohibit *any* keeping and transport of specimens of Annex IV(a) fauna species, even where such keeping and/or transport is not for the purposes of sale or exchange. However, the new section 45(1) only applies to persons who "keep for *sale*" or "transport for the purpose of *sale or exchange*". Secondly, the new section 45(1) exempts licensed wildlife dealers[23] from its provisions. Article 16 of the Directive which permits derogations from the Directive's *protection of species* provisions does not provide an basis for such a potentially wide exemption. It is possible that the exemption could be justified *in certain cases* under Article 16(d) where provision is made for derogations for the purpose of research and education, repopulation and re-introduction of protected species and associated breeding operations. Consequently, the Minister would be well advised to grant licences to wildlife dealers solely for those purposes.

6.3.7 Incidental Capture and Killing of Specimens

Regulation 23(4) restates requirement in Article 12(4) of the Directive that a system be established to monitor incidental capture and killing of the species listed in Part I of the First Schedule, i.e. the Annex IV(a) fauna species native to Ireland.[24] Having regard to information gathered, the Minister is obliged to take further research or conservation measures to ensure that incidental capture and killing does not have a significant negative impact on the species

---

[23] Such dealers are licensed under section 48 of the Wildlife Act, 1976 and have certain exemptions under the provisions of that Act.
[24] Article 12(4).

concerned. This Regulation is expressly stated to be in addition to section 23 of the Wildlife Act, 1976.

6.3.7 Measures in respect of Annex V(a) Fauna Species

Annex V species are not subjected to the strict protection requirements required for Annex IV species, but Article 14(1) requires a Member State if it deems it necessary after surveillance to take measures to ensure that the taking in the wild and exploitation of Annex V species is compatible with their maintenance at a favourable conservation status. The Annex V(a) fauna species native to Ireland are listed in Part II of the First Schedule to the Regulations.[25] Regulation 24(1) of the Habitats Regulations implements the requirements of Article 14(1) in respect of these fauna species in the same manner as it implements Article 14(1) in respect of Annex V(b) flora species. See section 6.2.5.

6.4 Prohibition of Indiscriminate Means of Capture and Killing

6.4.1 General Prohibition

Article 15 of the Habitats Directive applies to the capture or killing of specimens of the species of wild fauna in Annex V(a). In addition, where derogations are applied to allow the taking, capture and killing of species of wild fauna in Annex IV(a), Article 15 applies to the capture and killing of specimens of those species. Member States are required generally to prohibit the use of all indiscriminate means of capture and killing capable of causing local disappearance of, or serious disturbance to, populations of these species. In particular, they are required to prohibit:

(a) the use of the non-selective means of capture and killing listed in Annex VI(a) which contains a list of fourteen prohibited means of capture and killing of mammal species, and two prohibited means of capture and killing of fish species.

(b) any form of capture and killing from the modes of transport referred to in Annex VI(b).

---

[25] See Appendix II.

The Habitats Regulations do not contain provisions relating to the prohibition on indiscriminate means of capture and killing in Article 15 of the Directive. This area is however dealt with in Part II, Chapter IV (sections 28, 33-40) of the Wildlife Act, 1976, which is entitled "Restrictions to protect wildlife" and which covers many of the means of capture and killing listed in Annex VI(a), as well as capture and killing from the modes of transport in Annex VI(b).

The restrictions in Part II, Chapter IV of the Wildlife Act apply to the use of prohibited means for the purpose of hunting. "Hunt" is defined widely in section 2 of the Act to mean:

> stalk, pursue, chase, drive, flush, capture, course, attract, follow, search for, lie in wait for, take, trap or shoot by any means whether with or without dogs, and, . . . includes killing in the course of hunting,[26] but does not include stalking, attracting, searching for or lying in wait for any fauna by an unarmed person solely for the purpose of watching or of taking or making photographic or other pictures, and kindred words shall be construed accordingly

"Hunt" for purposes of Chapter IV of the Wildlife Act would appear to include the terms "capture" and "killing" as used in the Habitats Directive.[27]

The most straightforward way to approach this topic is to go through the list of prohibited means of capture and killing in Annex VI(a) of the Directive and link them to the relevant section(s) in the Wildlife Act, 1976 indicating the extent to which the section(s) fulfil the requirements of the Directive. It is possible that other legislation, e.g. fisheries legislation, can also be regarded as meeting the requirements of the Directive but this is not addressed here.

6.4.2 Prohibited Means of Capture and Killing of Wild Mammals

(i) *Blind or mutilated animals used as live decoys.* The use of a tethered, penned, blind, maimed or injured live *wild bird* for the purpose of hunting wild birds is prohibited in section 35(1)(b) of the

---

[26] Killing in the course of hunting is not included in the definition of "hunt" for the purposes of sections 28 and 29 of the Wildlife Act.

[27] These terms are not defined in the Habitats Directive.

Wildlife Act but this prohibition is not wide enough to cover the use of any blind or mutilated *animal.*

(ii) *Tape recorders.* Section 35(1)(d) prohibits the use of an electrical or other instrument or appliance (including recording apparatus) emitting or imitating bird-calls or the calls of wild mammals for the purpose of hunting any protected wild bird or protected wild animal which is a mammal.

(iii) *Electrical and electronic devices capable of killing or stunning.* There does not appear to be any provision in the Wildlife Act which prohibits the use of these devices.

(iv) *Artificial light sources;* (v) *Mirrors and other dazzling devices;* (vi) *Devices for illuminating targets.* Section 38 prohibits the use of any lamp, light, torch, mirror or other artificial light-reflecting or dazzling device or appliance in hunting any protected wild bird or protected wild animal unless such use is under and in accordance with a licence granted by the Minister. Such licences can only be granted for specific purposes, namely, the attaching a band, ring, tag or other marking device to the animal, or hunting for educational or scientific purposes.

(vii) Sighting devices for night shooting comprising an electronic image magnifier or image converter. There does not appear to be any provision in the Wildlife Act which prohibits the use of these devices.

(viii) *Explosives.* Section 33(2) prohibits use of a spring gun, or a tracer shot or a floating container containing an explosive substance to kill or injure any wild bird or wild mammal.

(ix) *Nets which are non-selective according to their principle or their conditions of use;* (x) *Traps which are non-selective according to their principle or their conditions of use.* Section 34(1)(a) prohibits the use of any trap, snare, net, line, hook, dart, spear or similar device, instrument or missile to hunt any wild bird or wild mammal. Section 34(2) provides that paragraph (1) does not apply to or render unlawful:

(a) the affixing of a trap, snare or net which is permitted by ministerial regulations
(b) the taking or killing by means of any such trap, snare, or net of any wild bird which is not a protected wild bird or any wild mammal which is not a protected wild mammal.

Section 34(3) provides that subsection (1) does not apply where any of the following are done pursuant to and in accordance with a licence granted by the Minister:

(a) the capture alive, on land specified in the licence by means of a trap, snare or net of any species of wild bird specified in the licence, for the purpose of propagating or of improving the quality of such species.
(b) the capture alive by means of nets of hares by or on behalf, or at the request, of a coursing club affiliated to the Irish Coursing Club.
(c) the capture alive by means of nets or other devices of hawks or falcons for the purpose of lawful falconry within the State
(d) the capture alive of wild birds or wild mammals, for research or other scientific or educational purposes or for removal to a new habitat or to a place specified in the licence.

(xii) *Poisons and poisoned or anaesthetic bait.* Section 34(1)(a) prohibits the use of any poisonous, poisoned or stupefying bait to hunt any wild bird or wild mammal. Section 34(1)(c) prohibits the laying of any poisonous or poisoned substance or stupefying bait, being a substance or bait which is calculated or is likely to injure, or facilitate the capture of, a wild bird or a wild mammal, in, or in the vicinity of any tree, pole, cairn or other structure in, or in the vicinity of, any place frequented by wild birds or wild mammals.

(xiii) *Gassing or smoking out.* There does not appear to be any provision of the Wildlife Act prohibiting this.

(xi) *Crossbows.* Section 34(1)(a) prohibits the use of, *inter alia*, any arrow, dart, spear or similar device, instrument or missile to hunt any wild bird or wild mammal.

(xiv) *Semi-automatic or automatic weapons with a magazine capable of holding more than two rounds of ammunition.* Section 33(3) provides that it shall be an offence for a person to kill or injure with a shotgun a protected wild animal other than a hare. Section 33(4) provides that the Minister may make regulations specifying the type and calibre of firearms and ammunition which may be used to hunt wild birds and wild mammals and ammunition of any other type and calibre shall not be used to hunt such birds or mammals.

6.4.3 Prohibited Means of Capture and Killing of Wild Fish
(i) *Poison.* There does not appear to be any provision of the Wildlife Act prohibiting the use of poison on fish species, but fisheries legislation should be consulted.

(ii) *Explosives.* There does not appear to be any provision of the Wildlife Act prohibiting their use, but again fisheries legislation should be consulted.

6.4.4 Prohibited Modes of Transport
(i) *Aircraft,* (ii) *Moving motor vehicles.* Section 36(1)(a) prohibits a person hunting, or disturbing for the purpose of hunting, any protected wild animal by means of a mechanically propelled vehicle, vessel or aircraft. The prohibition applies whether or not the vehicle is being propelled or is stationary. Section 36(1)(b) prohibits a person hunting or disturbing for the purpose of hunting any protected wild bird by means of a mechanically propelled vehicle, vessel or aircraft. In this case, however, the prohibition only applies while the vehicle is being so propelled. Section 36(2) enables the Minister to licence exceptions from the prohibitions in section 36(1) for limited and specified purposes.

6.5 Derogations

6.5.1 Power to Derogate
Article 16 of the Habitats Directive allows Member States to derogate from any or all of the provisions on *protection of species* contained in Articles 12 to 15. Article 16 closely follows the

derogation procedures in Article 9 of the Birds Directive. Although at first glance the derogation provisions in Article 16 may appear quite wide, in fact the scope for derogation is extremely limited.

6.5.2 Grounds for Derogations

Derogation is allowed only on certain specific grounds set out in Article 16(1), *viz.*:

(a) in the interest of protecting wild fauna and flora and conserving natural habitats;
(b) to prevent serious damage, in particular to crops, livestock, forests, fisheries and water and other types of property;
(c) in the interests of public health and public safety, or for other imperative reasons of overriding public interest, including those of a social or economic nature and beneficial consequences of primary importance for the environment;
(d) for the purposes of research and education, of repopulating and re-introducing these species and for the breeding operations necessary for these purpose, including the artificial propagation of plants;
(e) to allow, under strictly supervised conditions, on a selective basis and to a limited extent, the taking or keeping of certain specimens of the species listed in Annex IV in limited numbers specified by the competent national authorities.

These grounds are similar to those listed in Article 9 of the Birds Directive. The only difference is the addition of the grounds listed in Article 16(1)(c) which was adopted because it was considered that the prohibitions on development in the Birds Directive went too far and that not *all* development activities should be stifled. The Birds Directive did not permit derogations for imperative reasons of overriding public interest, including those of a social and economic nature in Article 9 of the Birds Directive. The change in Article 16 mirrors that in Article 6(4) of the Habitats Directive which declares that such reasons can be relied on to permit a plan or project to be carried out in a *Natura 2000* site despite a negative assessment of its implications.

6.5.3 Requirements for Derogation

In addition to having to come within one of the five stated grounds for derogation in the Directive, two other conditions which must be fulfilled before a derogation can be permitted, *viz.*:
(i) There must be no satisfactory alternative.
(ii) The derogation must not be detrimental to the maintenance of the species concerned at a favourable conservation status in its natural range.

The second condition was not contained in Article 9 of the Birds Directive. Its inclusion in Article 16 implies a policy of giving a higher level of protection to the species concerned and balances the slightly wider ground for derogation in Article 16(1)(c).

6.5.4 Report to Commission

Member States may permit derogations under Article 16 without obtaining prior Commission approval. However, as one of the ways of ensuring that derogations are not abused, Article 16(2) provides that Member States must forward a report to the Commission every two years on any derogations they have applied. The Commission must then give its opinion on the derogations within 12 months. Matters to be specified in the report are listed in Article 16(3). They are:

(a) the species which are subject to the derogations and the reason for the derogation, including the nature of the risk, with, if appropriate, a reference to alternatives rejected and scientific data used;
(b) the means, devices or methods authorised for the capture or killing of animal species and the reasons for their use;
(c) the circumstances of when and where such derogations are granted;
(d) the authority empowered to declare and check that the required conditions obtain and to decide what means, devices or methods may be used, within what limits and by what limits and by what agencies, and which persons are to carry out the task;
(e) the supervisory measures used and the results obtained.

This is intended to limit derogations to what is strictly necessary and to enable the Commission to supervise them.

6.5.5 Habitats Regulations

Regulation 25 reproduces the substance of Article 16 of the Directive. Responsibility for licensing derogations lies with the Minister. The grounds for derogation and necessary prerequisites are stated as in Article 16 of the Directive. The requirement to report to the Commission and the necessary contents of such report are also set out. The Commission has recently notified a Letter of Formal Notice to Ireland for failure to submit the required report which is due for the period 1994 to 1996.[28]

In *Commission v. Netherlands* (Case 339/87)[29] the European Court of Justice in deciding a case on Article 9 of the Birds Directive, held that the criteria which the Member States must meet in order to derogate from the provisions laid down in the Directive must be reproduced in *specific* national provisions because of the requirement for certainty as to the obligations to be complied with.[30] This obligation is met in the Habitats Regulations.

6.5.5 Consideration of the General Requirements in Article 2(3)

Article 2(3) of the Habitats Directive states that measures taken pursuant to the Directive shall take account of economic, social and cultural requirements and regional and local characteristics. The European Court of Justice has held in the context of Article 9 of the Birds Directive,[31] that general requirements of this nature do not constitute an autonomous derogation from the general system of protection in Articles 5 to 8 of that Directive above and beyond that permitted by the text of Article 9.[32] By analogy to this case, it is submitted that Member States cannot therefore justify a failure to implement the *protection of species* provisions of the Habitats Directive by reference to economic or social requirements etc., but must bring their case within the permitted derogations in Article 16.

---

[28] DGXI Press Release, 8 October 1998.
[29] [1990] ECR I-851; [1993] 2 CMLR 360.
[30] In response to the judgment of the European Court of Justice, express provision was made in Irish law for the derogations permitted under Article 9 of the Birds Directive. European Communities (Wildlife Act, 1976) (Amendment) Regulations, 1986, SI No. 254 of 1986.
[31] which is substantially similar to Article 16 of the Habitats Directive.
[32] *Association pour la Protection des Animaux Sauvages* (Case 435/92) [1994] ECR I-67.

Chapter 7
Financing Habitat Conservation

7.1 Introduction

Article 130s(4) of the Treaty of Rome provides that, with the exception of measures of a Community nature, the Member States are responsible for financing and implementing environmental policy. This is supplemented by the "polluter pays" principle,[1] which has become a cornerstone of Community environmental policy.[2] However, Article 130r(3) of the Treaty of Rome requires the Community to take account of the potential benefits and costs of action or lack of action in preparing its policy on the environment. Furthermore, Article 130s(5) provides that, if a measure adopted by majority decision in the Council of Ministers involves costs deemed disproportionate for the public authorities of a Member State, the Council shall, in the act adopting the measure, lay down appropriate provisions in the form of temporary derogations or financial support from the Cohesion Fund.[3]

The Eleventh Recital to the Preamble to the Habitats Directive states that the polluter pays principle can have only limited application in the "special case" of nature conservation. Furthermore, measures intended to promote the conservation of priority habitats and priority species are considered to be the common responsibility of all the Member States since such habitats and species constitute a common heritage. Accordingly, Article 8 of the Directive provides for Community co-financing. This ensures

---

[1] Treaty of Rome, Article 130r. See Council Recommendation 75/436/EEC of 3 March 1975 on cost allocation and action by public authorities on environmental matters, OJ L194/1, 25 July 1975.

[2] The principle can be found in all EC Action Programmes on the Environment adopted to date. See generally section 1.2.

[3] This provision was inserted into the Treaty to overcome complaints by some of the less developed Member States that EC environmental policy hindered their industrial and economic development.

that the cost of protecting SCIs and SACs is shared by all the Member States.[4]

Article 130r(2) of the Treaty of Rome, as amended by the Treaty on European Union, provides that environmental protection requirements must be integrated into the definition and implementation of other Community policies.[5] To this end, all Community co-funding should reflect the goal of achieving sustainable development. Many of the financial instruments through which co-funding will be provided are currently being reassessed to ensure that they are available to assist in the maintenance of the *Natura 2000* network.[6]

7.2 Procedural Requirements

Article 8 of the Directive provides that the Member States shall send, as appropriate, to the Commission their estimates of the Community co-financing they consider necessary in order to allow them to meet their obligations regarding priority species or priority natural habitat types when a site is designated as an SAC. The Commission, in agreement with the Member State, will then assess the co-financing needed. The Commission has the power to identify certain measures which must be undertaken in the site as a precondition for co-financing.[7] However, where a site hosts both priority and non-priority natural habitat types or species such conditions can only be imposed in relation to the priority natural habitat types or priority species. In assessing co-financing, the Commission must take into account the concentration on the Member State's territory of priority natural habitat types and/or

---

[4] Neither the Habitats Directive nor the Birds Directive provide specifically for Community co-financing of SPAs. However, existing financial instruments, e.g. LIFE-Nature, will continue to operate in relation to these sites.
[5] The Treaty of Amsterdam, when in force, will delete this provision and insert a new Article 6 into the Treaty to like effect.
[6] The *Progress Report on the Implementation of the Fifth Action Programme on the Environment* (COM(95) 624 final, 10 January 1996) noted some progress in the integration of environmental considerations into other policy areas, including into Community financial support mechanisms.
[7] Article 8(2).

priority species and the relative burdens which the required measures entail.[8]

Article 8 requires the Commission to adopt a prioritised framework of measures involving co-financing to be undertaken when the site has been designated as an SAC.[9] Measures which are not retained in the framework of measures due to insufficient resources may be postponed by the Member State pending a review of the framework of measures after two years.[10] Where measures are postponed the Member State must refrain from any activity likely to result in deterioration of the site. It is submitted that "measures", as used in Article 8, can refer both to positive action to maintain a species or habitat type at a favourable conservation status and to the prevention of activities in order to avoid a deterioration in the conservation status of a species or habitat type. Accordingly, finance obtained under a Community financial instrument could be used to compensate landowners whose activities are restricted because their lands host a priority species or habitat type if the conditions in Article 8 are met, i.e. the site is designated as an SAC and hosts a priority natural habitat type or priority species.[11] The financial instruments under which co-financing will be provided are discussed in the next section.

7.3 The Financial Instruments

7.3.1 The LIFE Programme

The LIFE programme is an EC financial instrument designed to contribute to the development and implementation of Community environmental policy and legislation through the support of innovative and demonstration-type environmental projects put forward by industry and local and regional authorities. At present, its role is to help in the implementation of Community

---

[8] Article 8(3).
[9] This is to be undertaken according to a procedure set out in Article 21 of the Directive.
[10] This is consistent with Article 130s(5) of the Treaty which provides for temporary derogations in instances where the costs involved are deemed to be disproportionate.
[11] The Rural Environment Protection Scheme (REPS) is likely to serve this purpose in most instances. See section 5.4.

environmental policy as outlined in the *Fifth Action Programme on the Environment*. The second phase of LIFE (LIFE II) began in 1996 and will run until 1999.[12] One of LIFE's priority areas is the protection of nature.[13] LIFE-Nature is the main financial instrument for *Natura 2000*.

Projects which receive funding under LIFE-Nature must contribute to the implementation of either the Birds Directive or the Habitats Directive and, in particular, to the maintenance or restoration of habitats or species at a favourable conservation status within *Natura 2000* sites. Financial support of up to 75% of eligible costs is available for actions taken in relation to priority natural habitats or priority species as defined in the Habitats Directive or species of bird in danger of extinction. All natural or legal persons established in the European Community are eligible to apply. Applications must be lodged with the Member State concerned. The applications are submitted to a Habitats Committee comprised of independent experts appointed by the Commission which delivers a technical opinion. The Commission then decides which projects to select and how much to award. Proposals must be for pilot schemes which are likely to bring about a measurable improvement in the environment. There are no funds for small projects, studies or infrastructure development.

In 1998, the EC Commission received 192 applications requesting a total of ECU 135 million. The available budget in 1998 was ECU 48 million. The Commission approved co-funding for 85 projects. There was a change in the nature of applications in 1998, as *Natura 2000* came on line, from bird protection projects to habitat and species (other than bird) protection projects. Seventy per cent of the LIFE-Nature budget was spent on on-site action, ten per cent was spent on awareness raising and information activities and the remaining funds went to various preparatory projects. Ireland received no funding whatsoever under LIFE-Nature for 1998. Only one application was submitted. This may be partly due to the fact that the national list of sites had yet to be formally submitted in

---

[12] Council Regulation 1973/92/EEC of 21 May 1992 establishing a financial instrument for the environment, OJ L206/1, 22 July 1992 amended by Council Regulation 1404/96/EEC, OJ L181/1, 20 July 1996.

[13] Forty-six per cent of LIFE II's total budget of ECU 450 million is destined for nature.

full,[14] thereby limiting the number of projects which could be submitted for funding. It should be noted that local authorities and NGOs are eligible to submit applications. While LIFE is the primary financial instrument for *Natura 2000*, an Informal Meeting of the European Council of Ministers held in Arles in June 1995 called for other EC financial instruments to be used for habitat conservation.

7.3.2 The Structural Funds

The Structural Funds are the Community's longest running financial instrument and form the core of its policy of economic and social cohesion. The Funds are governed by Framework Regulation 2052/88/EEC as amended and Co-ordination Regulation 4253/88/EEC as amended.[15] The integration principle in Article 130r of the Treaty of Rome is complemented by Article 7(1) of Regulation 2052/88/EEC which provides that measures financed by Community financial instruments must be in keeping with, *inter alia*, the provisions of the Treaty of Rome, with the instruments adopted pursuant thereto and with Community policy on environmental protection.[16] Accordingly, finance may be available

---

[14] See section 3.4.1.
[15] Council Regulation 2052/88/EEC of 24 June 1988 on the tasks of the Structural Funds and their effectiveness and on coordination of their activities between themselves and with the operations of the European Investment Bank and the other existing financial instrument, OJ L185/9, 15 July 1988, amended by Council Regulation 2081/93/EEC, OJ L193/5, 31 July 1993. Council Regulation 4253/88/EEC of 19 December 1988 laying down provisions for implementing Regulation 2052/88/EEC as regards coordination of the activities of the different Structural Funds between themselves and with the operations of the European Investment Bank and the other existing financial instruments, OJ L374/1, 31 December 1988 amended by Council Regulation 2082/93/EEC, OJ L193/20, 31 July 1993. Article 130d (renumbered Article 161) of the Treaty of Rome provides for the adoption of regulations for the purpose of defining the tasks, objectives and organisation of the Structural Funds.
[16] In December 1997, the European Commission suspended Structural Funds for the construction of a railway in the Scottish Cairngorms pending an investigation into whether the project complied with the Habitats Directive. The Commission withdrew funding from a waste water treatment plant for Mutton Island in Galway Bay because of environmental concerns. The Commission also threatened to withdraw funding for drainage works in Wexford Harbour until the Government designated the site as an SPA. In May 1998, the Minister for Arts, Heritage, the Gaeltacht and the Islands agreed to the designation. In April 1998, the Commission commissioned an independent study into a proposed road

for projects such as the restoration of damaged habitats or the introduction of sustainable and environmentally friendly agricultural practices in place of declining traditional agriculture. Questions have arisen concerning the effectiveness of Community attempts to "green" the Structural Funds. The central problem is inadequate monitoring of the actual environmental effects produced by the projects financed by such funding. The Community has attempted to tackle this problem in the current round of Structural Funding by requiring that all regional applications for aid be subject to prior appraisal and that national environmental authorities monitor the implementation of the programmes.

Structural Funds are distributed through either Community Support Frameworks (CSFs) or Single Programming Documents (SPDs) which set out the commitments and priorities for Fund expenditure for each region. The *Community Support Framework for Ireland 1994-1999* was agreed by the Government with the European Commission following the Government's submission of its *National Development Plan 1994-1999*. In order to receive funding, a project must normally form part of an Operational Programme within the CSF.[17] Operational Programmes may be funded from one or more of the Structural Funds. Ireland's Objective One status allows it to receive up to 75% co-funding for

---

development along part of the N21/N22 in County Kerry which would, if approved, run through Ballyseedy Wood, a priority natural habitat type under the Habitats Directive. The purpose of the study was to determine whether there was a need for the Commission to re-consider its decision to co-fund the project. The report, delivered in July 1998, concluded that the project did not comply with the provisions of the Environmental Impact Assessment Directive or the Habitats Directive and that the decision of the Commission to co-fund the project should be reconsidered. A revised decision has not, as yet, been delivered by the Commission. See also *An Taisce and WWF v. Commission,* Court of First Instance (Case T-461/93) [1994] ECR II-733, European Court of Justice (Case 325/94P) [1996] ECR I-3727.

[17] The *Community Support Framework for Ireland 1994-1999* includes an *Operational Programme for Environmental Services* which aims to meet the needs of industry, tourism and rural development through the provision of adequate water and waste infrastructure, coastal protection, environmental monitoring and research and development. The *Operational Programme for Tourism 1994-1999* includes a sub-programme for Natural/Cultural Tourism which can assist public bodies and other bodies to improve access to Ireland's natural and cultural heritage through investment in, *inter alia*, waterways, nature reserves and national parks.

public projects and 50% for private projects.[18] More than ECU 5.62 billion has been allocated to Ireland for 1994-1999. Part-financing by public authorities or the private sector is always required. The various Structural Funds are as follows.

(a) The European Social Fund
The European Social Fund (ESF) provides co-financing for vocational training schemes, job-creation schemes and other schemes aimed at adaptation to, and training for, technological change while paying particular regard to the protection of the environment.[19] The Fund is managed by the European Commission's Directorate-General for Employment, Industrial Relations and Social Affairs (DG V).

(b) The European Regional Development Fund
The objective of the European Regional Development Fund (ERDF) is to reduce disparities between levels of development in the regions of the Community by investing in, *inter alia*, productive

---

[18] Article 12(1) to (3), Council Regulation 2052/88/EEC as amended *supra*, fn 15. Objective One regions are those whose *per capita* GDP has amounted to less than 75% of the Community average over the past 3 years, as well as certain other regions whose *per capita* GDP is around that mark and for which there are special reasons for inclusion. It is unlikely that Ireland will retain Objective One status in forthcoming rounds of the Structural Funds, but discussions are ongoing to retain the status for western and border areas. On 19 March 1998, the Commission presented its proposals for regulations to govern the Structural Funds between 2000 and 2006: Commission Proposal for a Council Regulation laying down general provisions on the Structural Funds, OJ C176/1, 9 June 1998. These proposals will, if adopted, offer greater scope for financing nature conservation projects. Article 1 of the proposed regulation provides that "the Community, through the Funds, shall promote the harmonious, balanced and sustainable development of economic activities ...." Article 2 provides that the Commission and the Member States shall ensure that the operations of the Funds are consistent with other Community policies and operations, in particular in the areas of the incorporation of the requirements of environmental protection into the definition and implementation of the operations of the Funds." New regional rural development plans will include projects aimed at the preservation and promotion of sustainable agriculture respecting environmental requirements.
[19] Ninth Recital to the Preamble, Council Regulation 2084/93/EEC, OJ L193/39, 31 July 1993 amending Council Regulation 4255/88/EEC of 19 December 1988 laying down provisions for implementing Regulation 2052/88/EEC as regards the European Social Fund, OJ L374/21, 31 December 1988. See also Treaty of Rome, Article 123 (renumbered Article 146).

infrastructure, including infrastructure aimed at environmental protection where such investment is linked to regional development.[20] The Fund is managed by the European Commission's Directorate-General for Regional Policy and Cohesion (DG XVI).

(c) The Financial Instrument for Fisheries Guidance
The Common Fisheries Policy (CFP) came into being in 1983. Since 1994, the Community instruments providing funding for the CFP have been amalgamated in the Financial Instrument for Fisheries Guidance (FIFG).[21] The FIFG is managed by the European Commission's Directorate-General for Fisheries (DG XIV). Financial assistance can be granted under the FIFG, in accordance with the *Operational Programme for Fisheries 1994-1999*, for the implementation of measures which contribute to ensuring compliance with the requirements of the common fisheries policy and the development of alternative related industries. These measures may include the reduction of current over-capacity and the promotion of environmental protection.[22] Given that the Habitats Directive is applicable to the exclusive fishing limits of the State,[23] this Fund may be used to finance the protection of marine SACs.

(d) The European Agriculture Guidance and Guarantee Fund
The European Agricultural Guidance and Guarantee Fund (EAGGF) is the Community's financial instrument for the Common Agricultural Policy (CAP).[24] The Fund is managed by the European

---

[20] See Article 1(f), Council Regulation 2083/93/EEC of 20 July 1993, OJ L193/34, 31 July 1993 amending Council Regulation 4254/88/EEC of 19 December 1988 laying down provisions for implementing Regulation 2052/88/EEC as regards the European Regional Development Fund, OJ L374/15, 31 December 1988. See also Treaty of Rome, Article 130c (renumbered Article 160).
[21] Council Regulation 2080/93/EEC of 20 July 1993 laying down provisions for implementing Regulation 2052/88/EEC as regards the Financial Instrument for Fisheries Guidance, OJ L193/1, 31 July 1993.
[22] Regulation 2080/93/EEC *ibid.*, Articles 1 and 3(2) respectively.
[23] Habitats Regulations, Regulation 2. See section 4.3.2.
[24] Council Regulation 2085/93/EEC of 20 July 1993 amending Council Regulation 4256/88/EEC of 19 December 1988 laying down provisions for implementing Regulation 2052/88/EEC as regards the European Agricultural Guidance and Guarantee Fund (EAGGF), Guidance Section, OJ L193/44, 31 July 1993. See also Treaty of Rome, Article 40 (renumbered Article 34).

Financing Habitat Conservation 197

Commission's Directorate-General for Agriculture (DG VI). The EAGGF's Guidance Section includes measures for the renewal and adaptation of production techniques, the modernisation of farms and the protection and preservation of the environment, including provision for compensatory allowances for farms in mountain and hill areas. Regulation 951/97/EC provides that the Guidance Section of the Fund may contribute towards investments which facilitate the adoption of new technologies relating to environmental protection.[25] In addition, Regulation 950/97/EC provides co-financing for, *inter alia*, the conservation of natural resources.[26] The EAGGF's Guarantee Section finances measures directed at slowing down the increase in agricultural production, including setting land aside and the afforestation of agricultural land.[27] The *Progress Report on the Implementation of the Fifth Action Programme on the Environment* identified the continued incorporation of environmental elements into the CAP as a priority concern.[28] In Ireland, the Department of Agriculture and Food's *Operational Programme for Agriculture, Rural Development and Forestry 1994-1999* identified the environment as a priority area for support. The integration of environmental concerns into agricultural practices in Ireland to date is due, to a large extent, to the operation of the Rural Environment Protection Scheme. This scheme is discussed in section 5.4 above.

---

[25] Article 1(g), Council Regulation 951/97/EC of 20 May 1997 on improving the processing and marketing conditions for agricultural products, OJ L142/22, 2 June 1997.

[26] Article 1(d), Council Regulation 950/97/EC of 20 May 1997 on improving the efficiency of agricultural structures, OJ L142/1, 2 June 1997.

[27] See Council Regulation 2079/92/EEC of 30 June 1992 instituting a Community aid scheme for early retirement from farming, OJ L215/91, 30 July 1992 amended by Commission Regulation 2773/95/EEC, OJ L288/37, 1 December 1995; Council Regulation 2080/92/EEC of 30 June 1992 instituting a Community aid scheme for forestry measures in agriculture, OJ L215/96, 30 July 1992 amended by Commission Regulation 231/96/EEC, OJ L30/33, 8 February 1996; Council Regulation 2078/92/EEC of 30 June 1992 on agricultural production methods compatible with the requirements of the protection of the environment and the maintenance of the countryside, OJ L215/85, 30 July 1992 amended by Commission Regulation 2772/95/EEC, OJ L288/35, 1 December 1995, Commission Regulation 746/96/EEC, OJ L102/19, 25 April 1996 and Commission Regulation 1962/96/EEC, OJ L259/7, 12 October 1996 (See section 5.4).

[28] *Supra*, fn 6.

7.3.3 The Cohesion Fund

This instrument[29] is designed to bring about economic cohesion within the Community through the provision of finance for the development of the four least-prosperous countries in the Community: Ireland, Greece, Portugal and Spain.[30] The Fund is managed by the Commission's Directorate General for Regional Policy and Cohesion (DGXVI). The Fund provides direct co-financing for large-scale transport and environmental projects.[31] The latter may include sewerage, water and waste treatment projects which, in turn, may help to protect *Natura 2000* sites. Finance may also be available for direct conservation projects. ECU 1.3 billion has been committed to Ireland for the period 1994-99. The rate of assistance granted by the Fund ranges from 80% to 85%. By way of exception, preparatory studies and technical support measures may be financed at 100% of the total cost. All projects financed by the Fund must comply with, *inter alia,* Community policy on environmental protection.[32]

7.3.4 The Community Initiatives

Community Initiatives are programmes proposed by the Commission to Member States to help solve specific problems which are of concern to the Community as a whole.[33] Nine per cent of Structural Fund resources is allocated by the Community to Community Initiatives.[34] Community Initiatives of relevance to

---

[29] Council Regulation 1164/94/EC of 16 May 1994 establishing a Cohesion Fund, OJ L130/1, 25 May 1994. Article 130(d) of the Treaty of Rome, as amended by the Treaty on European Union, provides for the establishment of this Fund. On 19 March 1998, the Commission presented its proposal for a regulation to govern the Cohesion Fund between 2000 and 2006: Commission Proposal for a Council Regulation amending Regulation 1164/94/EC establishing a Cohesion Fund, OJ C159/7, 26 May 1998.

[30] These States have *per capita* GNP below 90% of the Community average.

[31] Regulation 1164/94/EC *supra,* fn 29, Article 3(1).

[32] *Ibid.,* Article 8(1).

[33] See Article 5(5), Council Regulation 2052/88/EEC, *supra,* fn 15 as amended by Article 1, Council Regulation 2081/93/EEC, *supra,* fn 15; Article 11, Council Regulation 4253/88/EEC, *supra,* fn 15 as amended by Article 1, Council Regulation 2082/93/EEC, *supra,* fn 15; and Article 3(2), Council Regulation 4254/88/EEC, *supra,* fn 20 as amended by Article 1, Council Regulation 2083/93/EEC, *supra,* fn 20.

[34] Regulation 2081/93/EEC *supra,* fn 15, Article 12(5). See Commission Notices laying down Guidelines for the Community Initiatives of 15 June 1994, OJ C180,

environmental protection include INTERREG, LEADER and the *Special Support Programme for Peace and Reconciliation in Northern Ireland and the Border Counties.*[35]

The INTERREG programme is designed to assist the populations of border areas to overcome the disadvantages of their relative isolation within national economies and the Community as a whole by stimulating local economic enterprises and cross-border activities. The programme, which was launched in 1990, has successfully enabled Ireland and the United Kingdom to pursue more effective cross-border co-operation. The latest phase of the initiative, INTERREG II (1994-1999) operates in Northern Ireland (except Belfast city) and the border counties of Ireland[36] and on the Ireland-Wales maritime border. Environmental protection projects, including the conservation and protection of fisheries and the marine environment and cross-border co-operation in agriculture, are eligible for funding.

The LEADER programme is the EC initiative for rural development. The programme allows approved groups to implement their own integrated business plans for the development of their areas. The latest phase of the programme, LEADER II (1994-1999) is administered in Ireland by the Department of Agriculture, Food and Forestry in accordance with the *Operational Programme for the Implementation of LEADER II in Ireland (1994-1999)*. Thirty-six groups have been selected to administer the programme throughout Ireland. Activities which the groups are authorised to undertake include habitat and landscape protection and

---

1 July 1994. Ireland has been allocated approximately £500 million from the Community Initiatives budget for the period 1994-1999.

[35] In addition, the URBAN Initiative 1994-1999, which assists socio-economically deprived urban areas, gives special attention to the environment in urban areas. Measures which may be undertaken under this initiative include the restoration of green areas and the reclamation of derelict and contaminated land. The PESCA initiative provides finance to assist communities dependant on fishing to diversify from traditional activities into alternative means of income generation including stock management, conservation programmes and marine tourism. An Bord Iascaigh Mhara has responsibility for implementing PESCA in Ireland. The ENVIREG programme, which operated for the period 1990-1993, financed measures for the protection of the environment of, *inter alia*, Objective 1 regions, including Ireland. This initiative was discontinued with the advent of increased integration of environmental protection requirements into other financial instruments.

[36] i.e. counties Donegal, Sligo, Leitrim, Cavan, Monaghan and Louth.

the preservation and improvement of the environment. The total funding allocated to approved groups in Ireland is £87.5 million.

The *Special Support Programme for Peace and Reconciliation in Northern Ireland and the Border Counties* 1995-1999 contains measures which can finance actions of a cross border nature between public bodies in the areas of agriculture, environmental research and development, and the improvement of the physical environment in, *inter alia*, rural areas.[37] The Erne Catchment Nutrient Management Scheme operates under this programme.

7.3.5 Other Sources of Funding

The environment is a priority area within the Community's Fourth Research Framework Programme.[38] The European Investment Bank (EIB) helps to finance investment in protecting the environment, particularly waste-water collection and treatment and the reduction of carbon dioxide emissions. Finance for measures with environmental benefits may also be available through Community technology, transport and energy programmes including SAVE, THERMIE, ALTENER and EURET. The *International Fund for Ireland* provides finance for projects which promote reconciliation and economic regeneration in Northern Ireland and the border counties of the Irish Republic. The Fund operates a variety of programmes and initiatives in pursuit of this aim, including a Rural Development Programme operated in conjunction with the Department of Agriculture, Food and Forestry, the Northern Ireland Department of Agriculture and the European Community's LEADER programme. Applications for finance for conservation projects which are consistent with or promote the Fund's central objectives of reconciliation and regeneration are eligible for consideration.

---

[37] See Commission Notice to the Member States laying down guidelines for an initiative in the framework of the special support programme for peace and reconciliation in Northern Ireland and the border counties of Ireland, OJ C186/4, 20 July 1995.

[38] The Fisheries, Agriculture and Agro-industry Research (FAIR) programme which operates within the Framework Programme may be of particular significance here. The Fifth Research Framework Programme will operate for the period 1998-2002.

Appendix I

COUNCIL DIRECTIVE 92/43/EEC[1]
of 21 May 1992
on the conservation of natural habitats
and of wild fauna and flora

THE COUNCIL OF THE EUROPEAN COMMUNITIES,

Having regard to the Treaty establishing the European Economic Community, and in particular Article 130s thereof,

Having regard to the proposal from the Commission[2],

Having regard to the opinion of the European Parliament[3],

Having regard to the opinion of the Economic and Social Committee[4],

Whereas the preservation, protection and improvement of the quality of the environment, including the conservation of natural habitats and of wild fauna and flora, are an essential objective of general interest pursued by the Community, as stated in Article 130r of the Treaty;

Whereas the European Community policy and action programme on the environment (1987 to 1992)[5] makes provision for measures regarding the conservation of nature and natural resources;

Whereas, the main aim of this Directive being to promote the maintenance of biodiversity, taking account of economic, social, cultural and regional requirements, this Directive makes a contribution to the general objective of sustainable development;

Whereas the maintenance of such biodiversity may in certain cases require the maintenance, or indeed the encouragement, of human activities;

---

[1] As amended by the Accession Act of Austria, Finland and Sweden (OJ L1/135, 1 January 1995).
[2] OJ C247/3, 21 September 1988, and OJ C195/1, 3 August 1990.
[3] OJ C75/12, 20 March 1991.
[4] OJ C31/5, 6 February 1991.
[5] OJ C328/1, 7 December 1987.

Whereas, in the European territory of the Member States, natural habitats are continuing to deteriorate and an increasing number of wild species are seriously threatened; whereas given that the threatened habitats and species form part of the Community's natural heritage and the threats to them are often of a transboundary nature, it is necessary to take measures at Community level in order to conserve them;

Whereas, in view of the threats to certain types of natural habitat and certain species, it is necessary to define them as having priority in order to favour the early implementation of measures to conserve them;

Whereas, in order to ensure the restoration or maintenance of natural habitats and species of Community interest at a favourable conservation status, it is necessary to designate special areas of conservation in order to create a coherent European ecological network according to a specified timetable;

Whereas all the areas designated, including those classified now or in the future as special protection areas pursuant to Council Directive 79/409/EEC of 2 April 1979 on the conservation of wild birds[6], will have to be incorporated into the coherent European ecological network;

Whereas it is appropriate, in each area designated, to implement the necessary measures having regard to the conservation objectives pursued;

Whereas sites eligible for designation as special areas of conservation are proposed by the Member States but whereas a procedure must nevertheless be laid down to allow the designation in exceptional cases of a site which has not been proposed by a Member State but which the Community considers essential for either the maintenance or the survival of a priority natural habitat type or a priority species;

Whereas an appropriate assessment must be made of any plan or programme likely to have a significant effect on the conservation objectives of a site which has been designated or is designated in future;

Whereas it is recognised that the adoption of measures intended to promote the conservation of priority natural habitats and priority species of Community interest is a common responsibility of all Member States; whereas this may, however, impose an excessive financial burden on certain Member States given, on the one hand, the uneven distribution of

---

[6] OJ L103/1, 25 April 1979. Directive as last amended by Directive 91/244/ECC (OJ L115/41, 8 May 1991).

Appendix I: Council Directive 92/43/EEC

such habitats and species throughout the Community and, on the other hand, the fact that the 'polluter pays' principle can have only limited application in the special case of nature conservation;

Whereas it is therefore agreed that, in this exceptional case, a contribution by means of Community co-financing should be provided for within the limits of the resources made available under the Community's decisions;

Whereas land-use planning and development policies should encourage the management of features of the landscape which are of major importance for wild fauna and flora;

Whereas a system should be set up for surveillance of the conservation status of the natural habitats and species covered by this Directive;

Whereas a general system of protection is required for certain species of flora and fauna to complement Directive 79/409/EEC;

Whereas provision should be made for management measures for certain species, if their conservation status so warrants, including the prohibition of certain means of capture or killing, whilst providing for the possibility of derogation's on certain conditions;

Whereas, with the aim of ensuring that the implementation of this Directive is monitored, the Commission will periodically prepare a composite report based, inter alia, on the information sent to it by the Member States regarding the application of national provisions adopted under this Directive;

Whereas the improvement of scientific and technical knowledge is essential for the implementation of this Directive;

Whereas it is consequently appropriate to encourage the necessary research and scientific work;

Whereas technical and scientific progress mean that it must be possible to adapt the Annexes; whereas a procedure should be established whereby the Council can amend the Annexes;

Whereas a regulatory committee should be set up to assist the Commission in the implementation of this Directive and in particular when decisions on Community co-financing are taken;

Whereas provision should be made for supplementary measures governing the reintroduction of certain native species of fauna and flora and the possible introduction of non-native species;

Whereas education and general information relating to the objectives of this Directive are essential for ensuring its effective implementation,

HAS ADOPTED THIS DIRECTIVE:

Definitions

Article 1

For the purpose of this Directive:

(a) *conservation* means a series of measures required to maintain or restore the natural habitats and the populations of species of wild fauna and flora at a favourable status as defined in (e) and (i);

(b) *natural habitats* means terrestrial or aquatic areas distinguished by geographic, abiotic and biotic features, whether entirely natural or semi-natural;

(c) *natural habitat types of Community interest* means those which, within the territory referred to in Article 2:
(i) are in danger of disappearance in their natural range; or
(ii) have a small natural range following their regression or by reason of their intrinsically restricted area; or
(iii) present outstanding examples of typical characteristics of one or more of the six following biogeographical regions: Alpine, Atlantic, Boreal, Continental, Macaronesian and Mediterranean.
Such habitat types are listed or may be listed in Annex I;

(d) *priority natural habitat types* means natural habitat types in danger of disappearance, which are present on the territory referred to in Article 2 and for the conservation of which the Community has particular responsibility in view of the proportion of their natural range which falls within the territory referred to in Article 2; these priority natural habitat types are indicated by an asterisk (*) in Annex I;

(e) *conservation status of a natural habitat* means the sum of the influences acting on a natural habitat and its typical species that may affect its long-term natural distribution, structure and functions as well as the long-termsurvival of its typical species within the territory referred to in Article 2.

Appendix I: Council Directive 92/43/EEC

The conservation status of a natural habitat will be taken as 'favourable' when:
– its natural range and areas it covers within that range are stable or increasing, and
– the specific structure and functions which are necessary for its long-term maintenance exist and are likely to continue to exist for the foreseeable future, and
– the conservation status of its typical species is favourable as defined in (i);

(f) *habitat of a species* means an environment defined by specific abiotic and biotic factors, in which the species lives at any stage of its biological cycle;

(g) *species of Community interest* means species which, within the territory referred to in Article 2, are:
(i) endangered, except those species whose natural range is marginal in that territory and which are not endangered or vulnerable in the western palearctic region; or
(ii) vulnerable, i.e. believed likely to move into the endangered category in the near future if the causal factors continue operating; or
(iii) rare, i.e. with small populations that are not at present endangered or vulnerable, but are at risk. The species are located within restricted geographical areas or are thinly scattered over a more extensive range; or
(iv) endemic and requiring particular attention by reason of the specific nature of their habitat and/or the potential impact of their exploitation on their habitat and/or the potential impact of their exploitation on their conservation status.
Such species are listed or may be listed in Annex II and/or Annex IV or V;

(h) *priority species* means species referred to in (g) (i) for the conservation of which the Community has particular responsibility in view of the proportion of their natural range which falls within the territory referred to in Article 2; these priority species are indicated by an asterisk (*) in Annex II;

(i) *conservation status of a species* means the sum of the influences acting on the species concerned that may affect the long-term distribution and abundance of its populations within the territory referred to in Article 2;

The *conservation status* will be taken as 'favourable' when:

- population dynamics data on the species concerned indicate that it is maintaining itself on a long-term basis as a viable component of its natural habitats, and
- the natural range of the species is neither being reduced nor is likely to be reduced for the foreseeable future, and
- there is, and will probably continue to be, a sufficiently large habitat to maintain its populations on a long-term basis;

(j) *site* means a geographically defined area whose extent is clearly delineated;

(k) *site of Community importance* means a site which, in the biogeographical region or regions to which is belongs, contributes significantly to the maintenance or restoration at a favourable conservation status of a natural habitat type in Annex I or of a species in Annex II and may also contribute significantly to the coherence of Natura 2000 referred to in Article 3, and/or contributes significantly to the maintenance of biological diversity within the biogeographic region or regions concerned.

For animal species ranging over wide areas, sites of Community importance shall correspond to the places within the natural range of such species which present the physical or biological factors essential to their life and reproduction;

(l) *special area of conservation* means a site of Community importance designated by the Member States through a statutory, administrative and/or contractual act where the necessary conservation measures are applied for the maintenance or restoration, at a favourable conservation status, of the natural habitats and/or the populations of the species for which the site is designated;

(m)*specimen* means any animal or plant, whether alive or dead, of the species listed in Annex IV and Annex V, any part or derivative thereof, as well as any other goods which appear, from an accompanying document, the packaging or a mark or label, or from any other circumstances, to be parts or derivatives of animals or plants of those species;

(n) *the committee* means the committee set up pursuant to Article 20.

Article 2

1. The aim of this Directive shall be to contribute towards ensuring biodiversity through the conservation of natural habitats and of wild fauna and

flora in the European territory of the Member States to which the Treaty applies.

2. Measures taken pursuant to this Directive shall be designed to maintain or restore, at favourable conservation status, natural habitats and species of wild fauna and flora of Community interest.

3. Measures taken pursuant to this Directive shall take account of economic, social and cultural requirements and regional and local characteristics.

Conservation of natural habitats and habitats of species

Article 3

1. A coherent European ecological network of special areas of conservation shall be set up under the title Natura 2000. This network, composed of sites hosting the natural habitat types listed in Annex I and habitats of the species listed in Annex II, shall enable the natural habitat types and the species' habitats concerned to be maintained or, where appropriate, restored at a favourable conservation status in their natural range.
The Natura 2000 network shall include the special protection areas classified by the Member States pursuant to Directive 79/409/EEC.

2. Each Member State shall contribute to the creation of Natura 2000 in proportion to the representation within its territory of the natural habitat types and the habitats of species referred to in paragraph 1. To that effect each Member State shall designate, in accordance with Article 4, sites as special areas of conservation taking account of the objectives set out in paragraph 1.

3. Where they consider it necessary, Member States shall endeavour to improve the ecological coherence of Natura 2000 by maintaining, and where appropriate developing, features of the landscape which are of major importance for wild fauna and flora, as referred to in Article 10.

Article 4

1. On the basis of the criteria set out in Annex III (Stage 1) and relevant scientific information, each Member State shall propose a list of sites indicating which natural habitat types in Annex I and which species in Annex II that are native to its territory the sites host. For animal species ranging over wide areas these sites shall correspond to the places within the natural range of such species which present the physical or biological factors essential to their life and reproduction. For aquatic species which

range over wide areas, such sites will be proposed only where there is a clearly identifiable area representing the physical and biological factors essential to their life and reproduction. Where appropriate, Member States shall propose adaptation of the list in the light of the results of the surveillance referred to in Article 11.

The list shall be transmitted to the Commission, within three years of the notification of this Directive, together with information on each site. That information shall include a map of the site, its name, location, extent and the data resulting from application of the criteria specified in Annex III (Stage 1) provided in a format established by the Commission in accordance with the procedure laid down in Article 21.

2. On the basis of the criteria set out in Annex III (Stage 2) and in the framework both of each of the five biogeographical regions referred to in Article 1 (c) (iii) and of the whole of the territory referred to in Article 2 (1), the Commission shall establish, in agreement with each Member State, a draft list of sites of Community importance drawn from the Member States' lists identifying those which lost one or more priority natural habitat types or priority species.
Member States whose sites hosting one or more priority natural habitat types and priority species represent more than 5 % of their national territory may, in agreement with the Commission, request that the criteria listed in Annex III (Stage 2) be applied more flexibly in selecting all the sites of Community importance in their territory.

The list of sites selected as sites of Community importance, identifying those which host one or more priority natural habitat types or priority species, shall be adopted by the Commission in accordance with the procedure laid down in Article 21.

3. The list referred to in paragraph 2 shall be established within six years of the notification of this Directive

4. Once a site of Community importance has been adopted in accordance with the procedure laid down in paragraph 2, the Member State concerned shall designate that site as a special area of conservation as soon as possible and within six years at most, establishing priorities in the light of the importance of the sites for the maintenance or restoration, at a favourable conservation status, of a natural habitat type in Annex I or a species in Annex II and for the coherence of Natura 2000, and in the light of the threats of degradation or destruction to which those sites are exposed

5. As soon as a site is placed on the list referred to in the third subparagraph of paragraph 2 it shall be subject to Article 6 (2), (3) and (4).

Article 5

1. In exceptional cases where the Commission finds that a national list as referred to in Article 4 (1) fails to mention a site hosting a priority natural habitat type or priority species which, on the basis of relevant and reliable scientific information, it considers to be essential for the maintenance of that priority natural habitat type or for the survival of that priority species, a bilateral consultation procedure shall be initiated between that Member State and the Commission for the purpose of comparing the scientific data used by each.

2. If, on expiry of a consultation period not exceeding six months, the dispute remains unresolved, the Commission shall forward to the Council a proposal relating to the selection of the site as a site of Community importance.

3. The Council, acting unanimously, shall take a decision within three months of the date of referral.

4. During the consultation period and pending a Council decision, the site concerned shall be subject to Article 6 (2).

Article 6

1. For special areas of conservation, Member States shall establish the necessary conservation measures involving, if need be, appropriate management plans specifically designed for the sites or integrated into other development plans, and appropriate statutory, administrative or contractual measures which correspond to the ecological requirements of the natural habitat types in Annex I and the species in Annex II present on the sites.

2. Member States shall take appropriate steps to avoid, in the special areas of conservation, the deterioration of natural habitats and the habitats of species as well as disturbance of the species for which the areas have been designated, in so far as such disturbance could be significant in relation to the objectives of this Directive.

3. Any plan or project not directly connected with or necessary to the management of the site but likely to have a significant effect thereon, either individually or in combination with other plans or projects, shall be subject to appropriate assessment of its implications for the site in view of the site's conservation objectives. In the light of the conclusions of the assessment of

the implications for the site and subject to the provisions of paragraph 4, the competent national authorities shall agree to the plan or project only after having ascertained that it will not adversely affect the integrity of the site concerned and, if appropriate, after having obtained the opinion of the general public.

4. If, in spite of a negative assessment of the implications for the site and in the absence of alternative solutions, a plan or project must nevertheless be carried out for imperative reasons of overriding public interest, including those of a social or economic nature, the Member State shall take all compensatory measures necessary to ensure that the overall coherence of Natura 2000 is protected. It shall inform the Commission of the compensatory measures adopted.

Where the site concerned hosts a priority natural habitat type and/or a priority species, the only considerations which may be raised are those relating to human health or public safety, to beneficial consequences of primary importance for the environment or, further to an opinion from the Commission, to other imperative reasons of overriding public interest.

Article 7
Obligations arising under Article 6 (2), (3) and (4) of this Directive shall replace any obligations arising under the first sentence of Article 4 (4) of Directive 79/409/EEC in respect of areas classified pursuant to Article 4 (1) or similarly recognised under Article 4 (2) thereof, as from the date of implementation of this Directive or the date of classification or recognition by a Member State under Directive 79/409/EEC, where the latter date is later.

Article 8
1. In parallel with their proposals for sites eligible for designation as special areas of conservation, hosting priority natural habitat types and/or priority species, the Member States shall send, as appropriate, to the Commission their estimates relating to the Community co-financing which they consider necessary to allow them to meet their obligations pursuant to Article 6 (1).

2. In agreement with each of the Member States concerned, the Commission shall identify, for sites of Community importance for which co-financing is sought, those measures essential for the maintenance or re-establishment at a favourable conservation status of the priority natural habitat types and priority species on the sites concerned, as well as the total costs arising from those measures.

3. The Commission, in agreement with the Member States concerned, shall assess the financing, including co-financing, required for the operation of the measures referred to in paragraph 2, taking into account, amongst other things, the concentration on the Member State's territory of priority natural habitat types and/or priority species and the relative burdens which the required measures entail.

4. According to the assessment referred to in paragraphs 2 and 3, the Commission shall adopt, having regard to the available sources of funding under the relevant Community instruments and according to the procedure set out in Article 21, a prioritised action framework of measures involving co-financing to be taken when the site has been designated under Article 4 (4).

5. The measures which have not been retained in the action framework for lack of sufficient resources, as well as those included in the above mentioned action framework which have not received the necessary co-financing or have only been partially co-financed, shall be reconsidered in accordance with the procedure set out in Article 21, in the context of the two-yearly review of the action framework and may, in the meantime, be postponed by the Member States pending such review. This review shall take into account, as appropriate, the new situation of the site concerned.

6. In areas where the measures dependent on co-financing are postponed, Member States shall refrain from any new measures likely to result in deterioration of those areas.

Article 9
The Commission, acting in accordance with the procedure laid down in Article 21, shall periodically review the contribution of Natura 2000 towards achievement of the objectives set out in Article 2 and 3. In this context, a special area of conservation may be considered for declassification where this is warranted by natural developments noted as a result of the surveillance provided for in Article 11.

Article 10
Member States shall endeavour, where they consider it necessary, in their land-use planning and development policies and, in particular, with a view to improving the ecological coherence of the Natura 2000 network, to encourage the management of features of the landscape which are of major importance for wild fauna and flora.

Such features are those which, by virtue of their linear and continuous structure (such as rivers with their banks or the traditional systems for marking field boundaries) or their function as stepping stones (such as ponds or small woods), are essential for the migration, dispersal and genetic exchange of wild species.

Article 11

Member States shall undertake surveillance of the conservation status of the natural habitats and species referred to in Article 2 with particular regard to priority natural habitat types and priority species.

Protection of species

Article 12

1. Member States shall take the requisite measures to establish a system of strict protection for the animal species listed in Annex IV (a) in their natural range, prohibiting:

(a) all forms of deliberate capture or killing of specimens of these species in the wild;

(b) deliberate disturbance of these species, particularly during the period of breeding, rearing, hibernation and migration;

(c) deliberate destruction or taking of eggs from the wild;

(d) deterioration or destruction of breeding sites or resting places.

2. For these species, Member States shall prohibit the keeping, transport and sale or exchange, and offering for sale or exchange, of specimens taken from the wild, except for those taken legally before this Directive is implemented.

3. The prohibition referred to in paragraph 1 (a) and (b) and paragraph 2 shall apply to all stages of life of the animals to which this Article applies.

4. Member States shall establish a system to monitor the incidental capture and killing of the animal species listed in Annex IV (a). In the light of the information gathered, Member States shall take further research or conservation measures as required to ensure that incidental capture and killing does not have a significant negative impact on the species concerned.

Article 13

1. Member States shall take the requisite measures to establish a system of strict protection for the plant species listed in Annex IV (b), prohibiting:

(a) the deliberate picking, collecting, cutting, uprooting or destruction of such plants in their natural range in the wild;

(b) the keeping, transport and sale or exchange and offering for sale or exchange of specimens of such species taken in the wild, except for those taken legally before this Directive is implemented.

2. The prohibitions referred to in paragraph 1 (a) and (b) shall apply to all stages of the biological cycle of the plants to which this Article applies.

Article 14

1. If, in the light of the surveillance provided for in Article 11, Member States deem it necessary, they shall take measures to ensure that the taking in the wild of specimens of species of wild fauna and flora listed in Annnex V as well as their exploitation is compatible with their being maintained at a favourable conservation status.

2. Where such measures are deemed necessary, they shall include continuation of the surveillance provided for in Article 11. Such measures may also include in particular:
- regulations regarding access to certain property,
- temporary or local prohibition of the taking of specimens in the wild and exploitation of certain populations,
- regulation of the periods and/or methods of taking specimens,
- application, when specimens are taken, of hunting and fishing rules which take account of the conservation of such populations,
- establishment of a system of licences for taking specimens or of quotas,
- regulation of the purchase, sale, offering for sale, keeping for sale or transport for sale of specimens,
- breeding in captivity of animal species as well as artificial propagation of plant species, under strictly controlled conditions, with a view to reducing the taking of specimens of the wild,
- assessment of the effect of the measures adopted.

Article 15

In respect of the capture or killing of species of wild fauna listed in Annex V(a) and in cases where, in accordance with Article 16, derogation's are applied to the taking, capture or killing of species listed in Annex IV (a), Member States shall prohibit the use of all indiscriminate means capable of causing local disappearance of, or serious disturbance to, populations of such species, and in particular:

(a) use of the means of capture and killing listed in Annex VI (a);

(b) any form of capture and killing from the modes of transport referred to in Annex VI (b).

Article 16

1. Provided that there is no satisfactory alternative and the derogation is not detrimental to the maintenance of the populations of the species concerned at a favourable conservation status in their natural range, Member States may derogate from the provisions of Articles 12, 13, 14 and 15 (a) and (b):

(a) in the interest of protecting wild fauna and flora and conserving natural habitats;

(b) to prevent serious damage, in particular to crops, livestock, forests, fisheries and water and other types of property;

(c) in the interests of public health and public safety, or for other imperative reasons of overriding public interest, including those of a social or economic nature and beneficial consequences of primary importance for the environment;

(d) for the purpose of research and education, of repopulating and re-introducing these species and for the breeding operations necessary for these purposes, including the artificial propagation of plants;

(e) to allow, under strictly supervised conditions, on a selective basis and to a limited extent, the taking or keeping of certain specimens of the species listed in Annex IV in limited numbers specified by the competent national authorities.

2. Member States shall forward to the Commission every two years a report in accordance with the format established by the Committee on the derogation's applied under paragraph 1. The Commission shall give its opinion on these derogation's within a maximum time limit of 12 months following receipt of the report and shall give an account to the Committee.

3. The reports shall specify:
(a) the species which are subject to the derogation's and the reason for the derogation, including the nature of the risk, with, if appropriate, a reference to alternatives rejected and scientific data used;

(b) the means, devices or methods authorised for the capture or killing of animal species and the reasons for their use;

(c) the circumstances of when and where such derogation's are granted;

(d) the authority empowered to declare and check that the required conditions obtain and to decide what means, devices or methods may be used, within what limits and by what agencies, and which persons are to carry but the task;

(e) the supervisory measures used and the results obtained.

Information

Article 17
1. Every six years from the date of expiry of the period laid down in Article 23, Member States shall draw up a report on the implementation of the measures taken under this Directive. This report shall include in particular information concerning the conservation measures referred to in Article 6 (1) as well as evaluation of the impact of those measures on the conservation status of the natural habitat types of Annex I and the species in Annex II and the main results of the surveillance referred to in Article 11. The report, in accordance with the format established by the committee, shall be forwarded to the Commission and made accessible to the public.

2. The Commission shall prepare a composite report based on the reports referred to in paragraph 1. This report shall include an appropriate evaluation of the progress achieved and, in particular, of the contribution of Natura 2000 to the achievement of the objectives set out in Article 3. A draft of the part of the report covering the information supplied by a Member State shall be forwarded to the Member State in question for verification. After submission to the committee, the final version of the report shall be published by the Commission, not later than two years after receipt of the reports referred to in paragraph 1, and shall be forwarded to the Member States, the European Parliament, the Council and the Economic and Social Committee.

3. Member States may mark areas designated under this Directive by means of Community notices designed for that purpose by the committee.

Research

Article 18

1. Member States and the Commission shall encourage the necessary research and scientific work having regard to the objectives set out in Article 2 and the obligation referred to in Article 11. They shall exchange information for the purposes of proper co-ordination of research carried out at Member State and at Community level.

2. Particular attention shall be paid to scientific work necessary for the implementation of Articles 4 and 10, and transboundary co-operative research between Member States shall be encouraged.

Procedure for amending the Annexes

Article 19

Such amendments as are necessary for adapting Annexes I, II, III, v. and VI to technical and scientific progress shall be adopted by the Council acting by qualified majority on a proposal from the Commission.

Such amendments as are necessary for adapting Annex IV to technical and scientific progress shall be adopted by the Council acting unanimously on a proposal from the Commission.

Committee

Article 20

The Commission shall be assisted by a committee consisting of representatives of the Member States and chaired by a representative of the Commission.

Article 21

1. The representative of the Commission shall submit to the committee a draft of the measures to be taken. The committee shall deliver its opinion on the draft within a time limit which the Chairman may lay down according to the urgency of the matter. The opinion shall be delivered by the majority laid down in Article 148 (2) of the Treaty in the case of decisions which the Council is required to adopt on a proposal from the Commission. The votes of the representatives of the Member States within the committee shall be weighted in the manner set out in that Article. The Chairman shall not vote.

2. The Commission shall adopt the measures envisaged if they are in accordance with the opinion of the committee.

If the measures envisaged are not in accordance with the opinion of the committee, or if no opinion is delivered, the Commission shall, without delay, submit to the Council a proposal relating to the measures to be taken. The Council shall act by a qualified majority.

If, on the expiry of three months from the date of referral to the Council, the Council has not acted, the proposed measures shall be adopted by the Commission.

Supplementary provisions

Article 22
In implementing the provisions of this Directive, Member States shall:

(a) study the desirability of re-introducing species in Annex IV that are native to their territory where this might contribute to their conservation, provided that an investigation, also taking into account experience in other Member States or elsewhere, has established that such re-introduction contributes effectively to re-establishing these species at a favourable conservation status and that it takes place only after proper consultation of the public concerned;

(b) ensure that the deliberate introduction into the wild of any species which is not native to their territory is regulated so as not to prejudice natural habitats within their natural range or the wild native fauna and flora and, if they consider it necessary, prohibit such introduction. The results of the assessment undertaken shall be forwarded to the committee for information;

(c) promote education and general information on the need to protect species of wild fauna and flora and to conserve their habitats and natural habitats.

Final provisions

Article 23
1. Member States shall bring into force the laws, regulations and administrative provisions necessary to comply with this Directive within two years of its notification. They shall forthwith inform the Commission thereof.

2. When Member States adopt such measures, they shall contain a reference to this Directive or be accompanied by such reference on the

occasion of their official publication. The methods of making such a reference shall be laid down by the Member States.

3. Member States shall communicate to the Commission the main provisions of national law which they adopt in the field covered by this Directive.

Article 24
This Directive is addressed to the Member States.

Done at Brussels, 21 May 1992

For *the Council*
The President
Arlindo MARQUES CUNHA

Annex I: Natural habitat types of Community interest whose conservation requires the designation of special areas of conservation.

Annex II: Animal and plant species of Community interest whose conservation requires the designation of special areas of conservation.

Annex III: Criteria for selecting sites eligible for identification as sites of Community importance and designation as special areas of conservation.

Annex IV: Animal and plant species of Community interest in need of strict protection.

Appendix II

FIRST SCHEDULE
FLORA AND FAUNA

PART I
Regulations 22, 23
1. MAMMALS
   Lutra lutra (Otter)
   Cetacean Species
   Bat Species

2. AMPHIBIANS
   Bufo calamita (Natterjack toad)

PART II
Regulations 7, 24, 25

1. MAMMALS
   Martes martes (Pine marten)
   Lepus timidus (Irish hare)
   Halichoerus grypus (Grey seal)
   Phoca vitinula (Common seal)

2. AMPHIBIANS
   Rana temporaria (Frog)

3. FISH
   Lampetra fluviatilis (Lampern)
   Coregonus autumnalis spp. (Pollan)
   Alosa alosa (Allis shads)
   Alosa fallax (Twaite shad)
   Salmo salar (Salmon) (only in freshwater)

4. MOLLUSCS
Helix pomatia (Edible snail)
Margaritifera margaritifera (Freshwater pearl mussel)

5. CRUSTACEANS
Austropotamobius pallipes (White-clawed crayfish)

6. LICHENS
Cladonia subgenus Cladina (Reindeer Moss)

7. MOSSES
Leucobryum glaucum
All Sphagna

8. FERNS AND RELATIVES
Lycopodium spp. (Clubmosses)

Appendix II: Schedules to the Habitats Regulations 221

SECOND SCHEDULE

PART I
ENACTMENTS REFERRED TO IN REGULATION 31

Regulation 31(7)

Number and Year	Short Title
No. 6 of 1965	Air Navigation and Transport Act, 1965
No. 3 of 1945	Arterial Drainage Act, 1945
No. 14 of 1996	Dumping at Sea Act, 1996
No. 15 of 1959	Fisheries (Consolidation) Act, 1959
No. 1 of 1980	Fisheries Act, 1980
No. 12 of 1933	Foreshore Act, 1933
No. 17 of 1992	Foreshore Act, 1992
No. 30 of 1976	Gas Act, 1976
No. 9 of 1946	Harbours Act, 1946
No. 31 of 1940	Minerals Development Act, 1940
No. 12 of 1979	Minerals Development Act, 1979
No. 15 of 1995	Minerals Development Act, 1995
No. 7 of 1960	Petroleum and Other Minerals Development Act, 1960

PART II
ENACTMENT (*sic*) REFERRED TO IN REGULATION 32

Regulation 32(7)

Number and Year	Short Title
No. 6 of 1987	Air Pollution Act, 1987
No. 7 of 1992	Environmental Protection Agency Act, 1992
No. 21 of 1990	Local Government Water Pollution (Amendment) Act, 1990
No. 10 of 1996	Waste Management Act, 1996
No. 1 of 1977	Water Pollution (Amendment) Act, 1977